GEORGE WASHINGTON

Also by James Morton Smith

Freedom's Fetters: The Alien and Sedition Laws and American Civil Liberties

Seventeenth-Century America: Essays in Colonial History (Editor)

Liberty and Justice: Forging the Federal Union (Editor with Paul L. Murphy)

Liberty and Justice: The Modern Constitution (Editor with Paul L. Murphy)

George Washington
A PROFILE

EDITED BY

JAMES MORTON SMITH

AMERICAN PROFILES

General Editor: Aïda DiPace Donald

HILL AND WANG : NEW YORK

To
M. J. and J. M.,
busy bees

Manufactured in the United States of America
by American Book–Stratford Press, Inc.

Contents

Introduction

George Washington was a living legend long before he retired from public life. For nearly a quarter of a century—from 1775 to 1799—he stood at the center of national affairs, his leadership indelibly imprinted on the three great achievements of the American people of the Revolutionary generation: the American Revolution itself, the Constitutional Convention, and the new Federal Republic devoted to popular government on a continental scale. Washington was a natural for hero worship, particularly in a new nation without national symbols or an extensive body of tradition. His military leadership in the war of the American Revolution had clearly made him the outstanding Continental leader, literally "first in war." His unanimous election as presiding officer at the Constitutional Convention and as President of the United States just as clearly marked him as "first in peace." A folk hero whose apotheosis was well under way in his own lifetime, Washington was obviously "first in the hearts of his countrymen," a mythic figure created at the same time that the nation was created, the charismatic leader who both legitimated and vindicated the American experiment in nationalism and republican rule.

For later generations, even more than for his own, Washington has remained as much myth as man, as much monument as human. His name is spread across the land, attached to one state, thirty-three counties, and one hundred twenty-one villages, towns, and cities, including the nation's capital. In the District of Colum-

bia the Washington Monument soars five hundred fifty-five feet
high, towering far above the memorials to Lincoln and Jefferson.
In Mount Rushmore Memorial Park in the Black Hills of South
Dakota, Washington is the first of four Presidents depicted in
gigantic granite busts. In 1901 he was the only unanimous choice
of the judges for the statuary Hall of Fame, New York University's
tribute to Great Americans. In a comparative analysis of coverage
in biographical dictionaries and encyclopedias in England, France,
Germany, and the United States, J. M. Cattell, a Columbia
University psychologist, compiled in 1903 a list of one thousand
outstanding persons in world history; the only Americans in the
top hundred were Washington, Lincoln, and Jefferson, in that
order. In the twenty-volume *Dictionary of American Biography,*
published between 1928 and 1936, Washington finished a close
second behind Jefferson in space allotted. In 1948 and again in
1962, Professor Arthur M. Schlesinger, Sr., polled a group of
historical experts who rated American Presidents on their performance in office; Washington ranked with Lincoln as the greatest,
although the historians gave Lincoln the edge. In 1966 Thomas A.
Bailey, after observing that "presidential polls are something of a
parlor game, and as such should not be taken too seriously,"
nonetheless took them seriously enough to write a book ranking
the Presidents from Washington to Johnson and promoted Washington "ahead of Lincoln in the premier position." And several
years earlier, Dumas Malone, the distinguished biographer of
Thomas Jefferson and the author of the Jefferson sketch in the
Dictionary of American Biography, agreed that Washington, not
Jefferson or Lincoln, was the greatest man in American history.

It is this very veneration which has made the task of Washington's biographers so difficult, for Washington has been obscured
almost from the beginning by hero worship and mythic magic. Nor
did the early biographers create the image of the hero; they simply
took the contemporary image and enshrined it. From his appointment as commander-in-chief in 1775, Washington became the
chief symbol of Continental union. Until the Declaration of Independence over a year later, there was no American nation to
defend. Indeed, at the moment of his commissioning on June 15,
1775, as a General "to command all the continental forces raised

or to be raised for the defense of American liberty," he was a one-man army, for all the other forces were yet "to be raised." On June 17, therefore, the delegates to the Continental Congress pledged that they would "maintain and assist him, and adhere to him, the said George Washington, Esqr., with their lives and fortunes" for the preservation of American liberty.

From that moment on, Washington was more than a military commander; he personified the American cause. John Adams and other New England delegates, happy to have a Continental commander take over the provincial troops besieging the British at Boston, sent off the first Revolutionary tributes praising Washington. Calling the General modest, virtuous, amiable, generous, and brave, Adams observed that "this appointment will have a great effect in cementing and securing the union of these colonies," and he urged Massachusetts to welcome Washington "with all that confidence and affection, that politeness and respect, which is due one of the most important characters in the world." Silas Deane of Connecticut, after observing that Washington was "Sacrificing private fortune, independent ease, and every domestic pleasure" by accepting "his Country's call," coined a phrase echoed in children's literature thenceforward: "Let our Youth look up to this man as a pattern to form themselves by; who unites the bravery of the soldier with the most consummate modesty and virtue."

When Washington's army forced the British to evacuate Boston in March, 1776, his fame was fixed with New Englanders; tributes from all parts of the colonies flooded him and the Continental Congress presented him with a gold medal in honor of the military feat. Thereafter, the scene of war shifted from New England, and the grateful people and their descendants, the most prolific of American literary groups, paid tribute to Washington. In 1794, during Washington's second term as President, the *New England Primer* substituted a new couplet under the letter *W*:

> By Washington
> Great deeds were done,

replacing the earlier jingle,

> Whales in the Sea
> God's Voice obey.

Even during the Revolution, Francis Hopkinson, a military aide to Washington, commented on the tendency to give the General a title of distinction: "To him the title of Excellency is applied with peculiar propriety. He is the best and greatest man the world ever knew . . . neither depressed by disappointment and difficulties, nor elated with temporary success. He retreats like a General, and attacks like a Hero. Had he lived in the days of idolatry, he had been worshipped as a God."

The days of idolatry came quickly. The first author to capitalize on the cultic worship of Washington was the Reverend Mason L. Weems, characterized by Albert J. Beveridge as "a delightful mingling of evangelist and vagabond, lecturer and politician, writer and musician" and by Daniel J. Boorstin as "an amiable and energetic charlatan," "a one-man market-research enterprise," "a supersalesman who had thoroughly mixed religion with salesmanship." In Weems's *Life of Washington*, first published in 1800 only months after the hero's death, the pious parson served up a mixture of anecdotal facts, moralistic myths, and patriotic phrases. When Washington had retired from the Presidency after two unanimous elections, he was at the peak of his fame, and Weems, the self-styled "former rector of Mount Vernon parish," had begun collecting materials for a biographical sketch. By the middle of 1799, he had informed his publisher that he had "The Beauties of Washington" (the tentative title) "nearly ready for the press." " 'Tis artfully drawn up," he added, "enlivened with anecdotes, and in my humble opinion marvellously fitted" for the American taste.

Seldom has an author better judged his readers. After Washington's death in December, 1799, Weems wrote his publisher that he was "very nearly primed and cocked" for the millions who "are gaping to read something about him." Published in 1800 as *The Life and Memorable Actions of George Washington*, Weems's brief biography was an instantaneous success, going through three and perhaps four editions that year. Not until the fifth edition, published in 1806, did the cherry tree story appear among the "number of very curious anecdotes" mentioned in Weems's subtitle. By 1808, the sixth edition had grown from an eighty-page pamphlet to a two-hundred-twenty-eight-page book filled with new anecdotes about Washington, all of them "perfectly in character, and equally honorable to himself, and exemplary to his young countrymen."

In canonizing the Hero of Mount Vernon, the parson-priest stressed Washington's major virtues: "1 his Veneration for the Diety [*sic*] or Religious Principles. 2 His Patriotism. 3d his Magninmity [*sic*]. 4 his Industry. 5 his Temperance and Sobriety. 6 his Justice, etc., etc." Others expanded the "et ceteras" into massive volumes, beginning with Chief Justice John Marshall, whose four volumes were published between 1804 and 1807. John Adams called Marshall's biography a mausoleum one hundred feet square at the base and two hundred feet high, and Weems himself dubbed it the "Washingtoniad." But Marshall's work was dwarfed by Jared Sparks's twelve-volume *Life and Writings of George Washington* (a one-volume biography by Sparks and eleven volumes of Washington's letters), published between 1834 and 1837, and by Washington Irving's five-volume *Life of George Washington*, published between 1855 and 1859.

Marshall's assessment set the reverential tone: "No man has ever appeared upon the theatre of public action, whose integrity was more incorruptible, or whose principles were more perfectly free from the contamination of those selfish and unworthy passions, which find their nourishment in the conflicts of party." And Irving, who traced Washington's descent from an ancestor with the unlikely name of William de Heartburn (a Norman noble of William the Conqueror, no less), made him a saintly patriot, a godlike hero who "stands apart from every other in history, shining with a truer luster and a more benignant glory." But the scholars and literary authors merely reflected the popular attitude towards Washington, one epitomized by a young Illinois politician, Abraham Lincoln, in a Washington birthday oration in 1842:

Washington is the mightiest name of earth—long since mightiest in the cause of civil liberty, still mightiest in moral reformation. . . . To add brightness to the sun or glory to the name of Washington is alike impossible. Let none attempt it. In solemn awe pronounce the name, and in its naked deathless splendor leave it shining on.

More than human, almost divine, Washington by the first quarter of the nineteenth century had become a demigod, and the parallel between Washington, the Savior of his Country, and Jesus Christ, the Savior of Mankind, was implicit. Finally, in 1832, Congressman Benjamin C. Howard of Maryland made it explicit in a speech in the House of Representatives on the eve of Washington's birthday celebration: "From the first ages of the world," he declared, "the records of all time furnished only two instances of birthdays being commemorated after the death of the individual: . . . the 22nd of February and the 25th of December." That view is echoed even today in Fredericksburg, Virginia, where a marker points pious pilgrims and tired tourists "This way to the Home of Mary the Mother of Washington."

Until the death and apotheosis of Lincoln, Washington held undisputed sway as the pre-eminent national hero, the model of perfection. But in the years following the Civil War, when Lincoln and Lee emerged as heroes and the old agrarian world of the eighteenth century gave way to industrialism, Washington became more remote, more unreal, and the myth more challengeable. Occasionally in the mid-nineteenth century, authors began to question the demigod theme of Washington historiography. Ralph Waldo Emerson in his immensely popular *Representative Men* warned that "every hero becomes a bore at last. . . . They cry up the virtues of George Washington—'Damn George Washington!' is the poor Jacobin's whole speech and confutation." And Mark Twain claimed that he was a greater man than Washington, for Washington couldn't tell a lie, but Twain could, though he added reassuringly that he wouldn't. Artemus Ward, another humorist, also jousted with the mythic Washington in a perfect parody of the usual eulogy: "G. Washington was abowt the best man this world ever sot eyes on. . . . He never slopt over! . . . He luved his country dearly. He wasn't after the spiles. He was a human angil in a 3 kornered hat and knee britches." And even the more severe Nathaniel Hawthorne, in one of his lighter moments, could raise questions sure to shock the pious: "Did anyone ever see Washington nude?" he asked. "It is inconceivable," he quickly answered, for it was clear that "he was born with his clothes on, and his hair powdered, and made a stately bow on his first appearance in the world."

By the second half of the nineteenth century there were increasing literary demands for more balanced biographies of Washington. At mid-century the editor of *Harper's Weekly* lamented that there were ideal studies of "the ideal Washington, but a lifelike picture of the man as he lived, spoke, acted, thought, and demeaned himself in private, we have none." As late as 1885 John Bach McMaster could still note that the outlines of Washington's biography were known "to every school-boy in the land. Yet his true biography is still to be prepared." Before the end of the nineteenth century, however, three historians—Henry Cabot Lodge, Woodrow Wilson, and Paul Leicester Ford—did try to write a "true biography," and Ford even entitled his *The True George Washington.* Lodge, who published two volumes on Washington in 1889 on the one-hundredth anniversary of Washington's inauguration as first President of the United States, attempted to "depict the very man himself," in order "to see what he really was and what he meant then, and what he is and what he means to us and to the world to-day." Aware that the whimsy of Weems had made Washington "a faultless prig" and had generated a reaction culminating in "an endless theme for joke and burlesque," Lodge sought to portray "a strong, vigorous man, in whose veins ran warm, red blood, in whose heart were stormy passions and deep sympathy for humanity, in whose brain were far-reaching thoughts, and who was informed throughout his being with a resistless will." Lodge's biography was a popularly written, often eloquent work, but it did not achieve its purpose. Lodge ultimately had to concede that "there is something about Washington, call it greatness, dignity, majesty, what you will, which seems to hold men aloof and keep them from knowing him. In truth," Lodge concluded, "he was a most difficult man to know." So Lodge ended up accepting the historical judgment which he had set out to explore: "When years after his death the world agrees to call a man great, the verdict must be accepted. . . . Whether the image be true or false is of no consequence: the fact endures."

Lodge's later political opponent, Woodrow Wilson, wrote a one-volume biography of Washington in 1896, but it was more a lifeless chronicle than a history, an account without evaluation, rather flat by comparison with Lodge's work. The most successful of the three ventures at "humanizing Washington, and making him a man rather than a historical figure," was Ford's *The True George Washington*, also published in 1896 and reissued in 1924 as *George Washington*. Ford's book is completely unpretentious. Starting with the assumption that it is curious for pragmatic Americans to "engage in the same process of hero building which has given us Jupiter, Wotan, King Arthur, and others," he suggested that the superheroic interpretation so stripped men of "human characteristics as to make us question even whether they deserve much credit for their sacrifices and deeds." He wanted to portray Washington not as a demigod but as a man who, like all men, was "limited by human limits, and influenced by human passions"; he wanted "to put the shadow-boxes of humanity round our historic portraits." In an attempt to capture Washington's personality, he let Washington speak for himself as often as possible. The result is not a biography but an engaging series of essays about important aspects of Washington's life and thought, on subjects as various as physique, education, and social life to master and employer, tastes and amusements, and friends and enemies. But after writing the book to humanize Washington, Ford confessed that restoring the marble statue to humanity "only served to make Washington the greater to him."

Between the Spanish-American War and World War II, writings about Washington fell into three broad categories: specialized studies by professionally trained historians belonging to either the "progressive" or the "imperial" schools of historical interpretation, popular books by the so-called debunkers, and the outpourings during the George Washington Bicentennial Celebration of 1932. Picking up where Ford had left off, Sydney George Fisher published early in the century three books whose titles indicate a desire to break with the heroic emphasis in early American history and biography: *The True Benjamin Franklin* (1900), *The True William Penn* (1900), and *The True History of the American Revolution* (1902). In 1912 his article on "The Legendary and Myth-Making Process in Histories of the American Revolution" demanded the substitution of "truth and actuality"—true histories—"for the mawkish sentimentality and nonsense with which we have been so long nauseated." So far as Washington is concerned, the switch from inconolatry to iconoclasm was inaugurated in 1913, when Charles A. Beard published *An Economic Interpretation of the Constitution of the United States* to demonstrate that the framers of the document were guided by "real economic forces" rather than divine inspiration. Beard listed five major economic interests of the Founding Fathers and noted that only Washington, "probably the richest man in the United States in his time," had holdings in as many as four of them. Washington and the other members of the Convention were not "disinterested," Beard concluded: "on the contrary, we are forced to accept the profoundly significant conclusion that they knew through their personal experiences in economic affairs the precise results which the new government that they were setting up was designed to attain." The Constitution "was an economic document drawn with superb skill by men whose property interests were immediately at stake."

If "progressive" historians did not place Washington at the head of the conservative reaction which forged the Constitution, as Beard did, they tended to relegate him to the sidelines. In his study of Washington's Presidency, entitled *Hamilton and Jefferson* (1925), Claude G. Bowers does not eliminate Washington as completely from the book as he does from the title, but neither does he make the President an effective figure in American political life. Bowers, who subtitled his book "The Struggle for Democracy," made Jefferson the democrat, Hamilton the autocrat-monocrat, and Washington a front man. In Vernon Louis Parrington's immensely influential *Main Currents of American Thought*, published two years after Bowers' book, Washington hardly appears at all.

More recent interpreters of early American history, though their emphases differ radically from those of the "progressive" historians, have usually continued to underrate or ignore Washington's role. This has been especially true of the work by historians of ideas and intellectual historians—those analysts of political thought and of literary and intellectual trends who have been writing during the last twenty-five years. In part their neglect of Washington springs from his failure to write any systematic or theoretical statement of his political and social philosophy until his Farewell Address, in part from the difficulty of classifying him as a liberal or a conservative thinker. The easy out is to omit him or to give him rather brief notice, as most intellectual histories have done (Merle Curti, *The Growth of American Thought*, 1943; Richard Hofstadter, *The American Political Tradition and the Men Who Made It*, 1948; Louis Hartz, *The Liberal Tradition in America*, 1955; Clinton Rossiter, *Conservatism in America: The Thankless Persuasion*, 1962; Arthur Ekirch, *The American Democratic Tradition: A History*, 1963). Saul K. Padover summarized the reaction of his friends and students in 1955 when they learned that he was preparing a documentary book on Washington's political and social ideas: "I was invariably asked the surprised and skeptical question: 'Why, did Washington have any ideas?'"

The tendency of the twentieth century to view Washington as a mindless man has been re-enforced by the tendency of the so-called imperial school of colonial historians to view him almost exclusively as a military man, a wartime commander interested in strategy and tactics rather than political issues, colonial rights, and independence. In Claude H. Van Tyne's short account of *The American Revolution, 1776–1783* (1905), all the references to Washington are to his military activities except one, which notes that "his efforts in the army to banish provincial distinctions did much to create fellow-feeling, which would make real union possible." In his later and longer appraisal of *The War for Independence* (1929), Van Tyne consistently discusses Washington as a military man except for six references: three times he lists Washington as a leader of the radical political forces in the colonies, though two of these are buried in footnotes; the other references mention his early appraisal of New Englanders, his opposition to independence in 1775, and his endorsement of Thomas Paine's *Common Sense* as a prelude to independence. Only in his volume on *The Causes of the War of Independence* (1922) did Van Tyne list Washington's attitudes towards Parliamentary measures, six of his eight references to Washington having political connotations.

Among present-day historians of the imperial school, Lawrence Henry Gipson is pre-eminent, and his work is the classic example of the tendency of this group to treat Washington only as a military man, without any interest in the political issues which ultimately separated the colonies from Great Britain. In his brief

book *The Coming of the Revolution, 1763–1775* (1954), Gipson
mentions Washington once in his introductory chapter but totally
ignores him in his analytical account, although it closes in 1775
when Washington was elected commander-in-chief. In his monumental thirteen-volume study of *The British Empire Before the
American Revolution* (1936–1967), Gipson devotes four volumes
to the pre-Revolutionary period but mentions Washington only
nine times in his 1,365 pages; his summary of the series in volume
XIII makes no reference to Washington at all.

The popular writers of the 1920's, reflecting the postwar mood
of disenchantment with Wilsonian idealism, turned to debunking
the legend of Washington. In a period when H. L. Mencken, the
most powerful and pungent writer during the decade dominated by
"The Lost Generation," ridiculed idealism, democracy, hypocrisy,
patriotism, organized religion, and the American "booboisie,"
William E. Woodward and Rupert Hughes led the revolt against
the Washington cult, striking out violently, as Professor Wesley
Frank Craven has observed, at what they "considered to be a false
image supporting some of the false values" in their own society. In
their attempts to destroy the myth and find the man—Woodward
subtitled his book "The Image and the Man," Hughes "The
Human Being and the Hero"—the debunkers stressed Washington's love affairs, his profanity and drinking habits, his materialism
and ambition, his indifference to religion, his passions and emotions, and his slaveholding. Whether or not Washington was
descended from a Baron de Heartburn, his less distant family,
according to Woodward, was "undistinguished, unless a persistent
mediocrity, enduring many generations, is in itself a distinction."
Instead of his low origins, Hughes stressed Washington's high
living as an eighteenth-century Virginia aristocrat; Washington's
life demonstrated "that one should dress as magnificently as
possible and indulge in every luxury available, including the dance,
the theatre, the ballroom, hunting, fishing, racing, drinking, and
gambling, observing in all of them temperance, justice, honesty
and pride, while avoiding excess and loss of dignity." Both Hughes
and Woodward gave the Sally Fairfax episode a big play in their
books; if Washington married Martha Custis while loving another
woman, who also happened to be the wife of his best friend,

George William Fairfax, then he must have been a passionate as well as a very human sort of man.

Nathaniel Wright Stephenson dubbed the debunkers of Washington "romantic biographers" who had made a sentimental discovery. "They phrase it by saying that they have proved him to be a 'human being.' What they mean is that they believe he was in love with his neighbor's wife. . . . Sally Fairfax—that is, Mrs. George William Fairfax, whose husband was perhaps his best friend." Romantics or not, even the debunkers fell under Washington's spell. "The more I study Washington," Hughes noted in an appendix to his final volume, published in 1930, "the greater and better I think him, yet I am not trying to prove him great or good. I am trying solely to describe him as he was and let him speak for himself. He was a man of such tremendous undeniable achievement that he does not need to be bolstered with propaganda, protected by a priestcraft of suppression, or celebrated by any more Fourth of July oratory."

But the biggest deluge of Fourth of July oratory was yet to come, for in 1932 impresario Sol Bloom, ex-showman turned Congressman, headed up an incredible nine-month celebration of the bicentennial of Washington's birth. Bloom had something going all the time, and it took five fat volumes to record the history of the celebration. Will Rogers, the Oklahoma humorist, wrote to the Congressman, "You are the only guy who ever made a party run nine months, and you did it in dry times, too. Sol, you made this whole country Washington conscious." Bloom boasted that on each day of the commemoration an average of sixteen thousand "individual Bicentennial programs—by churches, schools, civil bodies, patriotic societies, and fraternal orders—were held in all parts of the United States . . . totalling 4,760,345 separate and distinct programs." Although the final report of the Bicentennial Commission hit only the highlights of these celebrations, it could not omit mentioning that Director Bloom, besides taking over Mother's Day, Memorial Day, Independence Day, and even the anniversary of Goethe's death ("No statesman was ever greater than Washington. No poet . . . was greater than Goethe"), served as official starter of the Bicentennial Futurity, "perhaps the largest homing pigeon race held in America up till that time," according to

Bloom, who liberated ten thousand American and foreign birds, thus "giving the race an international significance."

Much of Bloom's activities was, like the pigeon Futurity, strictly for the birds, but there were some worthwhile achievements as well. The most significant aspect of the Bicentennial was the publication of Washington's *Writings*, edited in thirty-nine volumes by John C. Fitzpatrick between 1931 and 1944. On a smaller scale the brief but brilliant essay by Samuel Eliot Morison on "The Young Man Washington," reprinted in this volume, was prepared as a part of the Bicentennial. It remains to this day, along with the perceptive summary by Douglas Southall Freeman at the end of his second volume on Washington, the best analysis of Washington as a young man.

Between the boom of Washington material in 1932 and the end of World War II, there was surprisingly little written on Washington. For one thing the New Deal propelled Thomas Jefferson to the forefront as a hero, enshrining him in a new monument in Washington in 1943. By 1946 Curtis Putnam Nettels, in an astute appraisal of "The Washington Theme in American History," wrote that "the leading trend at the present time in historical studies concerning George Washington, if it may be called a trend, is one of neglect. . . . The professional historians have ignored him to the point that he is rapidly becoming the forgotten man of American history." The underlying explanation of the dearth of acceptable studies of his life and works, according to Nettels, is the hero worship of Washington. Modern historians have "hesitated to be caught in a cross fire of demands of sacred tradition on the one side and the exacting requirements of historical method on the other," which requires that Washington's writings be subjected to the rule that any statement must be verified by two or more independent witnesses.

Since Nettels wrote in 1946, he and other historians have begun a reappraisal of Washington and the remote times in which he lived. All of the essays reprinted in this volume except three have been written since 1948, and those earlier essays—by Morison, Dixon Wecter, and Harold W. Bradley—are representative of the best accounts published between the Washington Bicentennial and the end of World War II. Wecter's "President Washington and

Parson Weems" is a classic study of the historical figure and the heroic symbol which had come into existence even before Weems froze it for posterity. Morison's amiable account of the young Washington was first written in 1932, but the author revised it in 1953 following correspondence with John C. Fitzpatrick and Fairfax Harrison and after checking it against Freeman's volumes on Washington. Nettels' "Washington on the Eve of the Revolution" is a realistic portrayal of the Virginia leader's active participation in the American resistance movement against British policies from 1763 until his emergence as the unanimous choice of the Continental Congress as commander-in-chief. The most recent selection, from *George Washington in the American Revolution* (1968), is by James Thomas Flexner. His chapter, "Cincinnatus Assayed," is a balanced evaluation of Washington not only as a military commander but also as a political leader whose most fundamental greatness lay "in his ability to recognize the great principles," selecting "among the alternatives that were presented to him by the possibilities of his time and generation." Nor were the alternatives narrowly limited to military matters. "In many and in continually augmenting respects," Flexner concludes, "he became in 1775, twelve years before his official inauguration as President of the United States, the chief executive of an emerging nation. . . . This continuing activity forced Washington to face almost every type of problem he would eventually have to face as President. He found himself involved in naval affairs, in foreign affairs, in the use of rivers and highways, in politics, in commerce, in manufacturing."

Washington's wartime experiences gave him a Continental outlook, and his Circular Letter to the States in June, 1783, made it clear that he favored a strong and energetic national government, a point he reiterated in a toast the day before he surrendered his commission to Congress: "Competent powers to Congress for general purposes." When the Cincinnatus of the West returned to Mount Vernon, he found it impossible to retire within himself, as much as he might have hoped he could. Though he was reluctant to leave his retirement and participate in the Constitutional Convention in 1787, he finally decided to attend and served as president throughout the lengthy and exhausting sessions between

May and September. Freeman's chapter, "To Avert 'Some Awful Crisis,' " indicates that Washington's influence at the Convention and on the Constitution was enormous, even though he made only one speech during that decisive summer.

The position of President of the United States seemed shaped by the Convention on the assumption that Washington would be the first to occupy the office. In a day when executive power was suspect—when the creation of the Presidency, as Hamilton observed in *The Federalist,* was "attended with greater difficulty" than perhaps any other—the Constitution established an energetic and independent chief executive. Pierce Butler, one of the Founding Fathers, noted that the Convention would not have made the executive powers so great "had not many of the members cast their eyes toward General Washington as President, and shaped their ideas of the Powers to be given a President, by their opinions of his Virtue."

Although Washington believed in the need for an energetic executive, he also thought, with Madison, that different interests of society should be represented in a check-and-balance system that would insure as much popular rule as would be consistent with the protection of individual liberty. Three of the essays in this volume analyze Washington's thought on political and social issues. Bradley's "The Political Thinking of George Washington" is almost unique as an attempt to sort out and assess the central features of Washington's political thought. Paul F. Boller, Jr., in "George Washington and Religious Liberty," evaluates a little-explored aspect of the President's views on that profound freedom. For the American people, Washington wrote, it was "not only among the choicest of their *blessings* but also of their *rights.*" In a shorter piece on "Washington, the Quakers, and Slavery," Boller also discusses Washington's entrapment in the tragedy of slavery.

Nearly all observers agree that Washington's eight years as President demonstrated that executive power was completely consistent with the genius of republican government. Putting his prestige on the line in an untried office under an untried constitution, Washington was fully aware, as he pointed out in his First Inaugural Address, that "the preservation of the sacred fire of liberty and the destiny of the republican model of government are justly considered, perhaps, as *deeply*, as *finally*, staked on the experiment entrusted to the hands of the American people." In his book *Presidential Greatness . . . George Washington to the Present,* Thomas A. Bailey emphasizes Washington's role in launching this experiment in republicanism. "Although his every move could be deemed a potential precedent binding generations unborn, his foot did not slip once. He made no major mistakes—something that cannot be said of any of his successors who served long enough to make a mistake." Of the forty-three yardsticks which Bailey uses for measuring Presidential performance, Washington "not only passes most of the tests with flying colors, but in several significant respects is in a class by himself." Esmond Wright's "President of the United States (1789–1797)" summarizes the highlights of those precedent-setting years, analyzing both the domestic legislation and the foreign policy issues raised by the wars of the French Revolution.

Perhaps Washington's chief strength—the key to his success as a military and a political leader—was his realization that in a republic the executive, like all other elected representatives, would have to measure his public acts against the temper of public opinion. As military commander dealing with the Continental Congress and the state governments during the Revolution, Washington had developed a sensitivity to the importance of administrative skills as a means of building public support of the army fighting for popular government. As President he applied the same skills to win support for the new federal government. In his letter requesting Jefferson to serve as Secretary of State, he wrote: "I consider the successful Administration of the general Government as an object of almost infinite consequence to the present and future happiness of the Citizens of the United States." Leonard D. White's "George Washington as an Administrator" is an excellent account of the President's record.

Both White and Wright stress Washington's administrative genius more than his political legacy. This is in part due to the fact that Washington and the Founding Fathers did not foresee the rise of political parties. But despite the President's abhorrence of faction, his administrations and policies spurred the beginnings of the first party system, ultimately identifying Washington, the least partisan of Presidents, with the Federalist party, especially after the retirement of Jefferson from the Cabinet at the end of 1793. Washington's Farewell Address, though it was essentially a last will and political testament to the American people, inevitably took on political coloration in an election year. Warning against the divisiveness of excessive party spirit, which tended to separate Americans politically as "geographical distinctions" did sectionally, he stressed the necessity for an American character free of foreign attachments. Two thirds of his address dealt with domestic politics and the baleful influence of party; the rest of the document laid down a statement of first principles of American foreign policy. But even here, as Samuel Flagg Bemis has observed, Washington's warning against foreign entanglements was especially applicable to foreign interference in the domestic affairs of the United States. One of the more provocative interpretations of Washington's foreign policy is Alexander DeConde's "Washington's Farewell, the French Alliance, and the Election of 1796."

Washington's public service did not end with his retirement from the Presidency. During the Half-War with France, President John Adams appointed him commander-in-chief, a position he held when he died in 1799. At the time of his death, Congress unanimously adopted a resolution to erect a marble monument in the nation's capital "to commemorate the great events of his military and political life"; it also directed that "the family of General Washington be requested to permit his body to be deposited under it." The Washington Monument was not completed until 1884, and Washington's remains were never deposited under it. But the Washington myth flourished without monument or mausoleum, and Daniel J. Boorstin's "The Mythologizing of George Washington" traces the myth as an important feature of the national experience in the nineteenth century.

As the United States moves towards the Bicentennial of the American Revolution in 1976, biographers and historians will continue their attempts to remedy the recent neglect of Washington which Professor Nettels lamented in 1946. Most Americans, as Paul Leicester Ford suggested years ago, do not need or want a demigod; perhaps one of the reasons for Washington's fall from being first in the hearts of his countrymen is because he has been made in the past to seem so perfect—and so lifeless. The possibility of writing a more lifelike and a more lively biography of Washington will be greatly enhanced by the publication of a new and definitive eighty-volume edition of the complete correspondence of Washington, which will supersede the Fitzpatrick edition. The documentary project is sponsored by the University of Virginia; Donald Jackson will serve as editor-in-chief. On the biographical side, we may hope that a full-scale, one-volume life of Washington will soon appear. For the present, however, there is no such work. I have accordingly selected essays for this anthology which seem to me to give a relatively complete profile of Washington the man and a reasonably realistic understanding of the historical figure. Nevertheless, it is only an introduction to the mountain of material on Washington, most of it eulogistic. But as Abigail Adams said of Washington, "simple truth is his best, his greatest eulogy." Writing before the miasma of mythology had obscured the Washington she had known, President Adams' wife eschewed extravagant praise for precise appraisal: "He never grew giddy, but ever maintained a modest diffidence of his own talents. . . . Possessed of power, possessed of an extensive influence, he never used it but for the benefit of his country. . . . If we look through the whole tenor of his life, history will not produce to us a parallel."

JAMES MORTON SMITH

Ithaca, New York
June 28, 1968

George Washington, 1732–1799

George Washington was born at Bridges Creek, later known as "Wakefield," in Westmoreland County, Virginia, on February 22, 1732 (February 11, old style). His father died when he was nine years old, and the boy spent the next few years with his mother at Ferry Farm near Fredericksburg, with relatives in Westmoreland, and with his half-brother at Mount Vernon. By the time he was sixteen he had mastered a rudimentary education, studying mathematics, surveying, reading, and the usual subjects of his day. His half-brother Lawrence had married Ann Fairfax, daughter of Lord Fairfax, and Washington became a close friend of her brother George William. In 1748 the two young men helped survey Lord Fairfax's frontier land in the Shenandoah Valley. In 1749 Washington was appointed county surveyor for Culpeper County, and his experience in the frontier country led to his appointment as a major in the Virginia militia in 1752.

When Governor Dinwiddie decided to warn the French moving into the Ohio Valley not to encroach on English territory, he appointed the twenty-one-year-old Washington for the mission and later published the results of the expedition, including the French rejection of the ultimatum, in *The Journal of Major George Washington* . . . (1754). Dinwiddie then commissioned Washington a lieutenant-colonel with orders to dislodge the French at Fort Duquesne, but a superior French force besieged the Virginia troops at Fort Necessity until negotiations allowed the disarmed colonial troops to return to Williamsburg. This frontier conflict triggered the French and Indian War, and Great Britain dispatched regular troops under General Braddock in 1755 to oust the French. Braddock appointed Washington as aide-de-camp and marched for the Monongahela, where the British forces were routed, Braddock was killed, and Washington had two horses shot under him. Later in the year Dinwiddie promoted Washington to colonel and made him commander-in-chief of all Virginia troops. Throughout 1756 and 1757 Washington pursued a defensive policy, fortifying the frontier with twenty-seven stockades, recruiting men, and establishing discipline. In 1758, with the title of brigadier, he accompanied British regulars under General Forbes on the campaign which finally forced the French to abandon Fort Duquesne. With the threat of frontier violence removed, the twenty-six-year-old brigadier resigned his commission and shortly thereafter married the widow Martha Custis and devoted himself to life at Mount Vernon.

George found in Martha "an agreeable Consort for life," and she enjoyed "the pleasant duties of an old-fashioned Virginia house-keeper," describing herself as being "steady as a clock, busy as a bee, and cheerful as a cricket." Washington took seriously his role of stepfather and guardian of Martha's two children, Jacky (John Parke Custis), aged four, and Patsy (Martha Parke Custis), aged two; it was his duty, he wrote, to be "generous and attentive," and he was. Patsy's death at seventeen was an emotional shock to Washington, who wrote that "it is an easier matter to conceive than to describe the distress of this family." Jacky, whom Washington called "a remarkably fine" boy, became something of a problem, caring more for dogs, horses, and guns than for schooling. But when he died in 1781 at the age of twenty-five, after serving in the Virginia militia at Yorktown, Washington virtually adopted two of his four children, George Washington Parke Custis, whose *Recollections* are the source of many of the unprovable legends about Washington, and Eleanor Custis, whom he treated as a daughter. "It has always been my intention . . . ," he wrote in his will, "to consider the grandchildren of my wife in the same light as my own relations."

In 1758 Colonel Washington had been elected to the Virginia House of Burgesses, after unsuccessful attempts in 1755 and 1757. From 1760 to 1774 he served as a justice of Fairfax County, and he was a longtime vestryman of Truro Parish. His experience on the county court and in the colonial legislature molded his views on Parliamentary taxation of the colonies after 1763. He opposed the Stamp Act in 1765, arguing that Parliament "hath no more right to put their hands into my pocket, without my consent, than I have to put my hands into yours for money." As a member of the colonial legislature, he backed nonimportation as a means of reversing British policy in the 1760's, and in 1774 he attended the rump session of the dissolved Assembly which called for a Continental Congress to take united colonial action against the Boston Port Bill and other Intolerable Acts directed against Massachusetts. In July he presided at a county meeting in Alexandria which adopted the Fairfax Resolves he had helped George Mason write. These resolves influenced the adoption of the Continental Association, the plan devised by the First Continental Congress for enforcing nonimportation of British goods. They also proposed the creation in each county of a militia company independent of the Royal Governor's control, the idea from which the Continental Army developed. By May, 1775, Washington, who headed the Fairfax militia company, had been chosen to command the companies of six other counties. The only man in uniform when the Second Continental Congress met less than a month after the battles of Lexington and Concord, he was elected unanimously as commander-in-chief of all Continental forces. For over eight years, from June 15, 1775, until December 23, 1783, he commanded the Continental Army and, after the French alliance of 1778, the combined forces of the United States and France in the War of Independence against Great Britain.

Resigning "with satisfaction" the commission which he had accepted "with diffidence," Washington returned to Mount Vernon at the end of the Revolution. "I have not only retired from all public employments," he wrote Lafayette, "but I am retiring within myself." But there was little time, as he had hoped there would be, for sitting "under the shadow of my own vine and my own fig-tree." Instead, he kept constantly busy, devoting his attention to farming, western land interests, and navigation of the Potomac. In 1785 the Mount Vernon Conference between Virginia and Maryland met to discuss the future of the Potomac, and it set in motion a sequence of events—conventions at Annapolis and Philadelphia—which finally pulled Washington from retirement. He presided at the Federal Convention in 1787 and later supported ratification of the Constitution in order to "establish good order and government and to render the nation happy at home and respected abroad."

After his unanimous choice as President in 1789, Washington helped translate the parchment Constitution into a workable instrument of government: the Bill of Rights was added, as he suggested, out of "reverence for the characteristic rights of freemen"; an energetic executive branch was established, with the executive departments—State, Treasury, and War—evolving into an American cabinet; the federal judiciary was inaugurated; and the Congressional taxing power was utilized to pay the Revolutionary war debt and to establish American credit at home and abroad. As chief executive Washington consulted his Cabinet on public policy, presided over their differences—especially those between Jefferson and Hamilton—with a forebearance that indicated his high regard for his colleagues, and made up his mind after careful consideration of alternatives. He approved the Federalist financial program, both the Tariff and Tonnage duties enacted before Hamilton's appointment and the later Hamiltonian proposals—funding of the national debt, assumption of state debts, the establishment of a Bank of the United States, the creation of a national coinage system, and an excise tax. He agreed with the compromise locating the national capital on the Potomac, supported a national policy for disposition of the public lands, and presided over the expansion of the Federal Union from eleven states (North Carolina and Rhode Island ratified the Constitution after Washington's inaugural) to sixteen (Vermont, Kentucky, and Tennessee were admitted between 1791 and 1796). Washington's role as Presidential leader was of fundamental importance in winning support for the new government's domestic and foreign policies. "Such a Chief Magistrate," Fisher Ames noted, "appears like the pole star in a clear sky. . . . His Presidency will form an epoch and be distinguished as the Age of Washington."

Despite his unanimous elections, Washington expected that the measures of his administration would meet opposition, and they did. By the end of his first term the first American party system was in the early stages of development. When he mentioned the possibility of retirement in 1792, therefore, both Hamilton and Jefferson, though they could agree on little else, agreed that he was "the only man in the United States who possessed the confidence of the whole . . . no other person . . . would be thought anything more than the head of a party." "North and South," Jefferson urged, "will hang together if they have you to hang on."

Washington's second term was dominated by foreign policy considerations. Early in 1793 the French Revolution became the central issue in American politics when France abolished the monarchy, established a republican regime, declared war on Great Britain, and appointed Citizen Genêt Minister to the United States. Determined to keep "our people in peace," Washington issued a proclamation promising "a conduct friendly and impartial towards the belligerent powers." It was a proclamation of neutrality, although the word "neutrality" was not used. His purpose, Washington told Patrick Henry, was "to keep the United States free from political connections with *every* other country, to see them independent of all and under the influence of none. In a word, I want an *American* character, that the powers of Europe may be convinced we act for *ourselves* and not for *others*."

Citizen Genêt was not deterred by the proclamation of neutrality; he outfitted French privateers in American ports and organized expeditions against Florida and Louisiana. For his undiplomatic conduct, the Washington administration requested and obtained his recall. In the midst of the Genêt affair, Great Britain initiated a blockade of France and began seizing neutral ships trading with the French West Indies. Besides violating American neutral rights, the British still held posts in the American Northwest, and the Americans claimed that they intrigued with the Indians against the United States. Frontier provocations, ship seizures, and impressment made war seem almost inevitable in 1794, but Washington sent Chief Justice John Jay to negotiate a settlement of the differences between the two nations. Although Jay's Treaty was vastly unpopular—the British agreed to evacuate the Northwest posts but made no concessions on neutral rights or impressment—Washington overcame his reservations about it, finally accepting it as the best treaty possible at that time. The treaty also paved the way for Thomas Pinckney's negotiations with Spain, now fearful of an Anglo-American entente against her in the Western Hemisphere. Washington happily signed Pinckney's Treaty, which resolved disputes over navigation of the Mississippi, the Florida boundary, and neutral rights.

While attempting to maintain peace with Great Britain in 1794, the Washington administration had to meet the threat of domestic violence in western Pennsylvania. The Whisky Rebellion was a reaction against the first federal excise tax and a direct challenge to the power of the federal government to enforce its laws. After a federal judge certified that ordinary judicial processes could not deal with the opposition to the laws, Washington called out twelve thousand state militiamen "to support our government and laws" by crushing the rebellion. The resistance quickly melted before this display of power, and Washington showed that force could be tempered with clemency by pardoning the insurgents.

Near the end of his second term, Washington decided to retire from office and issued his Farewell Address, warning against "the fury of party spirit" and "the mischiefs of foreign intrigues." Called from retirement in 1798 during the Half-War with France, Washington accepted President Adams' appointment as commander-in-chief with the understanding that he would not take field command until the troops had been recruited and equipped. Since Adams settled the differences with France as Washington had with Great Britain—by diplomatic negotiations—Washington never assumed actual command of the provisional army raised against France. He continued to reside at Mount Vernon, where he died on December 14, 1799, after contracting a throat infection while inspecting his farms.

J.M.S.

servance of which you never suffer'd the least Deviation." phrases, as well as the closing ones about "Sentiments of Honor and Passion for Glory," are touched with the rhetor[ic] chivalry that Virginians have always loved. In his native prov[ince] therefore, and to lesser degree in the colonies at large, Washing[ton] early began to be admired as the perfect soldier.

But he was never the pure militaristic type. Even between yo[uth] and ripe age there was a marked difference—bridging the ti[me] when he assured Fitzhugh that "my inclinations are strongly be[nt] to arms," and the later day when he told his countrymen that th[e] deepest wish of his heart was to see the pestilence of war swep[t] from the earth. Under success, he reached the disenchantment with his first love that another Virginia soldier, Robert E. Lee, dis-covered in defeat. But at all times Washington had other keen interests. One of them was politics. He had been defeated for the House of Burgesses in 1755 and 1757, but won out in 1758 and was re-elected steadily thereafter. With his sense of public respon-sibility, he served from 1764 to 1770 as a justice of Fairfax County. In public life, Washington won everybody's respect, al-though he lacked fluent and brilliant gifts, and as a speaker never outgrew a heavy, somewhat clumsy manner. But his consuming passion was the soil. As a boy of sixteen he had bought, with his first surveying fees, the "Bullskin plantation"—even as a lad in the machine age might acquire his first flivver—and in the course of his life went on to accumulate some 62,000 acres. Mount Vernon, which came to him after the death of his half-brother Lawrence in 1752, was the proudest possession he ever had.

Sowing and reaping, planting and grafting, riding over the springy turf or along fields of green tobacco and rippling grain—these too were esthetic delights. "Agriculture has ever been the most favorite amusement of my life," he wrote after the Revolu-tionary campaigns were done, when visitors coming away from Mount Vernon were thinking that his chief pride was to be known as America's first farmer. A silver cup which he received at this time from an agricultural society in South Carolina, "as a premium for raising the largest jackass," is still displayed among his trophies in the museum of Mount Vernon. His tastes and sports—fishing, hunting deer and pheasants, riding to hounds, acting in amateur

---

DIXON WECTER

✪

President Washington and Parson Weems

Perhaps the reason little folks
 Are sometimes great when they grow taller,
Is just because, like Washington,
 They do their best when they are smaller.
                              —School recitation.

I

In his early twenties George Washington began to be talked about in Europe. In London in 1754, when he was a militiaman of twenty-two, was published the report he had made to Governor Dinwiddie after his journey to Fort Le Boeuf, through a wilderness of snows and black icy streams. He had mapped the country, given a matchcoat and a bottle of rum to an Indian queen, to build good will for England and Virginia against France. Again, in August of that year, readers of the *London Magazine* perused a boyish letter this Washington had written to his half-brother from Great Meadow, after a first skirmish with the French and Indians: "I heard the bullets whistle, and, believe me, there is something charming in the sound." According to Horace Walpole, George II read this letter of his young subject with the comment, "He would not say so, if he had been used to hear many."

In fact, the green soldier's exuberance was short-lived. Before his words were printed he had already tasted the first of many defeats. To the flag of France he had been forced to surrender Fort

Reprinted with the permission of Charles Scribner's Sons from *The Hero in America*, pp. 99–138, by Dixon Wecter. Copyright 1941 by Charles Scribner's Sons.

Necessity, and to sign a paper in which his ignorance of French betrayed him into admitting the "assassination" of an ensign named Jumonville, supposedly a peaceful scout, in the earlier skirmish. Washington had taken no chances with Jumonville, and from a military point of view his act was not unjustified. But in Paris, with great éclat, his captured journal was published after a little judicious doctoring—and "le cruel Washington" became a nine days' wonder. The British of course defended him stoutly, at least until the Revolution, when a Tory printer in New York named Rivington brought forth an epic poem recalling Washington's "assassination" of this fine young Frenchman. Propaganda is always a flexible sword.

The average American today has never heard of Jumonville, or how Washington at a precocious age provoked an international incident. The issue is too complex to fit readily into the Washington legend. Most people, however, know something of his next step into the limelight. That took place with Braddock's defeat in 1755. Popular tradition—always a little less than fair to a future hero's rivals—pictures Braddock as a fool in scarlet, swaggering through the forest, scornful of Washington's warning against ambush until too late. Braddock was a man of honest worth, and also very brave. But Washington, still weak from a bed of fever, was equally brave. Two horses were killed under him, and four bullets tore through his coat. Folklore says the Indians decided he was under the care of the Great Spirit; certainly Washington began to believe in his guiding Providence, holding fast to that faith through the Revolution's darkest days. At this early date, too, the exaggerations of myth entered Washington's life; promptly he had to write home to deny "a circumstantial acct. of my death and dying speech." A glimmer of the theatre already played about him.

Washington's part in salvaging Braddock's shattered troops left him with considerable prestige, especially among native Virginians. Here was a man who had come to the help of professionals from overseas. The Governor made him a colonel, and commander-in-chief of all Virginia troops—some three hundred men, whose task was to defend three hundred miles of frontier. He was clearly Virginia's best home-grown soldier, at a time when the military was supremely important. Thus responsibility settled early upon

his manly shoulders, giving him sober ways. Henceforth, it seemed, he was duty's man.

The British regulars were prone to be jealous of this rising youth, in his spotless buff-and-blue uniform of militia. Some tried to snub him, overriding his authority. To get his rights, Washington had to travel on horseback to Boston in 1756. His budding fame made New Englanders like the Adamses put him down as a Virginian worth watching. Restlessness was in the air, and some day they might need a Southern ally who could fight. Years later, after that day had come, Tories and personal enemies of Washington recalled his youthful friction with the redcoats, and hinted it was the mainspring of his zeal for Independence. Near the close of his Presidency, the editor William Duane sneeringly observed, to Washington, "that had you obtained promotion . . . after Braddock's defeat, your sword would have been drawn against your country." It was the closest that foes could come to impeaching the motives of Washington as patriot.

This young man loved soldiering. The cavalier traditions of Virginia had prepared him for it, as well as the passion for discipline and precision in his own soul. His orders from booksellers, in the years between Fort Necessity and the Revolution, show that he read chiefly two classes of books—those about war and those about practical farming. Young Washington was no saber-rattler, but in the pattern of military life—with its sense of mastery, its quiet planning of objectives, its scrupulosity of code and dress—he discovered an esthetic satisfaction which others found in music or mathematics. He had the serious-minded aristocrat's habit of taking charge of things, of looking after and worrying about those in his charge. Worry early became a trait of Washington's mind. But, with all his frosty young dignity and insistence on perfection, Colonel Washington inspired hero worship among his men. When in December, 1758, they heard he was retiring, in order to marry Mrs. Custis, they drew up a "humble Address" from "your most obedient and affectionate officers," revealing the role of foster father which this stalwart of twenty-six had already established: "In our earliest Infancy you took us under your Tuition, train'd us up in the Practice of that Discipline, which alone can constitute good Troops, from the punctual Ob-

theatricals, eating watermelons on the veranda of Mount Vernon, dancing with a stamina that sometimes lasted for three hours without pause—were those of a leisured rural society. Washington to the American mind has long represented "the country gentleman"—whose portrait by Gilbert Stuart is the perennial trademark of a magazine by that name.

With the passing years, Mount Vernon and Washington's nostalgia for it came to symbolize the purity of his patriotism. From his colonial campaigns, from the Revolutionary War, from eight years of the Presidency, he quit the life of power—the career of professional soldier, of potential dictator—to go back to his farm. Even as his military policy of watchful waiting gave Washington the title of "Fabius," so his character of farmer-patriot stamped him for that classical generation as "Cincinnatus." The ancient Roman left the furrow to take up arms for his country, and then with the selflessness unknown to all dictators, with duty fulfilled returned to the plow. The idea appealed deeply to America's distrust of the military idol, and her frank liking for a man ready to bow before popular self-government. The renunciation crowned the finished task. In the Renaissance, Sir Thomas Elyot in *The Governour,* after meditating on the example of Cincinnatus, had concluded that "nobility" is innate, that it is quite independent of election to office or the trappings of authority. This, Americans came eventually to feel about George Washington. Early and late, from the buckskin wilderness to the magistracy of a new republic, he showed that he used responsibility well. To its abuses he never succumbed. And thus—although the word "democracy" was foreign to his vocabulary—he set the pattern for romantic democracy in the United States. To a world which remembered other self-made leaders of empire like Alexander and Caesar, and even then looked upon the rising star of Bonaparte, this fact made Washington unique. It was the cardinal fact in his herohood. Byron drew that contrast, in writing of

> the first—the last—the best—
> The Cincinnatus of the West,
> Whom envy dared not hate,
> Bequeathed the name of Washington,
> To make man blush there was but one.

II

Certain glacial traits made Washington a rather surprising hero for a race whom Europeans are prone to think nervous and mercurial. Emerson, in 1852, after studying for some days the portrait of Washington that he had hung in his dining room, wrote in his Journal of its "Appalachian strength": "The heavy, leaden eyes turn on you, as the eyes of an ox in a pasture. And the mouth has gravity and depth of quiet, as if this MAN had absorbed all the serenity of America, and left none for his restless, rickety, hysterical countrymen." No doubt, in the noon of Emerson's life America had grown more febrile than in the eighteenth century—but even among his peers Washington was singular in his massiveness of character, his static rather than kinetic energy, his patient endurance and fixity of aim. Beside him, John Adams seemed fretful, Patrick Henry volatile, Thomas Jefferson impulsive. Like a glacier, Washington appeared at times to move slowly and also to be ice-locked in a reticence that inspired more admiration than love. To us, however, his reticence is more baffling than it was to his own time. Sentimentalists, cynics, and psychoanalysts have tried to penetrate Washington's "secret." This age of self-expression often mistakes reticence for apathy, assuming that Washington had no deep emotions or that he was hopelessly repressed. We fail to remember the standard of good form held up to eighteenth-century gentlemen, who practised certain arts of self-effacement now forgotten. And the Southern gentleman, like Washington, though less cramped in his social habits, was more shy of baring his soul than was the introspective Yankee.[1] His diaries—first published in 1925, to reveal the preoccupations of farm and social life, and an infrequency of church attendance that shocked some people—are quite different from the corresponding records of soul-probing, analysis of human motives, and eager pursuit of ideas penned by the great New Englanders. Spiritual nudism would have shocked Washington.

[1] Some excellent remarks by the late Carl Russel Fish, "George Washington, the Man," are in *Transactions Illinois State Historical Society*, 1932, p. 24.

Because of his slow dignity, joined to method, efficiency, and punctuality, Washington never appeared to be hurried. Some thought him a plugger, or downright lazy. But in good time he accomplished all things, with the same irresistibility of a glacier. This shows clearly in his attitude toward the Revolution. Herbert Agar and other moderns have remarked that on May 30, 1765, the day of Patrick Henry's fiery tocsin against George III, in the House of Burgesses, Washington's diary offers only the calm remark, "Peter Green came to me a gardener," and the next day observes, "Cut my clover for hay." They fail to note the fact that he did not even hear Henry's speech, having placidly left Williamsburg for Mount Vernon. But, as his correspondence reveals, he had clean-cut opinions about issues of the day. The Stamp Act he opposed, as a method of picking the citizen's pocket without his consent, but upon the hysterical violence of the Boston Tea Party he looked with disapproval. Similarly in April, 1768, on the day of "the great remonstrance" Washington was absent from the meeting of the Burgesses; he and Posey and other jolly companions were riding after a fox. But ten days later he did set forth for Williamsburg, and in his mind soon crystallized the decision—with a clarity unknown to many of his fellow patriots—that compromise was futile. He was always an authoritarian, to whom the civil power came first. But with single-mindedness Washington changed his sincere allegiance to the King for an equally staunch devotion to American freedom. Abruptly convinced that the Crown no longer fostered liberty in America, he did not hesitate to scrap the lesser for the greater loyalty. In liberty he had a simple, elemental faith, which became inwoven with his religious ideas. It was approved by God, and therefore must prevail. Hence his serenity in disaster, and the morale that Washington—a leader who lacked eloquence and thrilling personal charm—could still infuse into a shaky cause, and into an essentially minority movement that never enlisted more than one-eighth of all able-bodied Americans.[2]

After serving as a Virginia delegate to the First and then the Second Continental Congress, this silent man who sat quietly in uniform was made commander-in-chief on June 15, 1775. The

2 J. Franklin Jameson, *The American Revolution Considered as a Social Movement* (1926), p. 75.

choice was inevitable. Unlike Israel Putnam and other local sons, he was there in the flesh, and Washington's presence was always compelling. He was known to be America's best soldier, a man of solid judgment. He had the prestige of wealth, gained by his own efforts and by marriage. His selection would also consolidate the South behind a cause in which New England lawyers, merchants, and politicians had taken perhaps a too conspicuous part. Tradition says that Washington remarked to Patrick Henry, "This day will be the commencement of the decline of my reputation." He knew how invidious his position was, how brief might be the honeymoon of any leader in a republic. But for the time being, everybody except the secretly envious John Hancock was delighted with this tall, handsome, reassuring leader. Most of the Massachusetts men worked hard for his election. They were impressed with his riches, and his refusal to accept any salary. "There is something charming to me in the conduct of Washington," wrote his nominator, John Adams. "A gentleman of one of the first fortunes upon the continent, leaving his delicious retirement, his family and friends, sacrificing his ease, and hazarding all in the cause of his country!" These words were addressed to Elbridge Gerry, who from far away began to write of him as "the beloved Colonel Washington."

"Under the old elm" of song and story, at Cambridge on July 3, 1775, Washington took command of his troops. The unknown Tory satirist who wrote "The Trip to Cambridge" tried his best to make fun of the new leader, "the country's papa," "all clothed in power and breeches" as he rode up on a dappled donkey. But the arts of caricature—successful enough with the eccentricities of later heroes like Andrew Jackson and Lincoln and Jefferson Davis—fell flat before the smooth, well-groomed dignity of Washington. His features offered as little opportunity to ribald distortion as did those of Robert E. Lee.

It was fortunate that the Massachusetts men who had sponsored Washington were not able to read the fastidious Virginian's opinion, in a letter to Lund Washington, that the New Englanders "are an exceedingly dirty and nasty people." (Yet strangely enough, on August twenty-second in his General Orders, Washington at Cambridge had to reprimand these sons of Puritans for their careless bathing, "running about naked upon the Bridge, whilst passengers, and even Ladies of the first fashion in the neighbourhood, are passing over it.") Later, in 1777, British propaganda produced some forged *Letters from General Washington* in which he was made to praise New England soldiers at the expense of the Southerners—"cool, considerate and sensible, whilst we are all fire and fury"—with the intent of breeding dissension. The other tack might have been far more successful, for the issue of Washington's snobbery toward Yankeedom smoldered through the later years of the War. Meanwhile, Washington's triumph in forcing Howe to evacuate Boston in March, 1776, confirmed him, for a season, as the idol of the Bay State. Harvard made him a Doctor of Letters, and the Massachusetts legislature gave him a public dinner, with an address of thanks, at the Bunch of Grapes tavern.

He began to figure in poetry and drama, with associations of Roman heroism not unlike those of Addison's *Cato*—Washington's favorite play in amateur theatricals, one whose rhetoric he loved to quote.[3] His stiff integrity had a Roman quality, as artists and orators quickly sensed. And the cause for which he fought recalled those patriots who cradled the republicanism of early Rome. Philip Freneau wrote of Washington,

> Bold in the fight, whose actions might have aw'd
> A Roman Hero or a Grecian God.

David Humphreys and Jonathan Mitchell Sewall rhymed in the same vein, their favored epithet being "the god-like Washington," their tone an insistence upon his antique dignity. In John Leacock's turgid play *The Fall of British Tyranny,* written about the time of the fall of Boston, Washington is the majestic *deus ex machina,* though dull of speech in comparison with Ethan Allen, Putnam, and Charles Lee; only after five gouty acts does Washington warm to a little fervor and exclaim, "I have drawn my sword, and never will sheathe it, till America is free, or I'm no more." Patriot artists resented any lukewarm appreciation of Washington's excellence. A Boston play called *The Motley Assembly,* which has been ascribed to that republican bluestocking Mercy

---

3 John C. Fitzpatrick, *George Washington Himself* (1933), pp. 43, 112.

Warren, draws a scene from high life in which Mrs. Flourish
bridles at Captain Aid's toast to "godlike, glorious Washington":

> *Mrs. Flourish.* Why, he is no more than man, Captain Aid.
> *Aid.* Then all mankind beside are less, madam.
> *Mrs. F.* You have not seen all mankind, sir. I believe Mr. Washing-
> ton, or General Washington, if you please, is a very honest, good kind
> of man, and has taken infinite pains to keep your army together, and I
> wish he may find his account in it. But doubtless there are his equals—
> so say no more.
> *Aid.* If you meant that as a compliment, madam, it is really so cold
> a one, that it has made me shiver. I will, therefore, with your leave,
> drop the subject, and take another glass of wine.

Similarly, Francis Hopkinson wrote of a Tory lady who loved to
lisp the titles and dignities of the peerage, "whilst 'Captain A. the
tailor,' 'Colonel B. the tavern-keeper,' and even 'General Washington the farmer,' only created contempt. But I am persuaded, if
some Indian chief, with a long Cherokee or Mohawk name, had
commanded our armies, she would have thought much more
respectably of the American cause." Hopkinson himself, in January, 1777—after Washington had lost New York, but atoned by
the brilliant victories of Trenton and Princeton—wrote of his idol:

> To him the title of Excellency is applied with peculiar propriety. He
> is the best and the greatest man the world ever knew . . . neither
> depressed by disappointment and difficulties, nor elated with a tem-
> porary success. He retreats like a General, and attacks like a Hero.
> Had he lived in the days of idolatry, he had been worshipped as a God.[4]

Devotion to George Washington had already become a cult, a chip
on the shoulder.

To the public at large, and to Congress, Washington's prestige
fluctuated sharply. The withdrawal from Long Island in September, 1776, and the rout at Kips Bay—when, according to an
unreliable tradition begun by the Reverend William Gordon,
Washington in fury snapped his pistol and flourished his sword
against the cowardly Americans, while his aides had to drag him
back from advancing alone against the enemy—cost him some

---

[4] For these two quotations, see F. Hopkinson, *Miscellaneous Essays*
(Philadelphia, 1792), II, 55–56, and I, 120.

public confidence. The loss of Fort Washington, and the retreat through the Jerseys, added to the doubts of those for whom nothing succeeds like success. But through the gathering gloom, on Christmas night, 1776, Washington roused his dispirited army, crossed the Delaware, and fell upon the Hessians, reputed the best soldiers of Europe, with devastating effect. To clinch this victory of Trenton, he struck decisively again at Princeton, before settling into winter quarters. Trenton, though a battle of minor military results, has always stirred the American imagination. The true military hero, whether in success or failure, must have a sense of drama: Nelson and Napoleon both had it in transcendent degree, Lee had more of it than did Grant, Pershing has had almost none. Washington, at Trenton and at Yorktown, showed the careful preparation, electrified by audacity, of which he was capable at his best. An exultant country first sensed that a genius was in command. The ice and snow, the darkness and drunken stupor, the brilliant surprise attack, the panic of a thousand prisoners, make an incomparably good story. Poets quickly warmed to the occasion——

> Where the great chief, o'er Del'ware's icy wave,
> Led the small band, in danger doubly brave,

began the strains of Colonel Humphreys, while the Reverend Wheeler Case wrote:

> A storm of snow and hail the Lord sent down,
> A blessed season this for Washington:
> He now return'd, and thro' the storm he press'd,
> And caught twelve hundred Hessians in their nest.

Today, the episode is inseparable from Leutze's painting. Its accuracy, of course, leaves much to be desired. . . .[5]

Washington's glory was now on the crest of the wave. Congress, regaining its self-assurance after a hasty evacuation from Philadelphia, gave him the powers of a dictator for six months. Recruits now began to arrive in a steady stream. Washington tried to season this green timber into hardiness during the winter and spring. But summer and early autumn brought the wane. In September, 1777

---

[5] William Carlos Williams, *In the American Grain* (1925), p. 142.

—after Brandywine, most criticized of all Washington's maneuvers—his prestige plummeted to a new low. His temperament, like
that of Stonewall Jackson and Grant and other born soldiers, had a
curious rhythm: of inspiration and fierce energy followed by the
doldrums, of magnetic rages succeeded by moods of numbness.
That Washington could not always be at his best the public failed
to understand. Washington himself, fortunately, made no fetish of
success or omen of failure. He took both in his stride. Up to
Yorktown, in fact, the successes in his life were outnumbered by
the failures—as a young fighter in the French and Indian War
who never won a real battle, as a man disappointed in his dream of
empire-building in the West, as the loser of New York and
Philadelphia during the first two years of the Revolution. But he
had risen to prestige over failures. His doggedness, lack of bitterness against men and circumstance, and inner serenity were reassuring. Those who knew him best shared Washington's own faith
in himself. But those who knew him little, or whose eyes were
jaundiced by envy, began to doubt.

"O Heaven!" prayed petulant John Adams in his diary, "grant us
one great soul! One leading mind would extricate the best cause
from that ruin which seems to await the want of it." Even before
Washington's defeats at Brandywine and Germantown, on the
floor of Congress Adams had rebuked "the superstitious veneration that is sometimes paid to General Washington," with allusions
to graven images that came naturally to any scion of the Puritans.
Massachusetts, indeed, had heard whispers of Washington's private criticism of her soldiers. Now she turned against him. In the
later autumn of 1777, after the contrast of Gates's lucky victory at
Saratoga, Washington's standing dropped to the lowest in his
whole career. Among his subordinate officers, in Congress, and in
Anglo-American circles abroad, a dark intricate plot took shape,
the so-called Conway Cabal. To some it meant the elevation of
Horatio Gates to commander-in-chief, to others it hinted appease-
ment with England and a craven peace. And to all involved in
these backstairs intrigues, Adamses and Lees and other names
since revered in American patriotism, it promised the humiliation
of George Washington. Eventually the scheme collapsed, through
bungling and bad timing. But under fire Washington had remained

as calm, almost as free from vindictiveness, as did Lincoln in the most crucial days of the Civil War. And Washington, it might be remembered, lacked the safety valve of Lincoln's laughter. In a spirit of ironic politeness he treated with his enemies. Washington's naturally hot temper—which a few men saw, and others inferred from his sandy red hair and steel blue eyes—had been sublimated in the same school of discipline that had changed his innate vanity into a passion for perfection.

Through the same winter of 1777–1778 Washington and his men endured the ordeal of Valley Forge. Chilly smoky huts, half-starved and dying men, and bloody footprints in the snow make this episode unforgettable. Orators, artists, and pageant-makers cherish the name of Valley Forge, and visitors long ago made it a national shrine. Here, in Washington Chapel, services are always held on February twenty-second. The popular mind supposes that these hardships were necessary to the cost of the Revolution. But historians know better. Washington's soldiers starved and shivered, while food and clothing were abundant, largely because Congress quibbled with the Commissary Department.[6] The folklore of heroism is selective: it has chosen to forget the stupidity of Congress, as well as the very real but unromantic epidemic of the itch which plagued the continentals even more miserably than the lack of shoes. The true story of Valley Forge is fine enough, but myth has chosen to embroider it. Washington's known acts at Valley Forge—such as taking great pains for the health and cleanliness of his men, ordering inoculation for smallpox in the winter and the shaving of beards in the spring, arguing his men's welfare in patient letters to Congress, encouraging amateur theatricals and playing at wickets with his officers—are far more characteristic of the man than the one story everybody knows. This is the yarn that a Quaker, named Potts, came upon Washington on his knees in the snow, and listened while the commander prayed long and fervently. Parson Weems (whose veracity will be examined later) first told the incident in a newspaper article on March 12, 1804, in the Washington *Federalist,* called "The importance of religion." It caught the public eye, and was reprinted elsewhere. Seeing that he

---

[6] L. C. Hatch, *The Administration of the American Revolutionary Army* (1904), p. 122.

had a good story Weems incorporated it into the sixth edition of his life of Washington, in 1808. Henceforth it has been indestructible. That Washington apparently never knelt to pray even in church, but remained standing, did not affect the legend. It was carved in stone in a prominent place over the old Sub-Treasury building in New York City, and only a decade ago a federal postage stamp showed Washington on his knees at Valley Forge. On the latter occasion Doctor Isaac R. Pennypacker, chairman of the Valley Forge Park Commission, made a public protest against this commemoration of a falsehood—but it did no good.[7] . . .

During the last phase of the Revolution, homage to Washington followed a rising curve. "Every lip dwells on his praise," wrote young Colonel Alexander Hamilton in 1778, "for even his pretended friends (for none dare to acknowledge themselves his enemies) are obliged to croak it forth." In that year, in Francis Bailey's *Lancaster Almanack* for the coming twelvemonth, he was first called "The Father of His Country." In 1780 in London was published, "under the express sanction of the Duchess of Devonshire," *A Poetical Epistle to George Washington, Esquire*, by Charles Henry Wharton, an American Catholic priest living in England. The proceeds were to go for the relief of American prisoners of war. To Washington it offered a manly if stilted tribute—

> Great without pomp, without ambition brave,
> Proud not to conquer fellow-men, but save. . . .
> Such be my country!—what her sons should be,
> O, may they learn, great Washington, from thee!

More remarkable than the poem was the fact of its publication in a hostile capital. In 1781, Washington's birthday was publicly celebrated for the first time, when the French army paraded in his honor. The capture of Yorktown, the following October, crowned Washington's military career. That historic surrender contains two touches characteristic of Washington, which painting and popular history sometimes remember. The first was his appointment of a substitute to receive Cornwallis' sword, when the British commander on a plea of illness sent it by a substitute. Knowing the

[7] *Pennsylvania Magazine of History and Biography*, LVI, p. 105.

value of what the French term protocol, in setting the dignity of the new Republic, Washington insisted always upon wringing the last modicum of respect from the reluctant British. The second was his command that Cornwallis' sword be returned to the defeated general—a touch of gallantry, as we shall see, which folklore later invented for Grant at Appomattox.

For the next fifteen years, very few words were printed or spoken in public, in the United States, against George Washington. "All panegyrick is vain, and language too feeble to express our ideas of his greatness," exclaimed the *Pennsylvania Journal* soon after Yorktown. Everywhere he was hailed as "The Savior of His Country." Banquets, receptions, balls, triumphal arches, and the scattering of flowers followed him from Virginia to Philadelphia. In that city, where General and Mrs. Washington spent the winter, crowds cheered him through the streets whenever he left his door. Seeing too little of him, they gathered before Charles Willson Peale's house, where the painter had made an exhibit of "transparencies" to honor "the conquering Hero."[8] . . . In December of that year [1783], at Annapolis, on the night before Washington resigned his commission, the Maryland legislature gave a grand ball in his honor. Here Washington received a minor tribute—perhaps an anticlimax after the rhetoric of poets and divines—but one which a gallant Virginia gentleman, a lover of dancing and the company of fair women, may have found more to his taste. All the ladies asked permission to dance with him, and so, with each in turn, the tall grave soldier glided about the floor of the state-house—as an eyewitness says, so that every one "could get the touch of him."

III

One who dips into the panegyric of Washington, between the end of the War and his return to public life in 1787 as president of the Constitutional Convention, gains little impression of the man himself. All is unreal, nebulous, ecstatic. He remains "the godlike Washington."

[8] Quoted by N. W. Stephenson and W. H. Dunn, *George Washington* (1940), II, 172–173.

> Yea,—Fame shall ope for thee her hundred Gates
> While at her Shrine the aspiring Hero waits.
>   E'en to the frigid Pole
>   So far thy Deeds of Virtue shall extend,

he was assured in 1784 by a nameless poet whose tribute, in an unpublished manuscript, is now buried among the Washington Papers in the Library of Congress. Song-writers composed marches in his honor (one apparently converting "General Wayne's March" into "Washington's March") and painters visited Mount Vernon constantly. In a well-known letter in 1785, Washington wrote philosophically to Francis Hopkinson, who had been the means of setting another portraitist on his trail:

> *In for a penny, in for a pound,* is an old adage. I am so hackneyed to the touches of the painter's pencils, that I am now altogether at their beck; and sit 'like Patience on a monument' whilst they are delineating the lines of my face. It is a proof, among many others, of what habit and custom can accomplish. At first I was as impatient and as restive under the operation as a colt is of the saddle. The next time I submitted very reluctantly, but with less flouncing. Now no dray horse moves more readily to his thill than I do to the painter's chair.

Houdon, Sharpless, Charles Willson Peale, Gilbert Stuart, and other artists tried to capture the Washington of these latter years. But even here, in the physical man, he began to suffer the distortion of art. Between 1756 and 1790 he was slowly losing his teeth (frequent toothaches adding to his irritability during the Revolution), until all were gone and artificial dentures took their place. Gilbert Stuart's Washington, by far the most familiar image, owes its pursed severity of lips to these false teeth and to the cotton padding by which the painter tried in vain to restore the structure of gums and mouth. In early portraits Washington was not so grim, even though less brilliantly drawn than by the pink and gray suavity of Stuart. His visage then lacked what a newspaper wag called "the letter-box mouth." The effect of these teeth, and of Stuart's style, upon the Washington of legend is hard to exaggerate. Was he, indeed, a dour man?

"Let your countenance be pleasant but in serious Matters Somewhat grave," Washington as a boy had written, copying in his meticulous hand the well-known *Rules of Civility,* the Emily Post of his day. Gravity, deepened by cares, did make up a large part of Washington's nature. His reserved air, like his big-boned and masterful appearance, stamped him in any company as a silent leader. In comparison with Washington, some other American idols seem almost frivolous—like Jefferson with his gossip, or Lincoln with his droll stories. Washington's majesty no doubt concealed a measure of shyness, even as his deafness in later years encouraged an aloofness of manner. There was a defensive touch in both. He was prone to be forthright rather than tactful, strong of will rather than flexible of mind. He was far less the expedient man, the politician, than were Franklin and Jefferson and even Lincoln.

Washington's rigidity sprang in part from his aristocratic frankness and in part from his scrupulous honesty. Nothing ever made him more furious than an anonymous charge, in February, 1789, on the eve of inauguration, that he had located and laid claim to some of the Fairfax lands as his own. Recent debunking biographers, with very scant success, have tried to make him out a sharp businessman. The fairest evidence confirms Washington's aide Tilghman, who called him "the honestest man that I believe ever adorned human nature."

Most eulogists, in fact, have praised his character far more often than his intellect. With sincere modesty, Washington himself said he had inherited "inferior endowments from nature." In old age he tended to bore bright young men, even while they respected him deeply. Alexander Hamilton could not help comparing his own lightning calculations with the tortoise pace of Washington's mind. But, as in the fable, the tortoise had a free will to get there. In 1814 that shrewd observer, if not steady friend, Thomas Jefferson, wrote a private estimate of Washington as he knew him. "His mind was great and powerful, without being of the very first order," said Jefferson. He described him as brave, calm, deliberate, prudent, and just; a man of action rather than of reflection; a fluent writer of letters but a poor speaker. And, Jefferson added, he was the possessor of a heart "not warm in its affections."[9]

About Washington's coldness there are several opinions. One often hears the myth that he had no friends, and that through the

[9] Jefferson to Walter Jones, January 2, 1814.

Revolution he never smiled. Fact contradicts these statements.
They have arisen, no doubt, because his public life was and is
much better known than his private life. His best friends—the
Fairfaxes of his youth, Doctor James Craik and Benjamin Harrison in his middle age, Lafayette, Tilghman, Humphreys, and
Alexander Hamilton as the protégés of his riper years—were men
who shared something of Washington's personal reticence. More
casual acquaintances he held at arm's length. Virtually nobody
dared to call him George, up to the debunking biographers of the
twentieth century. A familiar story tells that Gouverneur Morris in
1787 boasted to Alexander Hamilton that "he could be as familiar
with Washington as with any of his other friends." To win his bet
of a supper and wine, Morris walked up to Washington at the next
reception, "bowed, shook hands, laid his left hand on Washington's shoulder, and said, 'My dear General, I am very happy to see
you look so well!' Washington withdrew his hand, stepped suddenly back, fixed his eye on Morris for several minutes with an
angry frown, until the latter retreated abashed, and sought refuge
in the crowd. The company looked on in silence. At the supper,
which was provided by Hamilton, Morris said, 'I have won the bet,
but paid dearly for it, and nothing could induce me to repeat
it.' "[10] Later times have felt a similar diffidence in striking an
attitude of intimacy toward Washington. His awesome character
has either frozen affection into icy admiration, or else has inspired,
by way of relief, the folksy tales of Weems or the slanders of
cynicism.

Yet in private life Washington played a different part, often
ignored by legend. From camp in 1777 a Virginia lady wrote to
one of her friends, that when "General Washington throws off the
Hero and takes up the chatty agreeable Companion, he can be
downright impudent sometimes, such impudence, Fanny, as you
and I like."[11] An unpublished letter from Washington to General
Walter Stewart, now in the possession of Mr. Philip Schuyler
Church, closes with a typical bit of Washington raillery: "Compli-
ments to Mrs. Stewart—tell her that if she dont think of me often, I
shall not easily forgive her & will scold & beat her soundly too—at

[10] James Parton, *Life of Thomas Jefferson* (1874), p. 369.
[11] Quoted by Fitzpatrick, p. 446.

49

Picquet—the next time I see her." The badinage is not brilliant, but at least is meant well. It belongs to the informal Washington, who loved to play cards and tease the ladies decorously, who spent great sums on silver lace for himself and toys for his stepchildren, who had an epicure's palate for madeira and at one stage of his life smoked long white clay pipes. He was no Puritan, no humorless abstraction of virtues—although his clerical biographers, and the schoolmasters of New England, did their best to make him so for several generations.

An anonymous writer in 1790 found that Washington's smile "was extraordinarily attractive."[12] Of his laughter we hear almost nothing. His sense of humor was neither jovial nor rich in vein; Washington was no Ben Franklin. But the conventional portrait has robbed him of such as he possessed. Among the few contemporaries of Washington who guessed that he enjoyed comic stories, and wrote him the good ones that came along, was the Benedict Arnold of happier days; later, of course, there was no time for comedy. In letters to Joseph Reed and a few other trusted friends, Washington indulged the dry irony, sometimes curling into sarcasm, which best expressed the humor of his mind. "Valiant New Englanders" who aspired to be "chiminey-corner heroes," or the antics of George III, "the best of Kings, so anxiously disposed to promote the welfare of his American subjects," were topics to which Washington's irony warmed. After the War, the one subject and virtually the only one upon which Washington wrote with humor was the breeding of jackasses. Like most agriculturists he had a Rabelaisian streak. In 1785 the King of Spain sent him a prize jackass, which Washington christened "Royal Gift." Through the months that followed, Washington regaled his good friends and relatives—Bushrod Washington, William Fitzhugh, Jr., Richard Sprigg, and Lafayette—with amusing bulletins on the conduct of this animal. A typical passage is that to Fitzhugh, on May 15, 1786:

At present, tho' young, he follows what one may suppose to be the example of his late Royal Master, who cannot, tho' past his grand climacteric, perform seldomer or with more majestic solemnity than he

12 *Ibid.,* p. 148.

does. However I have hopes that when he becomes a little better acquainted with republican enjoyments, he will amend his manners and fall into our custom of doing business; if the case should be otherwise, I shall have no disinclination to present his Catholic Majesty with as valuable a present as I received from him.

Similarly to Sprigg, on June 28, the solemn husband of petite Martha Washington wrote:

> I feel myself much obliged by your polite offer of the first fruits of your Jenny. Tho' in appearance quite unequal to the match, yet, like a true female, she was not to be terrified at the disproportionate size of her paramour, and having renewed the conflict twice or thrice, it is to be hoped the issue will be favourable.[13]

But these aspects of Washington—the ironist on one hand, the broad jester on the other—are unknown to the average American, although he has some glimmerings of the same qualities in Franklin and Lincoln. Officially, then, Washington is denied a sense of humor.

With Washington's domestic relationships, folklore, rumor, and officious meddling began to deal as soon as he became famous. Curiosity has continued ever since. . . .

The public also wants to know, who were the loves of George Washington? One painter, of the conventional school, shows Washington and the young widow Martha Custis in love at first sight, standing by the mantelpiece in sedate adoration of each other, while her two darling children play on the floor. But Washington's match in 1759 with her whom he called "an agreable Consort," the richest widow in Virginia as the realists never let us forget, is too bromidic for many tastes. Long ago it became sport to hang illicit passions upon him, the coldest and stateliest of American heroes. This began in London, in *The Gentleman's Magazine* for September, 1775. An authentic letter from General Benjamin Harrison to Washington, dated July 21, 1775, had been intercepted by the British and published correctly in the London *Daily Advertiser*. It was a dullish political news-letter, and some unknown writer for *The Gentleman's Magazine* decided to spice it

[13] John C. Fitzpatrick, ed., *The Writings of George Washington*, 39 vols. (Washington, D.C., 1931–1944), XXVIII, 426–427 and 471.

up, for republication, by the insertion of a paragraph which is not found in the original text as still preserved in official British archives. This paragraph made Harrison tell how he had lately met "pretty little Kate, the washerwoman's daughter . . . and but for the cursed antidote to love, Sukey, I have fitted her for my General against his return." Later, she became an octoroon slave-girl, whom Jefferson or Hamilton was proposing to share with Washington. In still other versions, Washington offers her as a dainty morsel to Jefferson or Hamilton or Lafayette. Even today, many people claim to know somebody who has seen the original letter. Thus propaganda echoes along the whispering-galleries of time. One of the recent debunkers of Washington, the businessman and amateur scholar William E. Woodward, swallowed this forgery—with the guileful comment, "Fitted her for what? for doing the laundry, of course."

In 1776 a pamphlet printed in London by one J. Bew, also grounded in forgery, stated that Washington had a Tory sweetheart named Mary Gibbons. She lived in Jersey, and the General was rowed across the Hudson every night by a discreet aide-de-camp. And there are at least three more canards, without the smallest benefit of proof. One declares that Washington at the age of eighteen left Virginia to go to Barbados with his consumptive half-brother because George was "in trouble." In his absence a neighbor girl bore his child, a boy whose surname was Posey. The proof is that Washington helped to pay the schooling expenses of a lad named Posey. But the case is somewhat weakened when we find that he gave such assistance to three Posey boys, and also to their sister Milly, as well as to at least five other deserving children. Were all these Washington's offspring? Then indeed, as has been suggested, a new meaning enters into the title Father of His Country. Still another yarn, often repeated but seldom printed, states that on this trip to Barbados in 1751 Washington, instead of running away from "trouble," ran into it. He had an affair with a married woman, and begat Alexander Hamilton, who, as everyone knows, was a bastard. The fact that Hamilton was born at Nevis in 1757 is not easy to explain. Stories of Washington's illegitimate son or sons seem to be pure fabrication; they spring either from political malice, or from the circumstance that Lund Washington, sometime manager of Mount Vernon, did have an illegitimate son, who lived in another state, and was said to resemble the Washingtons.[14] Medical men are interested in a youthful attack of mumps which may have rendered George Washington sterile for life. A final story, perhaps the most wanton of all, states that Washington's fatal illness was the result of his assignation in the snows of December with an overseer's wife. It resembles one of the earlier innuendoes of General Charles Lee, about Washington's liberties with his underlings at Mount Vernon. General Lee, who was something of a traitor and a coward, and had borne Washington's searing rage at Monmouth, had good reason to dislike his commander.

Many admirers of Washington, while rejecting these scandals with a shudder, are romantic enough to play up other stories whose texture is thin as moonshine. In 1748 young Washington wrote a letter mentioning his attraction to some "Low Land Beauty," whose identity is unknown. But at least a dozen Virginia families claim her as ancestress, telling how Washington courted her in vain. His banter about a little girl named Betsy Fauntleroy, and his visit in 1756 to Mary Philipse among the Knickerbocker gentry, have been made into fervent love affairs. A supposed letter from Washington to Sally Cary Fairfax, wife of his best friend, dated September 12, 1758, has caused excitement for two generations. It was printed in the New York *Herald* on March 30, 1877, and sold at auction the next day. The manuscript has never been heard of since, and no competent scholar ever examined it.* Its content is not very sensational. The writer makes "an honest confession of a simple Fact," namely that he is in love with a "lady known to you." Some have made the coy inference that this is the recipient herself, though others point out that he may mean his fiancée Martha Custis. Young Washington did admire the charming Mrs. Fairfax, and wrote her chatty letters from the frontier, touched here and there with a stiff style of compliment. And in old

---

[14] For an excellent résumé of the subject, see John C. Fitzpatrick, *The George Washington Scandals* (Alexandria, Va., 1929).

* The manuscript has been recently rediscovered and is now in the Houghton Library at Harvard University. It is printed in full in James Thomas Flexner, *George Washington: The Forge of Experience, 1732–1775* (Boston, 1965), pp. 197–199 [ed.].

age, on May 16, 1798, when she had long been living in England as the toast of London and Bath, he wrote her a letter speaking of "those happy moments the happiest in my life which I have enjoyed in your company." This nostalgia for the old days of visiting between Mount Vernon and Belvoir has been translated, by the romantic, into a sunset avowal of his *grande passion*. It has not been noticed before that, some years earlier, on February 27, 1785, Washington penned almost the same phrase to the lady's husband, George William Fairfax:

> But alas! Belvoir is no more! I took a ride there the other day to visit the ruins. . . . When I viewed them, when I considered that the happiest moments of my life had been spent there, when I could not trace a room in the house (now all rubbish) that did not bring to my mind the recollection of pleasing scenes, I was obliged to fly from them.[15]

In the entire record of Washington's friendship with the Fairfaxes there is nothing more incriminating than the passages here cited. Yet Mrs. Sally Nelson Robins, National Historian of the Colonial Dames, has written: "I consider his early romances but zephyrs to this one crimson whirlwind passion of his life."[16] Bernard Faÿ, that versatile Frenchman, in 1931 wrote a life of Washington built largely around Sally, "the queen of his thoughts," who "could converse in French" and taught him grace. She coddled him in illness, met "the wild surge of his heart" with wise understanding and a little teasing, and remained always "the great love" of his life. Frustrated and ever dreaming of Sally, Washington became a man of immense reserves and silences. Rupert Hughes likewise made much of the heartstricken man who had fallen desperately in love with his best friend's wife. In 1932 a whole novel, Bernie Babcock's *The Heart of Washington*, was devoted to the subject. But it, at least, did not claim to be other than fiction. The apparent truth of the matter is that Washington enjoyed the society of pretty women, polished the art of courtliness like a true Virginia gentle-

---

[15] *Writings of Washington* (Bicentennial ed.), XXVIII, 83. This still unpublished volume is here cited by kind permission of the editor, the late Dr. Fitzpatrick. See also N. W. Stephenson, "The Romantics and George Washington," *American Historical Review*, October 1933, pp. 274–283.

[16] *Love Stories of Famous Virginians* (Richmond, 1925), p. 21.

man, and found a satisfactory though hardly inspiring wife in
Martha Custis. In the major concerns of his life, it appears,
Washington was not much influenced by women. But to some, this
is a disappointing story.

About an equally personal matter, the religion of Washington,
there was speculation in his lifetime and much fabrication afterward. A weakness for lying is the occupational disease of many
clergymen—as the conduct of Weems, Jonathan Boucher, Bishop
Meade, and others bears witness, regarding Washington. Such men
may have thought that tinkering with truth, in a good cause,
carried its own absolution. We shall see the same temptation in
preachers who knew Lincoln, Grant and other unchurchly heroes.
Many spurious prayers have been written for Washington.[17] Baptists and other sectarians have claimed that he was immersed in the
Schuylkill, or sometimes the Delaware, River. One story tells how
when the army was encamped at Morristown he called on the
Presbyterian dominie, and asked to receive "the Lord's Supper" at
its semiannual observance: " 'Though a member of the Church of
England, I have no exclusive partialities.' The Doctor reassured
him of a cordial welcome, and the General was found seated with
the communicants the next Sabbath."[18] Ironically enough, Washington seems never to have received the Sacrament even in the
Episcopal Church. When his Philadelphia pastor scolded him
indirectly in a sermon, for this omission, Washington never again
"came on the morning of Sacrament Sunday."[19] Through all the
trials of his life Washington steadily believed that Providence
helped him. His diary shows that he attended church more often
in times of stress than of calm. His sense of truth, honor, and
justice were bound up with religion, although contrary to myth he
appears not to have been a deeply spiritual man. Beyond these
statements one cannot go. In public addresses he alluded to God,
but never mentioned Christ. How much of orthodox Christianity

[17] See Fitzpatrick, *George Washington Himself*, p. 528, n. 4 to Chap.
LXI; also R. Hughes, *George Washington*, I, Appendix II, "The Spurious
Prayers."
[18] Related in W. Hunt's *American Anecdotes* (1830), I, 166–167, on the
authority of Dr. David Hosack's *Memoir of DeWitt Clinton*.
[19] Quoted by P. L. Ford, *The True George Washington* (16th ed., 1896),
p. 82.

he accepted or rejected is Washington's secret. Here again his reticence baffles curiosity.

He was, however, singularly tolerant for his times. In drawing up instructions for the expedition against Canada in 1775, he forbade any ridicule of "Popery" among the French Canadians, or indulgence in that favorite Protestant sport of burning the Pope in effigy. "While we are contending for our own Liberty, we should be very cautious of violating the Rights of Conscience in others, ever considering that God alone is the judge of the Hearts of men and to him only, in this case, they are answerable."[20] On various occasions he attended the worship of Catholics, Presbyterians, Congregationalists, Lutherans, Dutch Reformed, and other sectarians. Yet Washington's old-time eulogists, who worked so hard to make him by their separate lights an orthodox Christian, curiously failed to pay homage to Washington the liberal. Not until the Bicentennial speeches and pamphlets of 1932 was much appreciation given to this trait.

IV

So much for the character of the living Washington. The panegyrics, myths, and misstatements already sprouting about it help us, perhaps, to understand the last decade of his life. These years saw the extremes of apotheosis and abuse. Only Lincoln among American heroes can match the full diapason of public emotions, from an angelic choir to hymns of hate, which Washington inspired.

From the green acres of Mount Vernon he was called in 1787 to the Constitutional Convention in Philadelphia. As the First Citizen of the Republic, he was promptly chosen its President. Washington's immense weight of approval had much to do with the ratification of the Constitution. It was inevitable, too, that he should be summoned to fill the first Presidency of the Republic. Years before, with horror, he had rejected Colonel Nicola's proposal of a military coup which should overthrow the politicians and give him a crown. To Washington, the civil was ever superior to the military

[20] Quoted by J. C. Fitzpatrick, *George Washington and Religion* (Bicentennial Pamphlet No. 5), p. 6.

power. Now, when the honor came in constitutional guise and with unanimous acclaim, he accepted it with the misgivings of a tired, ill, debt-ridden man. It was his purpose and duty to build prestige for the office. Washington's versatility was thus put to its final test. To his daring in planning the Revolution, and his tenacity in winning it, was now added the demand for his judgment and political skill in shaping the new nation. If he had failed at any of the three tests, his herohood would have been badly damaged if not destroyed.

With vast popular enthusiasm he was greeted en route to his inauguration, in the spring of 1789. Triumphal arches were erected, roses strewn in his path by girls dressed in white, and lyrics sung to Handel's "See the Conquering Hero Comes" and other tunes. The capital, New York City, gave him the first great ovation of the many in her history. When he took the oath of office, salutes were fired with such gusto that broken panes jingled merrily from scores of shopwindows. A silversmith named Forbes, whose thrift got the best of him, ran from his shop and begged the captain of artillery to cease firing. "Who," was the reply, "would refuse a salvo of artillery on such an occasion for a few paltry squares of window glass?"[21] A Boston girl wrote home:

> I have seen him! and though I had been entirely ignorant that he was arrived in the city, I should have known at a glance that it was General Washington: I never saw a human being that looked so great and noble as he does. I could fall down on my knees before him.[22]

A tour through New England in the autumn of 1789, and one through the South in 1791, offered contact with popular opinion by "a swing round the circle" such as later Presidents have made. Washington's diary shows his imperturbable cheerfulness under mass greeting; but in comparison with his notes on soils, harbors, and fortifications, little space is devoted to the songs of welcome, poems, dinners, and flower-strewings. Other things were more vital than the breath of cheers. With more than a touch of the aristocrat's pride, he later described himself as "a mind who always

21 *New York Spectator*, April 30, 1839, interview with Captain Van Dyck.
22 I. N. P. Stokes, *The Iconography of Manhattan Island* (1915 et seq.), V, 1242–1245.

walked on a straight line . . . without seeking any indirect or left-handed attempts to acquire popularity."[23] His own gauge of perfection, for George Washington, was more exacting than the public's.

As the first President, Washington was an object of curiosity. The people did not know what a President should be like, and often referred to him as "His Majesty." Washington in turn tended to be cold and stiff on state occasions; once, at least, he was publicly criticized for not bowing in the approved way.[24] His conduct of public affairs—the Indian problem, the Whisky Rebellion, Jay's treaty, and other issues—was firm and generally sagacious. With more tact than might have been anticipated, he maintained for several years the equilibrium of two brilliant but mutually hostile personalities in his Cabinet, Jefferson and Hamilton. Later, the teetering balance was lost. Jefferson secretly egged on Freneau and other journalists to attack the President, who in Jefferson's opinion was growing rigidly conservative, yielding with age to a kind of spiritual arteriosclerosis. In consequence, Washington began to lean heavily upon Hamilton as the staff of his weary steps. He accepted Hamilton's financial views, and ultimately submitted the draft of his Farewell Address to Hamilton's editorship. In a sense, he had become a partisan.

So-called liberals now felt that the Republic had outgrown Washington, that he was unable to keep pace with the march of democracy. The French Revolution he detested. Its minister Genêt, arriving in 1793, stirred masses of Americans to such frenzy that, as John Adams later recalled, "ten thousand people in the streets of Philadelphia day after day *threatened to drag Washington out of his house* and to effect a revolution in the government." Washington's second inaugural, in that year, was almost scandalously flat in comparison with his first.[25] Yet Washington, the supreme military hero, achieved probably the greatest moral victory of his career in 1795 in resisting the foolish war with Britain for which so many Americans were clamoring. He knew how disastrous another war and a military dictatorship would be to the fledgling

[23] *Writings* (Ford ed.), XIV, 143, under date January 20, 1799.
[24] Stephenson and Dunn, II, 269.
[25] Edward Stanwood, *A History of the Presidency* (1906), p. 41.

nation. Needless to say, this act stirred none of the old applause that had greeted Trenton and Yorktown. Only in retrospect does it seem great. At the time it was charged, by Jefferson and others, that Washington had sold out to England. Jay's treaty, whose shortcomings Washington saw as clearly as any but whose benefits he appreciated, earned hisses for the administration. The President himself, bearing the brunt, wrote of "such exaggerated and indecent terms as could scarcely be applied to a Nero, a notorious defaulter, or even to a common pickpocket."[26] This was the ingratitude of republics. In 1796 from Paris, Thomas Paine sent over his *Letter to George Washington*. He ridiculed "the pompous encomiums he so liberally pays to himself," and dismissed Washington's Revolutionary services as "the Fabian system of *doing nothing*. The *nothing* part can be done by anybody . . . he has not the talent of inspiring ardour in an army." In public and private relations, said Paine, Washington's chief traits were apathy and ungratefulness; the President was unwilling to help either France or Thomas Paine, who had languished awhile in the dungeons of the Terror. Among the posthumous papers of this firebrand was found "Advice to a statuary who is to execute the statue of Washington":

> Take from the mine the coldest, hardest stone,
> It needs no fashion: it is Washington.
> But if you chisel, let the stroke be rude,
> And on his heart engrave—Ingratitude.

Benjamin Franklin Bache, inspired by family resentment of Washington's supposed coolness to Franklin, attacked the President viciously in his newspaper the *Aurora*. "If ever there was a period for rejoicing, this is the moment," he announced in March, 1797, when Washington retired from office. "Every heart in unison with the freedom and happiness of the people, ought to beat high with exultation that the name of WASHINGTON from this day ceases to give a currency to political iniquity, and to legalize corruption." On the floor of Congress, while a committee was drafting a graceful reply to the Farewell Address, a group of dissenters (including the newly elected Andrew Jackson) sturdily refused to vote their

[26] *Writings* (Ford ed.), XIII, 76, 231.

thanks to Washington, indulging remarks on his "royal progresses" and snobbish delusions of grandeur. With the exception of Andrew Johnson, says one historian, "no President ever went out of office so loaded with odium as Washington."[27]

With far more weariness than resentment Washington returned to Mount Vernon. He had always driven himself too hard, and was now worn out. It was the good fortune of Lincoln the hero to die in office, at the high tide of success; but Washington's good fortune was to survive past his eight years of office, so that none could ever accuse him of planning to be a dictator. He thus closed a career, as soldier, counsellor, and statesman, that has influenced the pattern of American life more than that of any other man in history. "I am not afraid to go," he whispered in the anguish of a hard death, on December 14, 1799. . . .

The government ordered a day of mourning in all Christian churches, between Washington's death and his birthday in 1800. Memorial services are known to have been held in nearly two hundred towns, from Maine to Savannah and as far west as Lexington, Kentucky. Hundreds of tributes—newspaper obituaries, orations, essays, acrostics—found their way into print.[28] Before the Massachusetts legislature, Fisher Ames likened Washington to the purest and best heroes of antiquity. Seeking to crown him with martyrdom William Beers recalled, to the citizens of Albany, that Washington had once more accepted command of the American Army, in 1798, when trouble with France was brewing: "He came, my fellow-citizens—to die in your defence." Some praised him for "scrupulous accuracy [in] accounting for every cent that has ever passed through his hands"; others lauded his industry, his modesty, his selflessness in forswearing "the glow-worm glories of a Crown." The orator of Harvard College, Doctor Tappan, proclaimed that he belonged to the company "of GODS UPON EARTH." Timothy Dwight of Yale praised his self-sufficiency, citing as a rather curious example that in dying "General Washington closed his own eyes." . . . In the South, the land of classical oratory, Washington was likened most frequently to Cincinnatus, less often

[27] Moncure D. Conway, *Life of Thomas Paine* (1892), II, 176–177.
[28] Some 440 titles are given by Margaret B. Stilwell, *Washington Eulogies* (1916).

to Leonidas and Fabius. At Alexandria his old neighbors assembled in church on his birthday. A stand of colors under the portrait of Washington received tributes of wreaths from sixteen girls, who as they bestowed their flowers uttered a kind of litany.

1. Thus we offer our tribute to the memory of Washington.
2. The Daughters of America shall long lament thy loss.
3. He was acceptable as the return of Spring.
4. He was ornamental as the flowers of Summer.
5. He was beneficial as the fruits of Autumn.
6. He was terrible to oppressors as the storms of Winter.
7. Washington was a stately oak.
8. Washington as a sun illuminated the Western Hemisphere.
9. The Sun set, and gloom overspread the land.
10. Washington sleeps with his fathers.
11. Let the willow shade his grave.
12. Let the grass mantle it.
13. Let the fragrant herb perfume it.
14. Let the birds of the wood serenade it.
15. Let human voice chant a melancholy dirge.
16. Let the sons of Columbia emulate the character of Washington.

Only a few dissenting voices were heard in the land. Seth Williston, a missionary from Connecticut to the Indians of western New York, preached a sermon on February 22 warning against the idolatry of Washington. And in Brookfield, Massachusetts, the Reverend Peter Whitney did the same, in a discourse called *Weeping and mourning at the death of eminent persons a national duty.*

V

It was inevitable that George Washington should become "forever the model boy next door whom we are urged to emulate and for whom, therefore, affection is difficult and whose conduct we regard with suspicion."[29] His qualities were those of high competence and perseverance rather than brilliance. In business or politics— yesterday, today, tomorrow—Washington's gifts are those which make for success. His achievement seems more logical and less mysterious than that of the poetic, erratic Lincoln. Washington

[29] Fish, p. 40; to this essay I am indebted for suggestions in the following analysis.

offers us a somewhat attainable ideal. None of us, we know, could be Lincoln. But if we worked very hard and took infinite pains, and always did our duty, we might become little Washingtons. (Without a war and the foundation of a new republic we could not grow into great Washingtons.) He is therefore a silent reproach to our shortcomings. Some of us, especially in boyhood, were inclined to resent this fact.

Besides the perfectionism of Washington himself, there were other things that conspired unfairly to make him into a prig. His was an age of improving literature for the young. . . . Before the late eighteenth century, children had had scanty literature of their own and figured little in an adult world. Now, it was natural that the first attention paid them should be to harness their little lives in the leading-strings of morality. The good child and the bad child became stock types. Most people could not go all the way with M. Rousseau in avowing there was no such thing as a bad child, but felt that traits like truth-telling and cleanliness and obedience ought to be held up for admiration in the new literature. . . .

Furthermore, the clergy—whose vital role in fanning the flames of the American Revolution must not be forgotten—were strongly on the side of Washington. He was a great patriot, and a "safe" man rooted deep in the economic and ecclesiastical status quo. And so he remained in later years, when Mr. Paine and Mr. Jefferson were airing heresies dangerous to church and state. Schoolmasters and textbook writers were also prone to be on the side of General Washington. . . .[30]

In the spread of the new Washington lore there was still another factor. The cardinal acts of Washington's life—in the Revolution, the Federal Convention, the Presidency—were recent and fixed in sober history. Everybody knew them well. Moreover, Washington's deeds in battle or campaign were less spectacular than those of Greene, Wayne, or Marion. The embellishment dear to hero-legend had thus to seek other stuff than the *gestes* of a Charlemagne or Arthur. Instead, it turned to his childhood, the least known period of his life, and also to his character. Traits of honesty, truthfulness, courage, generosity, and piety as illustrated

[30] *Poems by Noah Webster* (1936), p. 9.

by anecdotes of youth made the ideal blend of myth and pane-gyric.[31] Hence, in the hands of a man like Weems, George Washington emerged not as a military idol or profound statesman, but as a Sunday-school hero.

Mason L. Weems, the nineteenth child of a Scotchman who had come down in the world, had to make his own way in life and knew it. Profit was never long absent from his thoughts. At first he had taken the unpromising path of the Episcopal ministry. Itinerant in his clerical calling, as well as in the side-line of book peddling, he contrived to preach several times at Pohick Church, not far from the Washingtons. So far as is known, he never met Washington, although Weems did receive from him in 1799 a polite acknowledgment for the dedication, to the General, of *The Philanthropist; or, A good twenty-five cents worth of political love powder.* (Beginning in 1809, Weems styled himself "Formerly Rector of Mt. Vernon Parish." On July 10, 1816, from New Holland, Pennsylvania, Weems wrote his friend Carey that he had preached "to a host of good Dutch People, who are mightily taken with me for having been Chaplain to the Great Gen[l] Washington, and the writer of his wonderful Life.") A jack-of-all-trades with a hungry look, Weems lived by projects and enthusiasms. In 1792 he had drawn some notoriety to himself with his first tract, entitled, *Onania;* Weems had a penchant for addressing himself to the moral problems of adolescence. On his travels he carried a puppet show and a violin, and was in demand at country dances. Later he wrote a temperance pamphlet, and sold it "like hot-cakes" in tavern bars after imitating the antics of a drunkard.

The most profitable idea of his life came to him in the summer of 1799. He resolved to write a book about the greatest living American, "artfully drawn up, enliven[d] with anecdotes, and in my humble opinion, marvellously fitted ad captandum gustum populi Americani!!!" as he wrote the publisher Carey. He sketched a crude frontispiece, with the inscription:

> Go thy way old George. Die when thou wilt
> We shall not look upon thy like again.

[31] For several profitable ideas on this topic I have consulted an unpublished Columbia M.A. thesis of 1920, Margaret Rowe's *George Washington: The Legend.*

Six months later Washington did die, and Weems hastily revised his manuscript, changing present to past tense. Promptly in 1800 it was published. "We may sell it with rapidity . . . it will be the first," he wrote Carey in January. With mounting excitement he saw it become a best seller, and swing into edition after edition. "The people are tearing me to pieces," he wrote frantically to his publisher, later pausing to mourn: "You know I let my Washingtons escape me 50 pr cent shorn of their retail fleeces." On another occasion he wrote solemnly: "God knows there is nothing I dread so as Dead stock, dull sales, back loads, and blank looks. But the Joy of my soul is quick & clean sales—Heavy pockets, and light hearts."[32] In all, there were fifty-nine editions before 1850, and seventy-nine up to 1921. It became the second best seller of its generation in the United States, and even Germany called for four editions.

Weems constantly tinkered with and amplified his text. The late Paul Leicester Ford showed how Weems tried out his Washington anecdotes in the newspapers—sometimes in advertisements for Chief Justice Marshall's ponderous four-volume life of Washington, which Weems boosted in the realization that it was no rival—and incorporated in the next edition those yarns which seemed to strike public fancy. . . .

In this classic he remarked that George Washington was the issue of a second marriage, "a circumstance which ought, in all conscience, to quiet the minds of those who have their doubts with respect to the lawfulness of second marriages." Without known proof, he told how young George threw stones or silver dollars across the Rappahannock. ("A physical impossibility," Congressman Sol Bloom announced at the Bicentennial, although Walter Johnson the baseball pitcher later convinced him he was wrong.) These feats—like Washington's taming of a wild horse, told in the doubtful memoirs of G. W. P. Custis—belong to the youth of any legendary hero. Hercules and Alexander were also stout lads. The mythical schoolmaster Hobby, who "between his knees laid the

[32] These sentences are quoted from P. L. Ford and Emily E. Ford Skeel, *Mason Locke Weems: His Works and Ways* (1929), and Randolph G. Adams, "The Historical Illustrations in Weems's Washington," *Colophon,* Part 8 (1931).

foundation of George Washington's greatness," appears to be a joint creation of Weems and of Jonathan Boucher. Boucher, a clergyman who held a grudge against the Washingtons because of their refusal to send "Jacky" Custis on a grand tour of Europe with him, added the detail that Hobby was a convict. Weems loved sentimental stories. One of his vivid scenes tells how little George's father reproved the boy for not sharing an apple with his cousin, by showing him an orchard which God's abundance had loaded with apples:

> Poor George could not say a word; but hanging down his head, looked quite confused, while with his little naked toes he scratched in the soft ground . . . then lifting his eyes, filled with shining moisture, to his father, he softly said, "Well, Pa, only forgive me this time; and see if I ever be so stingy any more."

In harmony with the code of grown-ups in Weems's time, rather than the boys' own code, the biographer told how George, when quite a big lad (just before he quitted school), would tell the teacher on his playfellows who got into fights. . . . Later generations, inclining to the boys' point of view in regard to tattling, have contrived to drop this fable from the remembered myths of Washington. Truth-telling, on the other hand, is perennially recommended; therefore Weems's most famous yarn is still current.

This of course is the cherry tree story, which first appeared in 1806 in the fifth edition. In this edition, for the only time, Weems calls the instrument of havoc a "little" hatchet. The boy did not fell the tree, but "barked [it] so terribly, that I don't believe the tree ever got the better of it." The scene between father and son is ever delightful.

> "I can't tell a lie, Pa; you know I can't tell a lie. I did cut it with my hatchet."
> "Run to my arms, you dearest boy," cried his father in transports, "run to my arms; glad am I, George, that you killed my tree; for you have paid me for it a thousand fold. Such an act of heroism in my son is more worth than a thousand trees, though blossomed with silver, and their fruits of purest gold."

The source of this, the most popular story in American biography, is a puzzle. Weems states that he had it of an "aged lady," "a distant relative." Of its factual truth there is no evidence whatever, and even in the school exercises, pageants, and poems of the Bicentennial in 1932 it was carefully suppressed—save in a few verses by Lydia Chatton.

> Let others echo Rupert Hughes
> And mix up motes and beams—
> The anecdotes that I peruse
> Were told by Parson Weems.
> Above iconoclastic views
> That little hatchet gleams!
> "I cannot tell a lie," I choose
> The Washington of Weems.

Up through the Civil War era, the anecdote seems to have been universally relished, even though sober historians might skirt the issue of its truth. A very popular boy's life of Washington, for example, first published in 1863 by Morrison Heady ("Uncle Juvinell"), told the story in a form more rococo than Weems's— starting with George's prayer, "Good Santa Claus, be kind to me while I am sleeping peacefully," and building up a subplot about suspicions thrown on a pickaninny named Jerry. To the Puritan mind, the story was a very good one. Moreover, the real Washington's refusal to flinch from the responsibilities of manhood, under his supreme sense of duty, lent a touch of veracity to the absurd yarn.

But eventually the higher criticism began to laugh this fable out of court. Mark Twain said he was sure he was a greater man than Washington: Washington couldn't tell a lie, whereas Mark Twain could, and wouldn't. That Weems could, and did, grew increasingly plain. . . .[33]

Weems's life of "the greatest man that ever lived" is filled with other revealing touches. He exaggerated Washington's poverty prior to marriage with rich Mrs. Custis ("Here was a proper rise for you!"), in the best traditions of the success story. His account of the Revolution had an enormous effect in shaping the heroism and jingoism of popular history, as Sydney G. Fisher pointed out

[33] Joseph Rodman, *The Critic*, February 1904, cited by R. Hughes, *George Washington* (1926), I, 501; and compare Allan Nevins, *The Gateway to History* (1938), p. 121.

some years ago. For generations, school texts were written (often unconsciously) in the shadow of this antic parson.[34] And his interpretation of the model Washington, from his cradle in Virginia to apotheosis in Heaven where seraphs embraced him with "tears of joy such as only angels weep," was powerful indeed in the making of American legend. "Let us believe as in the days of our youth," said one reader of Weems, Abraham Lincoln, "that Washington was spotless; it makes human nature better to believe that . . . human perfection is possible." The speaker could not foresee that after the Civil War new heroes would be made, with Lincoln himself as their captain, and that America's growing maturity would slowly put away the childish viewpoint of Parson Weems.

Until after the death of Lincoln, Henry Lee's claim for Washington, that he was first in the hearts of his countrymen, remained uncontested. For him were named uncounted thousands of Americans, ranging from the family intimacy of George Washington Parke Custis to the remoteness of Washington Roebling. The naming of places had begun in 1775–1776, with the christening of Washington, North Carolina (present population: 7,000). Washington Heights on Manhattan followed a few months later. In 1784 Jefferson proposed to create a State of Washington out of the eastern part of Ohio, but finally this region shrank to Washington County, Ohio. Not until 1853 did a portion of the Oregon Territory become the present State of Washington, giving the first President an honor unique among American heroes. In September, 1791, it was decided to call the unborn capital of the nation Washington City. The next year saw the naming of Mount Washington, in New Hampshire, thought to be the highest in the United States. Peaks in New York State, Montana, Oregon, Nevada, California and Alaska would later bear his name, and the sentimental would imagine "a wonderful likeness" of his profile in a great stone face near Harpers Ferry. In all, eight streams, ten lakes, thirty-three

[34] S. G. Fisher, "The Legendary and Myth-Making Process in Histories of the American Revolution," *Proceedings of the American Philosophical Society,* LI (1912); for an unconscious vindication of Fisher's conclusions, see Charles Altschul, *The American Revolution in Our School Text-books* (1917), a naïve but well-meant book by "a businessman," written apropos of America's entry into the World War.

counties, nine colleges and universities, and one hundred and twenty-one towns and villages have been named for him. From a great bridge in America's metropolis to hills in Morocco and the Fiji Islands, the patronymic fame of Washington extends.

✪

The Young Man Washington

Washington is the last person you would ever suspect of having been a young man, with all the bright hopes and black despairs to which youth is subject. In American folklore he is known only as a child or a general or an old, old man: priggish hero of the cherry tree episode, commander-in-chief, or the Father of his Country, writing a farewell address. By some freak of fate, Stuart's Athenaeum portrait of an ideal and imposing, but solemn and weary, Washington at the age of sixty-four has become the most popular. This year it has been reproduced as the "official" portrait, and placed in every school in the country; so we may expect that new generations of American schoolchildren will be brought up with the idea that Washington was a solemn old bore. If only Charles Willson Peale's portrait of him as a handsome and gallant young soldier could have been used instead! His older biographers, too, have conspired to create the legend; and the recent efforts to "popularize" Washington have taken the unfortunate line of trying to make him out something that he was not: a churchman, politician, engineer, businessman, or realtor. These attempts to degrade a hero to a go-getter, an aristocrat to a vulgarian, remind one of the epitaph that Aristotle wished to have carved on the tomb of Plato: *Hic jacet homo, quem non licet, non decet, impiis vel ignorantibus laudare* (Here lies a man whom it is neither permissible nor proper for the irreverent or the ignorant to *praise*).

Perhaps it is not the fault of the painters and biographers that we think of Washington as an old man, but because his outstanding qualities—wisdom, poise, and serenity—are not those commonly associated with youth. He seemed to have absorbed, wrote Emerson, "all the serenity of America, and left none for his restless, rickety, hysterical countrymen." The Comte de Chastellux, one of the French officers in the war, said that Washington's most characteristic feature was balance: "the perfect harmony existing between the physical and moral attributes of which he is made up." Yet Gilbert Stuart, after painting his first portrait of Washington, said that "all his features were indicative of the most ungovernable passions, and had he been born in the forests, it was his opinion that he would have been the fiercest man among the savage tribes." Both men were right. Washington's qualities were so balanced that his talents, which were great but nothing extraordinary, were more effective in the long run than those of greater generals like Napoleon, or of bolder and more original statesmen like Hamilton and Jefferson. Yet as a young man Washington was impatient and passionate, eager for glory in war, wealth in land, and success in love. Even in maturity his fierce temper would sometimes get the better of him. Here in Cambridge, at his headquarters in the Craigie House, he once became so exasperated at the squabbling of drunken soldiers in the front yard that, forgetting the dignity of a general, he rushed forth and laid out a few of the brawlers with his own fists; and then, much relieved, returned to his office. Under great provocation he would break out with a torrent of Olympian oaths that terrified the younger men on his staff. Tobias Lear, the smooth young Harvard graduate who became Washington's private secretary, admitted that the most dreadful experience in his life was hearing the General swear!

It was only through the severest self-discipline that Washington attained his characteristic poise and serenity. Discipline is not a popular word nowadays, for we associate it with schoolmasters, drill sergeants, and dictators; and it was certainly not discipline of that sort that made the passionate young Washington into an effective man. His discipline came in a very small part from parents, masters, or superiors; and in no respect from institutions. It came from environment, from a philosophy of life that he imbibed at an impressionable age; but most of all from his own will. He apprehended the great truth that man can only be free through mastery of himself. Instead of allowing his passions to spend themselves, he restrained them. Instead of indulging himself in a life of pleasure—for which he had ample means at the age of twenty—he placed duty first. In fact he followed exactly that course of conduct which, according to the second-hand popularizers of Freud, make a person "thwarted," "inhibited," and "repressed." Yet Washington became a liberated, successful, and serene man. The process can hardly fail to interest young men who are struggling with the same difficulties as Washington—although, I am bound to say, under the far more difficult circumstances of depression, machinery, and jazz.

Whence came this impulse to self-discipline? We can find nothing to account for it in the little we know of Washington's heredity. His family was gentle but undistinguished. George knew little of his forebears and cared less, although he used the family coat of arms. Lawrence Washington, sometime Fellow of Brasenose College, Oxford, was ejected from his living by the Roundheads as a "malignant Royalist." His son John came to Virginia by way of Barbados as mate of a tobacco ship, and settled there. As an Indian fighter, John Washington was so undisciplined as to embarrass the Governor of Virginia almost as much as did the Indians. His son Lawrence, father of Augustine and grandfather of George, earned a competence in the merchant marine and settled down to planting. Love of the land was a trait which all Washingtons had in common: they might seek wealth at sea or glory in war, but happiness they found only in the work and sport that came from owning and cultivating land.

Usually the Washingtons married their social betters, but the second marriage of George's father, Augustine, was an exception. Mary Ball, the mother of Washington, has been the object of much sentimental writing; but the cold record of her own and her sons' letters shows her to have been grasping, querulous, and vulgar. She was a selfish and exacting mother, whom most of her children avoided as early as they could; to whom they did their duty, but rendered little love. It was this sainted mother of Washington who opposed almost everything that he did for the public good, who wished his sense of duty to end with his duty to her, who pestered him in his campaigns by complaining letters, and who at a dark moment of the Revolutionary War increased his anxieties by strident complaints of neglect and starvation. Yet for one thing Americans may well be grateful to Mary Ball: her selfishness lost George an opportunity to become midshipman in the Royal Navy, a school whence few Americans emerged other than as loyal subjects of the King.

There is only one other subject connected with Washington upon which there has been more false sentiment, misrepresentation, and mendacity than on that of his mother, and that is his religion. Washington's religion was that of an eighteenth-century gentleman. Baptized in the Church of England, he attended service occasionally as a young man, and more regularly in middle age, as one of the duties of his station. He believed in God: the eighteenth-century Supreme Being, a Divine Philosopher who ruled all things for the best. He was certain of a Providence in the affairs of men. By the same token, he was completely tolerant of other people's beliefs, more so than the American democracy of today; for in a letter to the Swedenborgian church of Baltimore he wrote: "In this enlightened age and in the land of equal liberty it is our boast that a man's religious tenets will not forfeit the protection of the law, nor deprive him of the right of attaining and holding the highest offices that are known in the United States." But Washington never became an active member of any church. Even after his marriage to a devout churchwoman, and when as President of the United States the eyes of all men were upon him, he never joined Martha in the beautiful and comforting sacrament of the body and blood of Christ. Considering the pressure always placed on a man to conform by a religious wife, this abstention from Holy Communion is very significant. Christianity had little or no part in that discipline which made Washington more humble and gentle than any of the great captains, less proud and ambitious than most of the statesmen who have proclaimed themselves disciples of the Nazarene. His inspiration, as we shall see, came from an entirely different source.

Washington gained little discipline from book-learning; but like all Virginian gentlemen of the day he led an active outdoor life, which gave him a magnificent physique. When fully grown he stood a little over six feet, and weighed between 175 and 200 pounds. Broad-shouldered and straight-backed, he carried his head erect and his chin up, and showed a good leg on horseback. There is no reason to doubt the tradition of his prowess at running, leaping, wrestling, and horsemanship. The handling of horses, in which Washington was skilled at an early age, is one of the finest means of discipline that a youngster can have: for he who cannot control himself can never handle a spirited horse; and for the same reason fox-hunting, which was Washington's favorite sport, is the making—or the breaking—of a courageous and considerate gentleman. His amazing physical vitality is proved by an incident of his reconnaissance to the Ohio. At the close of December, 1753, he and the scout Christopher Gist attempted to cross the river just above the site of Pittsburgh, on a raft of their own making. The river was full of floating ice, and George, while trying to shove the raft away from an ice-floe with his setting-pole, fell overboard, but managed to climb aboard again. They were forced to land on an island and spend the night there without fire or dry clothing. Gist, the professional woodsman, who had not been in the water, froze all his fingers and some of his toes; but Washington suffered no ill effects from the exposure. For that, his healthy Virginia boyhood may be thanked.

His formal education was scanty. The colonial colleges provided a classical discipline more severe and selective than that of their successors, but George had none of these "advantages." There were no means to prepare him for William and Mary, the college of the Virginia gentry; his father died when he was eleven years old, and as a younger son in a land-poor family, his only schoolmasters were chosen haphazardly. Endowed with the blood and the instincts of a gentleman, he was not given a gentleman's education, as he became painfully aware when at adolescence he went to live with his half-brother at Mount Vernon.

In modern phrase, George was "parked" on the estate which would one day be his. Evidently there had been some sort of family consultation about what to do with him; and Lawrence good-naturedly offered to take his young brother in hand, if only to get him away from the termagant mother. Lawrence Washington, Augustine's favorite son and fondest hope, had been sent to England for his schooling, had served under Admiral Vernon in the war with Spain, and had inherited the bulk of his father's property, to the exclusion of George and the four younger brothers and sisters. The proximity of Mount Vernon to the vast estates of the Fairfax family in the Northern Neck of Virginia gave Lawrence his opportunity. He married a Fairfax, and was admitted to the gay, charmed circle of the First Families of Virginia. He was already a well-established gentleman of thirty when the hobbledehoy half-brother came to stay.

George was then a tall, gangling lad of sixteen years, with enormous hands and feet that were continually getting in his way. Young girls giggled when he entered a room, and burst out laughing at his awkward attempts to court them. He was conscious that he did not "belong," and made every effort to improve his manners. About three years before, a schoolmaster had made him copy out one hundred and ten Rules of Civility from a famous handbook by one Hawkins—a popular guide to good manners already a century and a half old; and George was probably glad to have this manuscript manual of social etiquette ready to consult. One of the most touching and human pictures of Washington is that of the overgrown schoolboy solemnly conning old Hawkins' warnings against scratching oneself at table, picking one's teeth with a fork, or cracking fleas in company, lest he commit serious breaks in the houses of the great.

These problems of social behavior no doubt occupied much space in Washington's adolescent thoughts. But he was also preparing to be a man of action. At school he had cared only for mathematics. He procured more books, progressed further than his schoolmaster could take him, and so qualified to be surveyor to Lord Fairfax. This great gentleman and landowner required an immense amount of surveying in the Shenandoah Valley, and found it difficult to obtain men with enough mathematics to qualify as surveyors, or sufficient sobriety to run a line straight and see a job through. So George at sixteen earned as Lord Fairfax's surveyor the high salary of a doubloon (about $7.50) a day, most of which he saved up and invested in land. For he had early decided that in the fresh lands of the Virginia Valley and the West lay the road to position, competence, and happiness. His personality as well as his excellent surveying earned him the friendship of the Fairfaxes, liberal and intelligent gentlemen; and this, as we shall see, was of first importance in Washington's moral and intellectual development.

That friendship, not the doubloon a day, was the first and most fortunate gain from this surveying job; the second was the contact which it gave young Washington with frontiersmen, with Indians, and with that great teacher of self-reliance, the wilderness. He had the advantage of a discipline that few of us can obtain today. We are born in crowded cities, and attend crowded schools and colleges; we take our pleasure along crowded highways and in crowded places of amusement; we are tempted to assert ourselves by voice rather than deed, to advertise, to watch the clock, escape responsibility, and leave decisions to others. But a hungry woodsman could not afford to lose patience with a deer he was trying to shoot, or with a trout he was trying to catch; and it did not help him much to bawl out an Indian. If you cannot discipline yourself to quiet and caution in the wilderness, you won't get far; and if you make the wrong decision in woods infested with savages, you will probably have no opportunity to make another. What our New England forebears learned from the sea, Washington learned from the wilderness.

His life from sixteen to twenty was not all spent on forest trails. This was the golden age of the Old Dominion, the fifteen years from 1740 to the French and Indian War. The old roughness and crudeness were passing away. Peace reigned over the land, high prices ruled for tobacco, immigrants were pouring into the back country; the traditional Virginia of Thackeray and Vachel Lindsay—"Land of the gauntlet and the glove"—came into being. Living in Virginia at that time was like riding on the sparkling crest of a great wave just before it breaks and spreads into dull, shallow pools. At Mount Vernon, on the verge of the wilderness, one felt the zest of sharp contrasts, and one received the discipline that comes from life. On the one side were mansion houses where young Washington could learn manners and philosophy from gentlefolk. He took part in all the sports and pastimes of his social equals: dancing and card-playing and flirting with the girls. When visiting a town like Williamsburg he never missed a show; and later as President he was a patron of the new American drama. He loved shooting, fox-hunting, horse-racing, and all the gentlemen's field sports of the day; he bet small sums at cards, and larger sums on the ponies, and was a good loser. He liked to make an impression by fine new clothes, and by riding unruly steeds when girls were looking on; for though ungainly afoot, he was a graceful figure on horseback. He belonged to clubs of men who dined at taverns and drank like gentlemen; that is to say, they drank as much wine as they could hold without getting drunk. Tobacco, curiously enough, made George's head swim; but he learned to smoke the peace-pipe with Indians when necessary without disgracing himself.

On the other side of Mount Vernon were log cabins, and all the crude elements of American life: Scots-Irish, Pennsylvania German pioneers, and other poor whites who as insubordinate soldiers would prove the severest test of Washington's indefatigable patience. The incidents of roughing it, such as the "one thread-bear blanket with double its weight of vermin, such as lice, fleas, etc." which he records in the journal of his first surveying trip, were not very pleasant, but he took it all with good humor and good sportsmanship. A little town called Alexandria sprang up about a tobacco warehouse and wharf, and young Washington made the first survey of it. There was a Masonic Lodge at Fredericksburg, and George, always a good "joiner," became brother to all the rising journalists and lawyers of the northern colonies. The deep Potomac flowed past Mount Vernon, bearing ships of heavy burden to the Chesapeake and overseas; you sent your orders to England every year with your tobacco, and ships returned with the latest modes and manners, books and gazettes, and letters full of coffee-house gossip. London did not seem far away, and young George confessed in a letter that he hoped to visit that "gay Matrapolis" before long.

It was probably just as well that he did not visit London, for he had the best and purest English tradition in Virginia. When Washington was in his later teens, just when a young man is fumbling for a philosophy of life, he came into intimate contact with several members of the Fairfax family. They were of that eighteenth-century Whig gentry who conformed outwardly to Christianity, but derived their real inspiration from Marcus Aurelius, Plutarch, and the Stoic philosophers. Thomas, sixth Lord Fairfax, was a nobleman devoted to "Revolution Principles"—the Glorious Revolution of 1688, in which his father had taken an active part. Of the same line was that General Lord Fairfax, commander-in-chief of the New Model Army, who of all great soldiers in English history most resembles Washington. The ideal of this family was a noble simplicity of living, and a calm acceptance of life: duty to the Commonwealth, generosity to fellow men, unfaltering courage, and enduring virtue; in a word, the Stoic philosophy which overlaps Christian ethics more than any other discipline of the ancients. A Stoic never evaded life: he faced it. A Stoic never avoided responsibility: he accepted it. A Stoic not only believed in liberty: he practiced it.

It is not necessary to suppose that young Washington read much Stoic philosophy, for he was no great reader at any time; but he must have absorbed it from constant social intercourse with the Fairfaxes of Belvoir, neighbors whom he saw constantly. At Belvoir lived George William Fairfax, eight years Washington's senior, and his companion in surveying expeditions. Anne, the widow of Lawrence Washington, was Fairfax's sister, and Sally, the lady with whom George Washington was so happy (and so miserable) as to fall in love, was his wife. Books were there, if he wanted them. North's Plutarch was in every gentleman's library, and it was Plutarch who wrote the popular life of Cato, Washington's favorite character in history—not crabbed Cato the Censor, but Cato of pent-up Utica. At the age of seventeen, Washington himself owned an outline, in English, of the principal Dialogues of Seneca the younger, "sharpest of all the Stoics." The mere chapter headings are the moral axioms that Washington followed through life.

An Honest Man can never be outdone in Courtesy
A Good man can never be Miserable, nor a Wicked man Happy
A Sensual Life is a Miserable Life
Hope and Fear are the Bane of Human Life
The Contempt of Death makes all the Miseries of Life Easy to us

And of the many passages that young Washington evidently took to heart, one may select this:

No man is born wise: but Wisdom and Virtue require a Tutor; though we can easily learn to be Vicious without a Master. It is Philosophy that gives us a Veneration for God; a Charity for our Neighbor; that teaches us our Duty to Heaven, and Exhorts us to an Agreement one with another. It unmasks things that are terrible to us, asswages our Lusts, refutes our Errors, restrains our Luxury, Reproves our avarice, and works strangely on tender Natures.

Washington read Addison's tragedy *Cato* in company with his beloved; and if they did not act it together in private theatricals, George expressed the wish that they might. At Valley Forge, when the morale of the army needed a stimulus, Washington caused *Cato* to be performed and attended the performance. It was his favorite play, written, as Pope's prologue says,

> To make mankind in conscious virtue bold,
> Live o'er each scene, and be what they behold.

Portius, Cato's son, whose "steddy temper"

> Can look on guilt, rebellion, fraud, and Caesar
> In the calm lights of mild Philosophy

declares (I, ii, 40–45):

> I'll animate the soldiers' drooping courage
> With love of freedom, and contempt of Life:
> I'll thunder in their ears their country's cause
> And try to rouse up all that's Roman in 'em.
> 'Tis not in Mortals to Command Success
> But we'll do more, Sempronius, we'll Deserve it.

These last two lines sound the note that runs through all Washington's correspondence in the dark hours of the Revolutionary struggle; and these same lines are almost the only literary quotations found in the vast body of Washington's writings. Many years after, when perplexed and wearied by the political squabbles of his Presidency and longing to retire to Mount Vernon, Washington quoted the last lines of Cato's advice to Portius (IV, iv, 146–154):

> Let me advise thee to retreat betimes
> To thy paternal seat, the Sabine field,
> Where the great Censor toil'd with his own hands,
> And all our frugal Ancestors were blest
> In humble virtues, and a rural life.
> There live retired, pray for the peace of Rome:
> Content thy self to be obscurely good.
> When vice prevails, and impious men bear sway,
> The post of honour is a private station.

From his camp with General Forbes's army in the wilderness Washington wrote to Sally Fairfax, September 25, 1758:

I should think our time more agreeably spent, believe me, in playing a part in Cato with the Company you mention, and myself doubly happy in being the Juba to such a Marcia as you must make.

Marcia was the worthy daughter of Cato, and Juba her lover, the young Numidian prince to whom Syphax says:

> You have not read mankind, your youth admires
> The throws and swellings of a Roman soul,
> Cato's bold flights, th' extravagance of Virtue.

And Juba had earlier said, (I, iv, 49–58):

> Turn up thy eyes to Cato!
> There may'st thou see to what a godlike height
> The Roman virtues lift up mortal man.
> While good, and just, and anxious for his friends,
> He's still severely bent against himself;
> Renouncing sleep, and rest, and food, and ease,
> He strives with thirst and hunger, toil and heat;
> And when his fortune sets before him all
> The pomps and pleasures that his soul can wish,
> His rigid virtue will accept of none.

So, here we have a young man of innate noble qualities, seeking a philosophy of life, thrown in contact during his most impressionable years with a great gentleman whom he admired, a young gentleman who was his best friend, and a young lady whom he loved, all three steeped in the Stoical tradition. What would you expect? Can it be a mere coincidence that this characterization of the Emperor Antoninus Pius by his adopted son Marcus Aurelius, the Imperial Stoic, so perfectly fits the character of Washington?

Take heed lest thou become a Caesar indeed; lest the purple stain thy soul. For such things have been. Then keep thyself simple, good, pure, and serious; a friend to justice and the fear of God; kindly, affectionate, and strong to do the right. Reverence Heaven and succour man. Life is short; and earthly existence yields but one harvest, holiness of character and altruism of action. Be in everything a true disciple of Antoninus. Emulate his constancy in all rational activity, his unvarying equability, his purity, his cheerfulness of countenance, his sweetness, his contempt for notoriety, and his eagerness to come at the root of the matter.

Remember how he would never dismiss any subject until he had gained a clear insight into it and grasped it thoroughly; how he bore with the injustice of his detractors and never retorted in kind; how he did nothing in haste, turned a deaf ear to the professional tale-bearers, and showed himself an acute judge of characters and actions, devoid of all reproachfulness, timidity, suspiciousness, and sophistry; how easily he was satisfied,—for instance, with lodging, bed, clothing, food, and servants,—how fond of work and how patient; capable, thanks to his frugal diet, of remaining at his post from morning till night, having apparently subjected even the operations of nature to his will; firm and constant in friendship, tolerant of the most outspoken criticism of his opinions, delighted if any one could make a better suggestion than himself, and, finally, deeply religious without any trace of superstition.

When Washington was twenty years old, his brother Lawrence died. George, next heir by their father's will, stepped into his place as proprietor of Mount Vernon. At this stage of his life, George did not greatly enjoy the exacting task of running a great plantation; he thirsted for glory in war. But he soon began to enlarge and improve his holdings, and in the end came to love the land as nothing else. . . .

It is clear from Washington's diaries that farming was a great factor in his discipline. For the lot of a Virginia planter was not as romance has colored it. Slaves had to be driven, or they ate out your substance; overseers had to be watched, or they slacked and stole; accounts had to be balanced, or you became poorer every year. There were droughts, and insect pests, and strange maladies among the cattle. Washington's life at Mount Vernon was one of constant experiment, unremitting labor, unwearying patience. It was a continual war against human error, insect enemies, and tradition. He might provide improved flails and a clean threshing floor in his new barn; when his back was turned the overseer would have the wheat out in the yard, to be trod into the muck by the cattle. His books prove that he was an eager and bold experimenter in that "new husbandry" of which Coke of Norfolk was the great exponent. There were slave blacksmiths, carpenters, and bricklayers; a cider press and a still-house, where excellent corn and rye whisky were made, and sold in barrels made by the slaves from plantation oak. Herring and shad fisheries in the Potomac provided food for the slaves; a grist-mill turned Washington's improved strain of wheat into flour, which was taken to market in his own schooner, which he could handle like any down-east skipper. Indeed, it is in his husbandry that we can earliest discern those qualities that made Washington the first soldier and statesman of America. As landed proprietor no less than as commander-in-chief, he showed executive ability, the power of planning for a distant end, and a capacity for taking infinite pains. Neither drought nor defeat could turn him from a course that he discerned to be proper and right; but in farming as in war he learned from failure, and grew in stature from loss and adversity.

Not long after inheriting Mount Vernon, Washington had an opportunity to test what his brother had taught him of military tactics and the practice of arms. Drilling and tactics, like surveying, were a projection of Washington's mathematical mind; like every born strategist he could see moving troops in his mind's eye, march and deploy them and calculate the time to a minute. He devoured accounts of Frederick's campaigns, and doubtless dreamt of directing a great battle on a grassy plain, a terrain he was destined never to fight on in this shaggy country. As one of the first landowners in the county, at twenty he was commissioned major of militia. He then asked for and obtained the post of adjutant of militia for the county. The settlement of his brother's affairs brought him into contact with Governor Dinwiddie, a shrewd Scot who knew a dependable young man when he saw one; and from this came his first great opportunity.

At twenty-one he was sent on a highly confidential and difficult thousand-mile reconnaissance through the back country from western Virginia to the Ohio, and almost to the shores of Lake Erie. This young man just past his majority showed a caution in wilderness work, a diplomatic skill in dealing with Indians, and a courteous firmness in dealing with French commanders that would have done credit to a man twice his age. But on his next mission, one notes with a feeling of relief, youthful impetuosity prevailed. Unmindful that one must always let the enemy make the first aggression, our young lieutenant-colonel fired the shot that began the Seven Years' War.

A phrase of the young soldier's blithe letter to his younger brother: "I heard the bullets whistle, and believe me, there is something charming in the sound," got into the papers, and gave sophisticated London a good laugh. Even King George II heard it and remarked: "He would not say so, if he had been used to hear many!" That time would come soon enough. Washington's shot in the silent wilderness brought the French and Indians buzzing about his ears. He retired to Fort Necessity, which he had caused to be built in a large meadow, hoping to tempt the enemy to a pitched battle. But the enemy was very inconsiderate. He swarmed about the fort in such numbers that Washington was lucky to be allowed to capitulate and go home; for this was one of those wars that was not yet a war; it was not declared till two years after the fighting began. The enemy was so superior in numbers that nobody blamed Washington; and when General Braddock arrived with an army of regulars, he invited the young frontier leader to accompany his expedition into the wilderness.

There is no need for me to repeat the tale of Braddock's defeat, except to say that the general's stupidity and the colonel's part in saving what could be saved have both been exaggerated. . . .

Shortly after Washington reached Alexandria, the annual electoral campaign began for members of the Virginia Assembly. In a political dispute the colonel said something insulting to a quick-tempered little fellow named Payne, who promptly knocked him down with a hickory stick. Soldiers rushed up to avenge Washington, who recovered just in time to tell them he was not hurt, and could take care of himself, thank you! The next day he wrote to Payne requesting an interview at a tavern. The little man arrived, expecting a demand for an apology, or a challenge. Instead, Washington apologized for the insult which had provoked the blow, hoped that Payne was satisfied, and offered his hand. Some of Washington's biographers cannot imagine or understand such conduct. One of them brackets this episode with the cherry tree yarn as "stories so silly and so foolishly impossible that they do not deserve an instant's consideration." Another explains Washington's conduct as a result of his defeat at Fort Necessity: "Washington was crushed into such meekness at this time that . . . instead of retaliating or challenging the fellow to a duel, he apologized." But the incident, which has been well substantiated, occurred after Braddock's defeat, not Washington's; and it was due to Stoical magnanimity, not Christian meekness. "It is the Part of a Great Mind to despise Injuries," says Seneca the younger, in the L'Estrange translation that Washington owned. The Payne affair was merely an early instance of what Washington was doing all his life: admitting he was wrong when he was convinced he was in the wrong, and doing the handsome thing in a gentlemanly manner. A man who took that attitude became impregnable to attack by politicians or anyone else. For a young man of twenty-three to take it meant that he had firm hold of a great philosophy.

During the next two years Washington had charge of the frontier defenses of Virginia, and a chain of thirty garrisoned stockades which followed the Shenandoah Valley and its outer bulwarks from Winchester to the North Carolina line. In the execution of this command he showed a prodigious physical activity, often riding thirty miles a day for several days over wilderness trails. His letters show a youthful touchiness about rank and recognition; he sorely tried the patience of Governor Dinwiddie, who, to Washington's evident surprise, accepted a proffered resignation; but he was soon reappointed and took a leading part in General Forbes's expedition against Fort Duquesne. It was merely to settle a question of precedence that Washington undertook a long journey to interview Governor Shirley, the commander-in-chief, at Boston. Two aides, and two servants clad in new London liveries of the Washington colors and mounted on horses with the Washington arms embroidered on their housings, accompanied their colonel; for George had a young man's natural desire to make an impressive appearance. He stopped with great folk at Philadelphia and New York and gave generous tips to their servants. At New London the exhausted horses had to be left behind, and the colonel and suite proceeded by sea to Boston, where George ordered a new hat and uniform, a mass of silver lace, and two pair of gloves. But Washington never made the mistake of wearing splendid clothes on the wrong occasion. In the French and Indian War he wore a plain, neutral-colored uniform instead of royal scarlet, and dressed his soldiers as frontiersmen, in buckskin and moccasins, so that they carried no superfluous weight and offered no mark to the Indians.

As a young officer he often became impatient with the frontier folk—their shortsighted selfishness in refusing to unite under his command, their lack of discipline and liability to panic, and the American militiaman's propensity to offer unwanted advice and sulk if it were not taken. But he found something to like in them as he did in all men, and learned to work with and through them. Militia deserted Washington as they deserted other officers, despite the flogging of sundry and the hanging of a few to encourage the rest. Here is plenty of material for a disparaging biographer to describe Washington as a military martinet who had not even the merit of a notable victory; and some of the "debunkers," who have never known what it is to command troops, have said just that. A sufficient reply to them, as well as striking proof of the amazing confidence, even veneration, which Washington inspired at an early age, is the "Humble Address" of the twenty-seven officers of his regiment, beseeching him to withdraw his resignation.

Sir,
We your most obedient and affectionate Officers, beg leave to express our great Concern, at the disagreeable News we have received of your Determination to resign the Command of that Corps, in which we have under you long served. . . .

In our earliest Infancy you took us under your Tuition, train'd us up in the Practice of that Discipline, which alone can constitute good Troops, from the punctual Observance of which you never suffer'd the least Deviation.

Your steady adherence to impartial Justice, your quick Discernment and invariable Regard to Merit . . . first heighten'd our natural Emulation, and our Desire to excel. . . .

Judge then, how sensibly we must be Affected with the loss of such an excellent Commander, such a sincere Friend, and so affable a Companion. . . .

Fully persuaded of this, we beg Leave to assure you, that as you have hitherto been the actuating Soul of the whole Corps, we shall at all times pay the most invariable Regard to your Will and Pleasure, and will always be happy to demonstrate by our Actions, with how much Respect and Esteem we are,

Sir,

Fort Loudoun   Your most affectionate
Decr 31st 1758   and most obedient humble Servants
[Followed by twenty-seven signatures]

There stands the young man Washington, reflected in the hearts of his fellows. As one reads this youthfully sincere composition of the officers' mess at Fort Loudoun, one imagines it addressed to a grizzled veteran of many wars, a white-whiskered colonel of fifty. Colonel Washington was just twenty-six.

A farewell to arms Washington was determined it must be. Fort Duquesne was won, and his presence at the front was no longer needed. Virginia, the colony which had received the first shock of the war, could justly count on British regulars and the northern colonies to carry it to a glorious conclusion on the Plains of Abraham.

In four years Washington had learned much from war. He found it necessary to discipline himself before he could handle men. He had learned that the interminable boredom of drill, arguing about supplies, and begging for transportation was ill rewarded by the music of whistling bullets; that war was simply hard, beastly work. The sufferings of the border people, the bloody shambles on the Monongahela, the frozen evidence of torture on the road to Fort Duquesne, cured his youthful appetite for glory, completely. When Washington again drew his sword, in 1775, it was with great reluctance, and only because he believed, like Cato (II, v, 85):

The hand of fate is over us, and Heaven
Exacts severity from all our thoughts.

> It is not now a time to talk of aught
> But chains, or conquest; liberty, or death.

From one woman he learned perhaps as much as from war. Sally Cary, his fair tutor in Stoicism and the love of his youth, was eighteen and married to his friend and neighbor George William Fairfax, when at sixteen he first met her. Beautiful, intelligent, and of gentle birth, Mrs. Fairfax took a more than sisterly interest in the callow young surveyor; and as near neighbors they saw much of each other. Cryptic jottings in his diary for 1748 show that he was already far gone in love. His pathetic letter to her from Fort Cumberland in 1755, begging for a reply to "make me happier than the day is long," strikes a human note in the midst of his businesslike military correspondence. No letters from her to him have been preserved, but from the tone of his replies I gather that Sally was somewhat more of a tease than befitted Cato's daughter. Whatever her sentiments may have been toward him, Washington's letters leave no doubt that he was passionately in love with her; yet gentlemanly standards were then such that while her husband lived she could never be his wife, much less his mistress. What anguish he must have suffered, any young man can imagine. It was a situation that schooled the young soldier-lover in manners, moderation, and restraint—a test case of his Stoical philosophy. His solution was notable for its common sense: when on a hurried visit to Williamsburg in the spring of 1758, to procure clothes for his ragged soldiers, he met, wooed, and won a housewifely little widow of twenty-seven named Martha Custis. She wanted a manager for her property and a stepfather for her children; he needed a housekeeper for Mount Vernon. It was a *mariage de convenance* that developed into a marriage of affection. But Martha well knew that she was not George's first or greatest love, nor he hers.

Thirty years later, when Mrs. Fairfax was a poor and childless widow in London, crushing the memories of a Virginia springtime in her heart, there came a letter from Washington. The First Citizen of the World writes that the crowded events of the more than a quarter-century since they parted have not "been able to eradicate from my mind the recollection of those happy moments, the happiest in my life, which I have enjoyed in your company." Martha

Washington enclosed a letter under the same cover, in order to show that she, too, understood.

Let us neither distort nor exaggerate this relation, the most beautiful thing in Washington's life. Washington saw no visions of Sally Fairfax in the battlesmoke. He did not regard himself as her knightly champion, or any such romantic nonsense; Walter Scott had not yet revived the age of chivalry. Women occupied a small part in Washington's thoughts, as in those of most men of action. No more than Cato did he indulge in worry or bitter thoughts about his ill fortune in love. Suppose, however, Washington had turned out a failure or shown some fault of character at a critical moment, instead of superbly meeting every test. Every yapping biographer of the last decade would have blamed the three members of this blameless triangle. Since he turned out otherwise, we can hardly fail to credit both women with an important share in the formation of Washington's character. And who will deny that Washington attained his nearly perfect balance and serenity, not through self-indulgence but through restraint?

What of other women?—a subject that cannot be shirked in any honest account of the young man Washington. Many of you must have heard the story of that so-called letter of Washington inviting someone to Mount Vernon, and setting forth the charms of a certain slave-girl. No investigator has ever managed to see this letter, or even found a person who has seen it—but that man for some peculiar reason is always sick, dead, or nonexistent when you look for him, or else he refers you to another man, who knows the man, who knows the man that has it. John C. Fitzpatrick, who has spent much time on the trail of the seductive if mythical octoroon of Mount Vernon, believes that all stories of this sort were started by a spurious sentence in a letter from Benjamin Harrison to Washington during the war, which was intercepted by the British and printed in England. Fortunately the original, a plain letter of military information, has been preserved. But when it was given out for publication to the *Gentleman's Magazine* (of all places), the editor interpolated a jocularly bawdy description of "pretty little Kate the washerwoman's daughter," whose charms the commander-in-chief was invited to share. Of similar origin are the stories of Washington's illegitimate children. Of course one cannot prove a negative to every rumor. I can only state my opinion that, in view of the fact that Washington fell deeply in love at sixteen, and remained in love with the same lady until his marriage; in view of his reputation under pitiless publicity, he led a clean life, in every sense of the word.

Plutarch wrote of Cato: "He had not taken to public life, like some others, casually or automatically or for the sake of fame or personal advantage. He chose it because it was the function proper to a good man." That was why Washington allowed himself to be elected in 1758 to the Virginia Assembly, an office proper to a gentleman of his station. He had no gift for speaking or for wire-pulling; he showed no talent or desire for political leadership. But he learned at first hand the strange behavior of *homo sapiens* in legislative assemblies. Everyone marvels at the long-suffering patience shown by Washington in his dealings with Congress during the war; few remember that he had been for many years a burgess of Virginia, and for several months a member of the very Congress to which he was responsible.

So at twenty-seven George Washington was not only a veteran colonel who had won the confidence and affection of his men, but a member of the Virginia Assembly, a great landowner, and a husband. His youth was over, and he had the means for a life of ease and competence; but the high example of antique virtue would not let him ignore another call to duty. When it came, his unruly nature had been disciplined by the land and the wilderness, by philosophy and a noble woman, and by his own indomitable will, to become a fit instrument for a great cause. There were other colonial soldiers in 1775 who from better opportunity had gained more glory in the last war than he; but there was none who inspired so much confidence as this silent, capable man of forty-three. So that when the political need of the moment required a Virginian, there was no question but that Colonel Washington should be commander-in-chief.

If he had failed, historians would have blamed the Continental Congress for a political appointment of a provincial colonel with an indifferent war record. If he had failed, the American Revolution would have been something worse than futile—a Rebellion of '98 that would have soured the American character, made us another Ireland, with a long and distressful struggle for freedom ahead. If, like so many leaders of revolutions, he had merely achieved a personal triumph, or inoculated his country with ambition for glory, the world would have suffered from his success. His country could and almost did fail Washington; but Washington could not fail his country, or disappoint the expectations of his kind. A simple gentleman of Virginia with no extraordinary talents had so disciplined himself that he could lead an insubordinate and divided people into ordered liberty and enduring union.

CURTIS P. NETTELS

✪

Washington on the Eve of the Revolution

> Certain it is, our whole substance does already in a manner flow
> to Great Britain and whatsoever contributes to lessen our impor-
> tations must be hurtful to their manufactures.[1]
> —WASHINGTON TO FRANCIS DANDRIDGE, SEPTEMBER 20, 1765

I

Before the summer of 1774 Washington had not been one of the
more conspicuous opponents of the British measures which inspired the colonial resistance. For ten years after 1763, the contest
had been fought mainly with the weapons of argument and debate.
This polemical warfare had brought into the foreground a group of
men who were versed in the constitutional history of England. It
had popularized writers and orators—men like James Otis, John
Dickinson, and Patrick Henry. By reason of writings published in
1774, John Adams, Thomas Jefferson, and James Wilson gained
sudden distinction. Franklin owed his eminence in the cause of
resistance largely to his pen. In the port towns, leaders like Samuel
Adams had achieved renown as organizers and directors of the
common people.

Washington was not a writer, an orator, a constitutional lawyer,
or an organizer of urban masses. He was a planter and a business-

[1] John C. Fitzpatrick, ed., *The Writings of George Washington*, 39 vols.
(Washington, D.C., 1931–1944), II, 426 (hereafter cited as *Writings of
Washington*).

man—and not a particularly articulate one. Consequently, he had not gained notoriety during the years of agitation and discussion. However, by May, 1775, the great debate was nearing its end, and the time for action had come. Suddenly he moved to the center of the stage. A hurried glance at his early career might give the impression that he stumbled into the leadership of the American cause without knowing why. The fact is that in May, 1775, he was one of the most forward and determined of the leaders—fully the equal of Samuel Adams in fixity of purpose and maturity of conviction. His military uniform was an arresting expression of his forwardness. He alone among the members of the Congress outwardly proclaimed his willingness to take up arms and to levy war against the king's agents. His attitude in 1775 was not hastily assumed or superficial. It was the result of personal experiences reaching as far back as 1755. Many things had happened which explain why he became one of the most determined opponents of Britain's rule.

Early in May, 1755, on the eve of the French and Indian War, he joined the army of General Edward Braddock, in the capacity of aide-de-camp to the British commander. Washington was then twenty-three; the general was about sixty. A month had not passed before the two were engaged in heated arguments. Braddock had some disagreeable experiences with local contractors which moved him to denounce the colonists as a whole. Washington defended his compatriots, fearing, as he said, that the general would represent them "in a light we little deserve." Instead "of blaming the individuals as he ought, he charges all his disappointments to a public supineness, and looks upon the country, I believe, as void of both honor and honesty." "We have frequent disputes on this head," continued the youthful patriot, "which are maintained with warmth on both sides, especially on his, who is incapable of arguing without [it], or giving up any point he asserts, let it be ever so incompatible with reason."[2]

Then followed disappointments arising from the British management of the campaign. Washington urged a rapid advance to the French post, Fort Duquesne, at the forks of the Ohio. Brad-

2 Washington to William Fairfax, June 7, 1755, *ibid.,* I, 133.

dock agreed, but his slowness dismayed his energetic aide, who complained in June: "All my sanguine hopes [were] brought low when I found that instead of pushing on with vigor, without regarding a little rough road, they were halting to level every mold hill, and to erect bridges over every brook, by which we were four days getting twelve miles."[3]

Soon came the defeat of Braddock on the Monongahela, within seven miles of Fort Duquesne. Praising the conduct of the British officers and the Virginia troops, Washington blamed the British regulars for the disaster. "The dastardly behavior of the English soldiers," he wrote, "exposed all those who were inclined to do their duty to almost certain death; and at length, in despite of every effort to the contrary, [they] broke and ran as sheep before hounds, leaving the artillery, ammunition, provisions, and every individual thing we had with us a prey to the enemy; and when we endeavored to rally them in hopes of regaining our invaluable loss, it was with as much success as if we had attempted to have stopped the wild bears of the mountains."[4]

After Braddock's defeat, Governor Dinwiddie placed Washington in command of Virginia's frontier defenses, with the rank of colonel. The British government had adopted a rule for military operations in America to the effect that an officer (usually an Englishman) who had received his commission directly from the king should outrank an officer (usually a colonist) who had received his commission from a colonial governor. This rule meant that Englishmen controlled military affairs in the colonies. In 1755, Governor Sharpe of Maryland placed Fort Cumberland under the command of a certain Captain Dagworthy, who claimed that he held his commission directly from the king. Dagworthy ignored orders from Washington and insisted that the Virginian serve under him. Washington emphatically refused and appealed to Governor Dinwiddie, who consented that Washington should go to Boston for a conference with Governor William Shirley of Massachusetts, then commander-in-chief of the British forces in America. Early in 1756 Washington made the journey and secured from Shirley an order which authorized him to take command at Fort

[3] Washington to John Augustine Washington, June 28, 1755, *ibid.*, 144.
[4] Washington to Governor Dinwiddie, July 18, 1755, *ibid.*, 149.

Cumberland. Later in the year, when he was being censured in Virginia for the loose conduct of soldiers at the fort, he wrote: "The unhappy differences which subsisted so long about the command did, I own, prevent me from going to Fort Cumberland, to enforce those orders, which I never failed to send there; and caused, I dare say, many gross irregularities to creep into that garrison. . . . But whose fault was that? Ought it not to have been attributed to the officer commanding there [Captain Dagworthy], whose business it was to suppress vice in every shape?"[5]

Once the command at Fort Cumberland had been settled, it soon involved Washington in other troubles with the royal government. His superiors insisted on garrisoning the fort with considerable force. He objected to this, pointing out that only a very few people lived in its vicinity. It was so isolated, "lying quite out in a corner, quite remote from the inhabitants"—so far from "where the Indians always repair to do their murders"—that it did not afford protection to the settlements.[6] When raids occurred, the frontiersmen fled toward Winchester, about fifty miles to the southeast, and the Indians pursued them thither, without interference. Since the garrison usually did not learn of such forays until a month afterward, it offered no succor. It was worse than useless because it immobilized troops who were needed where the frontiersmen were being attacked.

Washington urged that most of the soldiers be withdrawn from the fort and that Winchester be made the chief center of operations. During a visit to Williamsburg he endeavored to win Governor Dinwiddie to his views. The latter's response was noncommittal. Washington wrote in August, 1756: "Now whether I am to understand this [as] ay or no to the plain simple question asked, vizt. 'Is the fort to be continued or removed?' I know not. But in all important matters I am directed in this ambiguous and uncertain way."[7]

Dinwiddie went so far as to authorize Washington to get the views of his officers as to the retention or abandonment of the fort. The Virginian evidently construed this as an official approval of

[5] Washington to John Robinson, December 1755, *ibid.*, 532–533.
[6] Washington to Robinson, August 5, 1756, *ibid.*, 428.
[7] *Ibid.*, 428.

his plans. Thereupon he withdrew most of the garrison in order to place the men where they could defend the settlers. But just at this time there arrived in the colonies a new British commander in chief, Lord Loudoun. Though ignorant of conditions on the Virginia frontier, he rejected Washington's plan and ordered the garrison to return. A withdrawal from Fort Cumberland, he thought, would "not have a good appearance at home."[8] Imperial strategy, it seems, transcended for the moment the safety of the families on the Virginia frontier. Washington sided with the latter. For the sake of maintaining Fort Cumberland, he wrote in December, "the best lands in Virginia are laid open to the mercy of a cruel and inhuman enemy." The people, he continued, "have long struggled with the dangers of savage incursions, daily soliciting defense, and willing to keep their ground. . . . The disposition I had made of our small regiment gave general satisfaction to the settlements, and content began to appear everywhere. The necessary measures for provision and stores were agreeably concerted, and every regulation established for the season. But the late command reverses, confuses, and incommodes everything. . . . Whence it arises, or why, I am truly ignorant; but my strongest representations of matters relative to the peace of the frontiers are disregarded as idle and frivolous; my propositions and measures, as partial and selfish; and all my sincerest endeavors for the service of my country perverted to the worst purposes." The orders he received were "dark, doubtful and uncertain; today approved, tomorrow condemned." He lamented that he was left "to act and proceed at hazard, accountable for the consequence, and blamed without benefit of defense."[9]

In November, 1758, a force of Americans and British, of whom Washington was one, advanced to the site of Fort Duquesne, which they found deserted and in ruins. The Indian allies of France had fallen away and her cause in the Ohio valley had collapsed. A new British stronghold, Fort Pitt, soon rose upon the ruins of Fort Duquesne. These events made the frontiers of Virginia secure. In December, 1758, Washington gave up his duties as commander-in-chief of the colony's forces and retired to private

[8] Loudoun to Dinwiddie, November or December, 1756, *ibid.*, 491–492 n.
[9] Washington to Robinson, December 19, 1756, *ibid.*, 528.

life at Mount Vernon, which estate he had acquired by virtue of
the death of his half brother, Lawrence.

II

For the next fifteen years Washington devoted his energy to the
management of his farms and other business affairs. In these pursuits he soon ran into difficulties with British merchants which
remind one of his earlier disagreements with the British army.

At first he concentrated on the production of tobacco. As a
planter, he found himself involved in the network of laws and
commercial relations which bound the colonies to Britain. In large
measure the colonial policies of Britain had been shaped with an
eye to regulating the trade which was carried on by planters like
Washington. He therefore came into contact with British colonial
policy at its most essential points.

That policy decreed, first of all, that the tobacco which Washington produced could not be sent from Virginia directly to a
foreign country. It must be carried first into a British port, even
though the final market for two thirds of Virginia's crop was on
the European continent. Nor could he sell his tobacco to a foreign
buyer, inasmuch as a British act prohibited foreign merchants
from trading with Britain's colonies. He must transport his tobacco
across the Atlantic only in British vessels: foreign ships could not
legally visit British colonial ports. He must buy his supplies of
European goods in Britain, for Parliament had decreed that all
European goods en route to America must be carried into Britain
and unloaded there before they could be transshipped to the
colonies.

The planters who, like Washington, lived in the tidewater area
of Virginia commonly depended upon British merchants for the
sale of their tobacco. Ships from England went up the rivers of
the colony, visiting the various plantations, where they took on
board that part of the year's crop which the planters chose to
export. Such tobacco, while on shipboard, remained the property
of the planter, and he assumed all the risks which attended the
voyage across the Atlantic. Ordinarily, the ship belonged in whole
or in part to a merchant who resided in London or in another

English town. To such a merchant the planter consigned his tobacco shipment, with instructions regarding its sale. After the merchant had sold the tobacco, the proceeds technically belonged to the planter. However, he was obliged to pay a number of charges that had been incurred either in transit or at the English port. The merchant deducted such charges from the gross proceeds before any cash was credited to the planter's account.

Import duties payable in England composed the first charge which the planter had to pay. He must also pay to the merchant the costs of the shipment: freight charges, insurance premiums, and a commission for handling the tobacco. Other expenses involved warehouse and inspection fees and the cost of unloading and carting the consignment, while the planter bore all losses which arose from shrinkage or deterioration of the tobacco, if such loss occurred before the merchant made a sale.

In a vessel which carried the tobacco to England the planter usually sent a written order which told the merchant how to use that part of the proceeds which would belong to the planter after all charges had been deducted. From shops and warehouses in England the merchant selected goods which the planter had ordered. All sorts of manufactured articles, thus purchased, went out to Virginia in the vessels which sailed to fetch the next year's tobacco crop.

It often happened that bad market conditions in Europe depressed the price of tobacco, and that the gross proceeds from a shipment failed to pay both the English charges and the cost of the manufactured goods which the planter had ordered. In such a case, the merchant might fill the order, thereby supplying the goods on credit and protecting himself by taking a lien on the planter's next crop. The gravest difficulty, however, befell the planter in time of severe depression, when the sale of tobacco in England did not yield enough money to meet all the English charges. On such occasions, the merchant had to pay, first of all, the import duties, in full. This meant that the remaining part of the gross proceeds would not pay the sums due to the merchant on account of freight, insurance, and commission. For such unpaid charges the planter then became indebted to the merchant. In prosperous times the planter often borrowed money outright in order to purchase land, slaves, or plantation stock. By reason of these underlying conditions, the debts of the planters became larger, year after year, as short-term loans secured by crops were converted into mortgages on their estates.

The debtor planter experienced many troubles. He must pay the merchant a yearly interest charge—a sum which, when deducted from the proceeds of his tobacco sales, cut down his buying power for manufactured goods. In addition, he had to send his tobacco to one merchant—his creditor—in order to pay existing debts and to obtain new credit. Compelled thus to trade with a single firm, he lost the benefit of competitive bidding for his crop. Debtor planters appreciated the truth of Franklin's maxim that necessity never drives a good bargain. In hard times many a planter would regard himself as "in the clutches" of his merchant creditor.

III

Washington bought and sold in England through the firm of Robert Cary and Company. His letters to that house abound with allusions to his disappointments and distress. Once his tobacco could not be exported because vessels failed to arrive from England. On another occasion he objected that he had to pay higher freight rates than other shippers. Protesting against the cost of insurance he observed that "a person had better risk the loss . . . than part with so large a proportion of the year's produce to secure the rest."[10] When some of his tobacco was damaged on shipboard he wrote that he could "prove that the craft which received it had twelve or fifteen inches of rain water in her bottom entirely discolored by the juice of the tobacco; nothing but a miracle therefore could save it from destruction."[11]

The price which Cary secured for his tobacco in England frequently did not satisfy him. He heard that his neighbors' tobacco brought higher prices than his own. The crop of one year he thought had been sold for a third of its value, and another went at a price so low "that the freight and other incident charges swallowed up the sales and rendered me very unprofitable returns,

[10] Washington to Robert Cary, October 12, 1761, *ibid.*, II, 368.
[11] Washington to J. Pollard, August 22, 1766, *ibid.*, 441.

much less so than I could have had in this country without risking the hazard of a boisterous element."[12] In 1768 he wrote: "I have lost (at least) four years out of five by my consignments, having better prices offered in this country than my tobacco has sold for in England."[13]

Nor did the services of Cary and Company as a buyer satisfy him. The goods he ordered were numerous and varied: all kinds of plain and fashionable clothing, drugs, wines, fruits, notions, tools, household utensils, paper, handkerchiefs, playing cards, and snuff. A carriage and harness for four horses cost him £352. He wanted to secure busts of Alexander the Great, Julius Caesar, and other military leaders; for his library he sought busts of Sallust, Terence, Horace, and Erasmus; for his chimney piece he purchased statuary and ornamental pottery.

At different times he objected to the high prices, to the poor quality, and to the inferior style of the goods which he received. In 1760 he noted that "woolens, linens, nails, etc. are mean in quality but not in price, for in this they excel indeed, far above any I ever had."[14] A set of hoes he found to be worthless, "for they are scarcely wider or bigger than a man's hand."[15] A dozen scythes did not suit him—"some of one length, some of another; some crooked and some straight."[16] A shipment of 1766 included some wheat riddles so worthless that one would either have to send them back or keep them as "useless lumber. . . . I expressly desired sand sieves for the purpose of sifting out the dust and retaining the wheat, instead of which the wicker is so open that not only the dust but all the wheat passes through likewise . . . which renders them of no service." . . .[17]

Such were Washington's business troubles when the news of the Stamp Act shook the colonies. His cup of bitterness became exceedingly bitter. He thought that the colonies had been contributing enough to Britain through the channels of trade. "For certain it is," he wrote, "that our whole substance does already in a manner

12 Washington to Cary, July 20, 1767, *ibid.*, 461.
13 Washington to Cary, June 20, 1768, *ibid.*, 491.
14 Washington to Cary, June 23, 1766, *ibid.*, 437–438.
15 Washington to Cary, September 27, 1763, *ibid.*, 405–406.
16 Washington to Cary, July 21, 1766, *ibid.*, 439.
17 Washington to Cary, August 22, 1767, *ibid.*, 440.

flow to Great Britain." The immediate purpose of the new taxes was to maintain in America a British army, ten thousand strong. For the first time in peace the colonies were to be filled with the sort of military men he had encountered during the late war. He denounced the act as "an unconstitutional method of taxation," and pointed out that the colonies simply did not have the money that was required by the act. Since it taxed most legal documents, the courts would have to close, whereupon they would be unable to protect the rights of creditors. If that should be the result of the act, "the merchants of Great Britain trading to the colonies will not be among the last to wish for the repeal of it."[18]

In the opposition to the Stamp Act Washington was not surpassed by any other American leader. But since he was neither an orator nor a writer, his influence was exerted behind the scenes, and he did not gain thereby a continental reputation. However, it was not then necessary for him to address the world because one of his colleagues at Williamsburg in the Virginia assembly did that for him. He was content to have his views and indignation expressed by a young orator of "bold, grand, and overwhelming eloquence"—Patrick Henry.

IV

As a painstaking, systematic businessman, Washington kept exact accounts of the cost and profit of raising tobacco. They told him that it did not pay. Consequently, in the mid-1760's, he decided to abandon tobacco as a large-scale, commercial crop. Thereby he sought to escape his thralldom to British merchant monopolists and creditors—a bondage that was enforced by British law. This was perhaps the most important decision of his life, for it led him into conflict with the British government at several critical points. He now sought to achieve economic independence and to develop new sources of income that would free him from the entanglements of British trade.

It is highly probable that Washington was strongly influenced in this decision by the Stamp Act. He perceived in 1765 that the centering of American trade in Britain permitted the British gov-

[18] Washington to Francis Dandridge, September 20, 1765, *ibid.*, 425–426.

ernment to tax it at will. Only by means of diversified industries, he thought, could the colonies free themselves from the danger. In September he wrote: "The eyes of our people, already beginning to open, will perceive that many luxuries which we lavish our substance to Great Britain for, can well be dispensed with whilst the necessaries of life are (mostly) to be had within ourselves. This consequently will introduce frugality, and be a necessary stimulation to industry. If Great Britain therefore loads her manufactures with heavy taxes, will it not facilitate these measures? They will not compel us, I think, to give our money for their exports, whether we will or no; and certain I am none of their traders will part from them without a valuable consideration."[19]

The margin of profit in the tobacco industry was so slight that parliamentary taxation of the planters threatened to consume their surplus. Washington was farsighted when in 1765 he anticipated that Britain might impose taxes on manufactured goods sent to the colonies. That was exactly what Parliament did by levying the Townshend duties of 1767. Washington then entered into a non-importation association and in 1769 directed his London merchant not to send him any articles subject to such taxes ("paper only excepted").[20]

If Washington was to discontinue the exportation of tobacco, he must also find another means of supplying himself with manufactured goods. He therefore undertook to produce them at Mount Vernon. His spinners and weavers were soon making considerable quantities of linens, woolens, cottons, and linsey-woolsey. His records proved that such goods could be produced at lower cost than the price he had to pay for comparable articles obtained from England.

Such domestic industries in America did not serve the welfare of the empire, as viewed by British officials. Their first rule of policy decreed that the colonies should provide a profitable market for British wares, of which cloth ranked first in importance. To this end the imperial authorities had, by various legal devices, endeavored to check the growth of American industries that threatened to produce the sort of things that Britain desired most

[19] *Ibid.*, 426.
[20] Washington to Cary, July 25, 1769, *ibid.*, 512.

urgently to sell to the colonies. Numerous acts and orders, extending backward to the seventeenth century, aimed to deter the Americans from manufacturing iron and steel products, hats, leather goods, and cloth of all varieties.

The imperial trade resembled a tennis game in which Britain sent over manufactured goods and the colonists returned raw materials. Britain made the rules and acted as referee. Finding that so many of his returns were called out of bounds and that they did not yield him credit on the financial score, Washington decided to quit the game. When he abandoned tobacco as an export crop he took himself out of the imperial trade. He practically withdrew from the empire, since it was first and last a commercial organization. If the other planters had followed his example, one major branch of the imperial trade would have been lopped off. British manufactures would have lost a market; British shipowners would have lost business; British merchants would have lost an important source of profit. And the Crown would have suffered seriously, for in the 1760's it derived about £400,000 a year from taxes levied on the tobacco shipments of the colonies.

To manufacturing, Washington added another enterprise—the fishery. Again he utilized the resources of the plantation, for his hands made their catches in the Potomac, taking large quantities of whitefish, herring, and shad. On the farm he replaced tobacco with wheat. His yield of that crop increased nearly twentyfold in a period of four years. At his mill he ground his wheat into flour which, along with the fish, he exported to the West Indies. Thereby he obtained sugar, molasses, rum, coffee, fruits, and nuts, as well as money which he used to buy the finer goods that could not be manufactured at Mount Vernon.

As a producer of wheat and fish, Washington did not act as British officials thought a good Virginian ought to act. Britain did not favor an increased production of those commodities. Pennsylvania, New York, New Jersey, and New England already supplied all the wheat and fish that the empire needed. Perhaps those colonies were producing too much. The surplus had to be sold largely in the West Indies. Britain's islands there, having passed the peak of their development, could not provide a market sufficient to take off all the current output. If more was to be produced, it would have to be sold to the West Indian possessions of France, Holland, and Spain. That would merely serve Britain's competitors. It would supply them with cheap provisions and enable them to cut their production costs and thereby to undersell their British rivals. Thus at a second point Washington's new activity did not serve the welfare of the empire, as it was viewed in London.

V

A third enterprise with which Washington busied himself proved to be exceptionally absorbing—his speculations in western lands. The society of his day lived by a process of expansion. Pioneers opened a clearing in the forest; farmers moved in with their families; young men took younger wives; the settlement quickly swarmed with children who were soon seeking farms of their own. After two or three generations, these vigorous replenishers of the earth had occupied all the good land in their vicinity and a farther frontier beckoned to landless sons and daughters. In 1767 Washington urged a friend in distress to go west, "where there is a moral certainty of laying the foundations of good estates to your children." To men of wealth the great west afforded the means of acquiring more. "The greatest estates we have in the colony," continued Washington, were made "by taking up . . . at very low rates the rich back lands which were thought nothing of in those days but are now the most valuable lands we possess."[21] For fortunate promoters who amassed large holdings there were various ways to wealth. One might sell on a rising market, or rent to industrious tenants, or work one's land with imported servants.

The colonists, said Lord Dunmore, "do and will remove as their avidity and restlessness incite them. They acquire no attachment to place, but wandering seems engrafted in the nature; and it is a weakness incident to it that they should ever imagine that the lands farther off, are still better than those upon which they are already settled."[22]

By 1763 the tide of settlement had overflowed the great valley

[21] Washington to John Posey, June 24, 1767, *ibid.*, 459.
[22] Quoted in R. C. Downes, "Dunmore's War," *Mississippi Valley Historical Review,* XXI (December 1931), 319.

of Virginia and was ready to surge across the mountains into the lands adjoining the southern tributaries of the Ohio. Virginians had participated in the late war in order to clear the way for the occupation of this fertile area. Soil, climate, and the needs of the settlers all decreed that it should be a wheat and cattle land—not an extension of the tobacco country of the seaboard. The Potomac, flowing with majestic sweep past Mount Vernon, offered a natural highway to link an old Virginia with a new. The prospectus of a plan for improving the navigation of the river urged that thereby "we might . . . greatly increase our exports of wheat, gently lead our people off from tobacco . . . and render a vast extent of back country useful to trade."[23] In the upper Ohio Valley Washington saw a land ideally suited to the type of settlement in which he was now most interested—one devoted to diversified farming and to domestic manufacturing.

Unhappily for all concerned, this vision of a great interior commonwealth was not attractive to the king's principal advisers in London. They had quite a different conception of the destiny of inland America. It is true that shortly before and during the French and Indian War they had acted on ideas akin to Washington's views of a future appropriate to the west. They had then sought to extend settlements beyond the mountains. The advance of the pioneers strengthened the hold of Britain on the territory claimed by the French. Since the frontier farmers were also soldiers, the Crown encouraged them to go into border zones where they met the vanguards of the Spaniards and the French. To encourage such pioneers the king's officials offered them land in the upper Ohio Valley. In March, 1749, the Privy Council authorized a grant of 200,000 acres to a group of Virginians who organized the Ohio Company. The scene of this grant was the land about the forks of the Ohio. Many leading Virginians took part in the adventure, among them three Washingtons (including George), Robert Carter, George Mason, Thomas Nelson, and four members of the Lee family. In the negotiations that produced this grant there appeared a source of future conflict between the Virginians and the Crown. British officials conceived of the new company as a

[23] Grace L. Nute (ed.), "Washington and the Potomac," *American Historical Review*, XXVIII (April 1923), 510.

club with which to beat the French. The Virginians regarded it mainly as an agency through which the Ohio country might be occupied by settlers.

A few years later, the governor, Robert Dinwiddie, when seeking soldiers for the war, offered land to volunteers and promised that 200,000 acres in the west would be set aside for that purpose. As the leading soldier of Virginia, Washington became entitled to a share of this proffered bounty.

During the period of the French war, the short-run aim of the British government had harmonized with the objectives of the Virginians. Both desired to encourage settlement. The Crown wished to use the pioneers mainly to drive out the French. The colonists desired to open the west to farmers who would overspread the land and build new communities. This difference of aims quickly became apparent after the expulsion of the French had removed the menace which, for a time, had held the Crown and the Virginians together in an artificial partnership.

Once the French had been expelled from the Ohio Valley the British government dropped its earlier policy of encouraging settlement there, and adopted a new one which tended to discourage it. The Crown no longer needed to extend a frontier zone of farmer-soldier settlers into an area claimed by an enemy. Now it appeared that the occupation of the Ohio Valley would not promote the welfare of the empire. The settlers would produce grain and livestock—commodities with which the empire was already overstocked. Moreover, new communities in the west would not be accessible to British traders. To transport goods across the mountains would be so expensive as to prevent the settlers from buying British products. They would be obliged to make most of the things they needed. Isolated in the interior, they would not contribute to the growth of British trade.

On the other hand, the interior produced commodities that influential men in England deemed to be far more valuable than additional supplies of wheat and meat products. Such were the furs and deerskins of the Indian trade. They did not compete with British goods; in fact, they afforded a market, inasmuch as they were obtained from the Indians in return for manufactured articles. The fur trade was the great prize that Britain had gained through the conquest of Canada, eastern Louisiana, and Florida. The incompatibility of fur trade and settlement was an old story. The settlers drove back the Indians and destroyed the fur-bearing animals.

Britain's plans for the utilization of the resources of North America did not assume their full form until the middle of 1774. The final decision was not reached until after a good deal of experimentation. The matured policy exhibited two main features. First, it decreed that the larger part of the interior should be closed to settlement and reserved to the Indians and the fur trade. The Crown established a western limit of settlement by making a line to divide the lands reserved to the Indians from those open to settlers. This "dividing line" or "boundary line" was drawn in agreement with the Indian tribes. The red men ceded to the king their claims to the land east of the line and retained full title and possession to the land lying west of it. By this means the two parties designated an Indian country into which settlers were not allowed to enter.

While the king's advisers were working out this policy, they recognized that the rapidly increasing population of the thirteen colonies could not safely be excluded from unoccupied land, without room for expansion. To relieve the pressure of expanding settlement, the government offered a special outlet. Land-hungry farmers might move to certain seacoast areas—to Florida, Nova Scotia, Cape Breton Island, or Prince Edward Island. The development of those areas promised to benefit the empire. They might produce such things as wine, silk, and fruits (in Florida) or timber and naval stores (in the north). Britain needed such commodities, and none of them would compete with the products of established industries. Settlements on or near the seacoast would be easily accessible to British traders. For such reasons the king's advisers chose to settle the seacoast areas in preference to the Ohio Valley. The former were opened freely to settlement, and liberal grants of land were made to British promoters who would people them with workers.

If Britain's plans of 1774 had been realized, the growth of North America would have produced a belt of settled territory, semicircular in shape, extending along the Atlantic seacoast and the Gulf of Mexico, from the mouth of the St. Lawrence to the mouth of the Mississippi. The interior beyond the mountains would have remained an Indian country, closed to settlement and reserved to the fur trade.

VI

When Washington found that tobacco-growing was unprofitable, he decided to supplant it with operations in western lands, using the bounty claims as a wedge to open to settlement the valley of the Great Kanawha. To this end he originated a project and enlisted the interest of other veterans. He purchased many bounty claims, "as a lottery," at low prices, since the royal government was slow in making good its promises and the claims for a time had little value. He embarked upon this course in 1767.

His efforts soon bore fruit. In December, 1769, the Council of Virginia authorized him to locate 200,000 acres for the benefit of the veterans. He met with other claimants at Fredericksburg, where they chose him as their agent and decided to locate their grants on the Great Kanawha. Late in 1770 he made a trip to that river, explored the country, and selected a site for the grants. At another meeting at Winchester his associates decided to survey the site he had chosen. In November, 1771, he reported that "we have surveyed ten of the largest tracts we can find in the district allowed us, and have been able to get 61,796 acres."[24]

The chosen site on the Great Kanawha was then well to the westward of the fringe of settlement. At the start, Washington hoped to find tenants to work his land. This interest raised the question of a government for the area; and that in turn magnified the importance of the Crown, as the recognized creator of such authority. British policy did not at the time countenance the establishment of a government in the Kanawha country. The better sort of independent settlers would not occupy an area devoid of a civil authority; only those would be attracted who had little or no respect for an organized government. But persons of that sort made the worst possible tenants, for they were such as would

[24] Washington to George Mercer, November 7, 1771, *Writings of Washington,* III, 68.

desert a landlord at their pleasure "without paying any rents."[25] This handicap obliged Washington to postpone his tenancy plans and to engage bonded servants to make the initial improvements on his tract. Even so, the problem of government remained, for the settlement could not prosper without an effective civil authority. The British government, claiming as it did the supreme power over the west, would hold the whip in its hand, as long as its pretensions were recognized by the colonists.

In April, 1774, Washington's agent, John Floyd, surveyed for him two thousand acres, located on the west bank of the Great Kanawha, forty miles above its junction with the Ohio. About a year later Washington completed plans for the development of his land. Having obtained servants, he engaged an overseer, whom he directed to go to the site and begin improvements. "Use every diligence in your power," he advised, "to get as much land as possible ready for corn, and continue planting even with ripe rare corn, as long as you think it shall have time to come to perfection. You may, in the meanwhile, be putting up houses for the convenience of yourselves to live in, but do not spend any time fencing in the field till it is too late to plant, as the corn can take no injury till some time after it is up which will be time enough to begin fencing."[26]

At the critical point he received a rude shock, for on March 21, 1775, Lord Dunmore, the governor of Virginia, suddenly canceled his claims. Washington registered a strong protest. On the very day that the British army at Boston prepared to march to Concord the governor at Williamsburg replied, confirming the invalidation of the Kanawha grant, on the pretext that Washington's surveyor was not qualified to make surveys.

By this time Washington was deep in the activities of the American resistance. He had come forward in the summer of 1774 to take a leading part in the opposition to the punitive acts. He spoke with considerable asperity of the Quebec Act, which aimed a mortal blow at his western plans. That act detached from the

[25] Richard Thompson to Washington, September 30, 1775, Washington Papers, Library of Congress, XIV.

[26] Instructions for William Stevens, March 6, 1775, Writings of Washington, III, 269.

thirteen colonies the land west of Pennsylvania, north of the Ohio, and east of the Mississippi, and added it to the royal province of Quebec. The authors of this drastic measure intended that the land thus severed from the thirteen colonies should be reserved to the Indians and the fur trade. It did not interfere, directly, with Washington's Kanawha tract. But indirectly it did. Presumably, the Indians were to continue to live on the north bank of the Ohio, with the sanction and protection of the Crown. If so, could the settlement of the lands along the south bank proceed with safety?

If there was one law that governed the peopling of the colonies, it was the rule that settlement should advance inland along a river and that the pioneers should simultaneously occupy both banks. It was not comfortable to dwell with hostile Indians on an opposite shore, adept as they were in the art of slipping noiselessly across a stream. On the north bank of the Ohio, opposite the mouth of the Great Kanawha, the situation was especially serious. There dwelt the Shawnee nation, traditional foes of the colonists. Most disconcerting was the fact that these warriors claimed the ownership of the land across the river from their villages, and insisted that it be preserved as their hunting domain. They wished to be free to roam at will over the very land that Washington had chosen for his settlement. Back in 1769 a Shawnee chief had warned a band of intruders led by Daniel Boone: "Now, brothers, go home and stay there. Don't come here any more, for this is the Indians' hunting ground, and all the animals, skins, and furs are ours; and if you are so foolish as to venture here again you may be sure the wasps and yellow-jackets will sting you severely."[27]

The strife between the Shawnee and the pioneers exploded in Dunmore's War of 1774. It arose from friction between the whites and the Indians who passed to and fro across the Ohio River. The chief engagement, the battle of Point Pleasant, occurred in October at the mouth of the Great Kanawha. The war had begun in earnest after it became known on the frontier that the Quebec Act had extended the province of Quebec so as to include within it the Shawnee villages, and had, by inference, sanctioned the Shawnee claims to the valley of the Great Kanawha. Dunmore's zeal in pressing for war gave color to the charge that he had provoked it

[27] Quoted in Downes, *Mississippi Valley Historical Review*, XXI, 312.

in order to weaken the colonists at the onset of their renewed struggle with the British government.

Washington's experience with Britain's policies was such as to exasperate a patient man. Before 1760 those policies had encouraged him to suffer hardship and to risk his life in the struggle against the French, on the supposition that victory would open the west to settlement. No one had done more to expel the French. For this service the royal government promised him a land bounty in the west. After the war he devoted much arduous labor to his Kanawha project. He kept within the legal bounds set by Britain, for his proposed settlement was located east of the dividing line, as it was drawn in 1770. Then, in 1774, Parliament unceremoniously detached from Virginia the land north of the Ohio, and in so doing created a condition unfavorable to the development of his Kanawha tract. At this time, also, the British colonial secretary, Lord Dartmouth, instructed Dunmore to stop the granting of western lands. Washington protested vigorously against the Quebec Act and the other punitive measures. For such opposition, presumably, he was penalized by the invalidation of a title he had acquired at no little hazard, expense, and labor.

VII

In mid-May the Second Continental Congress was called upon to consider an absorbing question. Should it establish an American army and incorporate into it the thousands of militiamen who surrounded the British troops in Boston? Affirmative action would endorse the resistance of April 19 and approve the view of Massachusetts that the British troops had begun the war by shooting down innocent citizens, almost within sight of their homes. Every member of Congress who should vote for such military assistance would give aid and comfort to armed men, branded as rebels, who were levying war against the British state. . . .

The *Journals of the Continental Congress* do not record a formal resolve for the creation of a Continental army. The question was: should the members vote to levy war against the British state and thereby expose themselves to the penalty for the crime of treason? As early as May 21 John Adams ventured to "guess" that an army would be posted in Massachusetts, "at the continental expense."[28] Three days later Congress selected as its president the "arch-traitor," John Hancock, and on the twenty-sixth it condemned Britain as the aggressor in the engagement of April 19. About this time it received word that the trade of South Carolina, Virginia, Maryland, Pennsylvania, and New Jersey had been subjected to the vengeance of Parliament. On June 3 the delegates approved the borrowing of £6,000 for purchasing powder "for the continental army."[29] Such is the first official notice that the critical step had been taken. But even yet it was not decisive, for there was no reference to the inclusion in the Continental force of the New England troops at Boston. The final arrangements were evidently completed by June 7. On the eighth a great celebration was staged in Philadelphia. Early in the afternoon the members gathered on the Common to watch a "parade of the three battalions [of] militia of the city and liberties, with the artillery company . . . a troop of light horse, several companies of light infantry, rangers, and riflemen, in the whole above two thousand men, who joined in one brigade, and went through their manual exercises, firings, &c. &c."[30]

The final decision is recorded in the *Journal* for June 10 in a resolve which, for the first time, used the expression, "the American army before Boston."[31] On that day Congress made provision for obtaining an adequate supply of powder. It was then, also, that John Hancock, in official capacity, notified the authorities of Massachusetts and New York of the fateful decision. Writing to James Warren that day Samuel Adams pointedly alluded to "the American Army before Boston."[32] Other arrangements were soon announced. On the fourteenth a Virginia delegate reported: "We

28 John Adams to James Warren, May 21, 1775, Edmund C. Burnett, ed., *Letters of Members of the Continental Congress,* 8 vols. (Washington, 1921–1936), I, 95.

29 Worthington C. Ford and others, eds., *Journals of the Continental Congress,* 34 vols. (Washington, 1904–1937), II, 79.

30 William Duane, Jr., ed., *Passages from the Remembrancer of Christopher Marshall* (Philadelphia, 1839), 32–33.

31 *Journals of Continental Congress,* II, 85.

32 Samuel Adams to James Warren, June 10, 1775, Burnett, *Letters,* I, 121.

have determined to keep ten thousand men in Massachusetts Bay, and five thousand in different parts of the New York government, at the expense of the continent."[33] Congress then authorized the printing of $2 million in paper currency (bills of credit) to be used for paying the troops and for purchasing army supplies. The climax was reached on June 15 when Washington was unanimously elected commander-in-chief. . . .

On June 20 the newly elected commander-in-chief wrote to his brother: "I am embarked on a wide ocean, boundless in its prospect and from whence perhaps no safe harbor is to be found."[34]

Washington's activities during the twelve months before June, 1775, led naturally to his acceptance of the army command. Early in May, 1774, he had attended the regular session of the Virginia House of Burgesses at Williamsburg. The electrifying news of the Boston Port Bill spurred the members to devise resolves in protest. Suddenly, the governor dissolved the house, it having adopted a resolve which urged resistance and intimated the possibility of civil war. The members met immediately at Raleigh Tavern, there to propose the assembling of a Continental Congress, on the theory that the British measures against Massachusetts imperiled all the colonies. Soon afterward, dispatches from the north told of insurgent activities in Maryland, Philadelphia, and Boston. Twenty-five of the burgesses then issued a call for a provincial convention to assemble on August 1. Washington was one of the signers of this appeal. The impetus for it arose from a Boston proposal for a "general association against exports and imports, of every kind, to and from Great Britain."[35]

Early in July Washington, back at Mount Vernon, busied himself with plans for the August convention. The citizens of Fairfax County appointed him to a committee to prepare a set of resolutions on the unfolding crisis. One of the other members, George Mason, visited Mount Vernon on Sunday, July 17. There the two men whipped into shape a paper containing twenty-four resolves.

34 Washington to J. A. Washington, June 20, 1775, *Bicentennial,* III, 299.

35 Statement of May 31, 1774, signed by Washington, Washington Papers, Library of Congress, XV.

Washington took it to a second meeting at the Fairfax County courthouse, where the citizens approved it on July 18. Hence the name, "the Fairfax Resolves."

Washington was later accused of something akin to "railroading" the Resolves through the meeting. As the presiding officer, he refused to read a letter submitted by his friend, Bryan Fairfax, to whom he explained: ". . . as no person seemed in the least disposed to adopt your sentiments . . . except a Mr. Williamson . . . I forbore to offer it."[36] Fairfax replied: "Mr. Williamson told me the other day that he found afterward that there were a great many of his opinion in the court house who did not care to speak because they thought it would be to no purpose. . . ."[37] Washington evidently was not to be deterred by timid souls who shrank from attending a public meeting, or—if present—feared to speak.

The Fairfax meeting having selected him as one of its delegates to the August convention, he returned to Williamsburg, armed with the Fairfax Resolves. They provided the substance of a program adopted by the convention. The members also chose him as one of seven delegates to present the plan to the forthcoming Continental Congress. Washington's continental fame was enhanced by his militant stand in Williamsburg. A South Carolinian informed a Bostonian "that Colonel Washington made the most eloquent speech at the Virginia convention that ever was made. Says he, 'I will raise one thousand men, subsist them at my own expense, and march myself at their head for the relief of Boston.' "[38] When John Adams learned of the action of the Virginia convention he wrote: "The spirit of the people is prodigious; their resolutions are really grand."[39] The convention voted to pay the expense of its delegates to the Philadelphia Congress. Washington's assessment amounted to more than £90.

The most important influence of the Fairfax Resolves appears in one of the principal measures of the First Congress—the Conti-

[36] Washington to Bryan Fairfax, July 20, 1774, *Bicentennial*, III, 231.
[37] Bryan Fairfax to Washington, August 5, 1774, Washington Papers, Library of Congress, XV.
[38] Diary entry for August 31, 1774, Charles Francis Adams, ed., *The Works of John Adams. . .*, 10 vols. (Boston, 1850–1856), II, 360.
[39] Diary entry for August 23, 1774, *ibid.*, 352.

nental Association. This was a plan for establishing an independent government in the colonies—one that was to function in opposition to the British government, for the purpose of nullifying British laws.

Both the Fairfax Resolves and the Continental Association provided for nonimportation of goods from Britain, to be effective about six weeks after approval. Both proposed a ban on the importation of slaves. Both suggested an embargo on American exports to Britain, to take effect about one year after adoption. Washington insisted on this delay to avoid any charge of a plot to default on colonial debts due to British merchants.

The unique feature of the Fairfax Resolves, which gave unusual importance to the work of the First Continental Congress, was a plan for enforcing the nonimportation agreements. In every community, an extralegal committee was to be authorized to stand watch over local merchants and other importers. If a committee should detect a violator of the nonimportation agreements, it was to compel him either to send back his goods or to place them in its custody. It was also to publish the names of all violators, in order that they might be boycotted and exposed to public contempt.

If the First Congress had merely recommended nonimportation agreements, on a voluntary basis, its activities would not have appeared unduly serious to British authorities. But when the Congress introduced the idea of compulsion, its work assumed, in British eyes, a most offensive aspect. Merchants were required to conform, whether they approved or not. They were to be subjected to a supervising authority, armed with coercive powers. The earlier nonimportation agreements had been private and voluntary. Individuals merely pledged to act for themselves; there was no organized official means of enforcement. When the Congress undertook to create the machinery to enforce its measures, and to authorize penalties and punishments, it ceased to be a recommending body and became a legislature. Its acts now acquired the force of law. It had set up a new government. And for what purpose? That British laws might be nullified; that the British government might be rendered futile; that British authorities might be forced to bow to the will of Congress.

It is not known whether Washington or Mason originated the Fairfax Resolves. The only manuscript copy, in Mason's handwriting, is in Washington's papers. The Resolves were given their final form at Mount Vernon. Washington presided at the meeting which adopted them. As a delegate of Fairfax County, he presented them to the Virginia convention at Williamsburg. There they were incorporated into the plan which the Virginia delegation submitted to the First Continental Congress. At Philadelphia the Virginians held a commanding position. Washington was their most important leader. Two of his fellow delegates, Patrick Henry and Richard Henry Lee, were of his mind at this time.He also had the confidence of three of the other members, as indicated by the fact that on October 24 Benjamin Harrison, Peyton Randolph, and Richard Bland authorized him to sign their names "to any of the proceedings of Congress."[40] The work of Washington and Mason at Mount Vernon in July blossomed in the most decisive action taken by the First Continental Congress in October.

Equally important, the Fairfax Resolves contained the seed from which the Continental Army developed. It was evident at once that local committees charged with the duty of enforcing nonimportation agreements would need the assistance of an organized military force. Hence, when the Virginia convention of August, 1774, adopted the essential feature of the Fairfax Resolves, it also authorized the establishment, in each county, of an independent military company. Independent, that is, of the royal governor, who commanded the regular militia organization.

Before he left to attend the First Continental Congress, Washington took a hand in the preparations for establishing the Fairfax company. During the following winter he devoted his attention mainly to the task of placing Virginia on an independent military footing. He continued to collaborate with George Mason, who assisted in devising plans for the new organization. For various companies Washington acted as purchasing agent, ordering military equipment through a Philadelphia merchant, William Milnor. The articles purchased included sashes, epaulettes, colors, fifes,

[40] Harrison, Randolph, and Bland to Washington, October 24, 1774, *Journals of Continental Congress,* I, 52–53.

drums, muskets, bayonets, powder boxes, and treatises on military discipline. The planners envisaged a formal, disciplined army to be used in conventional warfare—not a band of Indian fighters. Each company was to consist of sixty men, with seven elected officers and four corporals appointed by the captain. When enough companies had been established they were to be formed into a regiment. The uniform included a hunting shirt, cap, and gaiters. Each soldier furnished his own musket and powder.

Late in December the governor, Lord Dunmore, described the progress of the resistance. "The associations," he wrote, "first . . . recommended by the people of this colony, and adopted by what is called the Continental Congress, are now enforcing throughout this country with the greatest vigor. A committee has been chosen in every county, whose business it is to carry the association of the Congress into execution, which committee assumes to inspect the books, invoices, and all other secrets of trade and correspondence of merchants, to watch the conduct of every inhabitant without distinction, and to send for all such as come under their suspicion . . . to interrogate them respecting all matters which, at their pleasure, they think fit objects of their inquiry; and to stigmatize, as they term it, such as they find transgressing what they are hardy enough to call the laws of Congress, which stigmatizing is no more than inviting the vengeance of an outrageous and lawless mob to be exercised upon the unhappy victim. Every county, besides, is now arming a company of men, whom they call an Independent Company, for the avowed purpose of protecting their committees, and to be employed against government if occasion require."[41]

The evolution of the companies pointed to a final colony-wide organization to be headed by Washington. By May, 1775, he had been chosen to command the companies of seven counties. His new activities added to his fame abroad. From England a friend wrote to him early in March, 1775: "It is reported in London, that you are training the people of Virginia in the use of arms."[42] He informed his brother about this time that ". . . it is my full inten-

[41] Dunmore to Dartmouth, December 24, 1774, *Bicentennial,* III, 248 n.
[42] G. W. Fairfax to Washington, March 2, 1775, Washington Papers, Library of Congress, XV.

tion to devote my life and fortune to the cause we are engaged in. . . ." The uniform of buff and blue which made him so conspicuous at the Second Congress was that of the Fairfax company. He wore it throughout the Revolutionary War.

✪

Cincinnatus Assayed:
Washington in the Revolution

Arguments on Washington's skill as a soldier are as old as the
history of the United States, and extreme positions have been
taken. A school which insists that he would have been igno-
miniously defeated by any general except the dullards the incompetent English ministry sent against him has a fantastic fringe which
believes that what happened can only be explained by assuming
that General Howe (as a British Whig) purposely avoided crushing Washington's army. However, two distinguished military historians have recently stated that by 1781 Washington had "developed a competence worthy of favorable comparison beside
Alexander at Granicus, Caesar at the Rubicon, Hannibal at the
Alps, Genghis Khan at the Great Wall, Frederick the Great at
Prague, or Napoleon at Montenotte."[1]

An intelligent comparison between Washington and the celebrated soldiers of the past is greatly impeded by a fact too often

[1] R. Ernest Dupuy and Trevor N. Dupuy, *The Compact History of the
Revolutionary War* (New York, 1963), pp. 474–475; Thomas J. Fleming,
"The Enigma of General Howe," *American Heritage*, XV (1964), 6–11,
96–103.

overlooked: Washington was never truly a military man. He remained to the end of the war a civilian serving half-reluctantly in uniform.

If we read Washington's writings beside those of any dedicated warrior—say, Light Horse Harry Lee—it is instantly clear how little the basic bent of his mind was military. The numerous metaphors he wrote down in armed camps are almost never drawn from warfare: they recall the fields and forests, the mounting and sinking suns of a peaceful home. He never wrote of a Revolutionary battle in terms of sanguinary exultation; he never, in all his exhortations to his troops, appealed to bloodlust or glorified carnage. Such happy visions of military adventure as he had enjoyed as a younger man and in an earlier war had faded from him. "It is time," he admonished Chastellux, "for the age of knight-errantry and mad heroism to be at an end." The French staff officer Barbé-Marbois wrote, "I have been told that he preserves in battle the character of humanity which makes him so dear to his soldiers in camp."[2]

Washington would take military risks to protect what he referred to as "the essential interests of any individual." He wrote, "The misfortunes of war, and the unhappy circumstances frequently attendant thereon to individuals, are more to be lamented than avoided: but it is the duty of everyone to alleviate these as much as possible." Although recognizing the military genius of Harry Lee, he was horrified by the cruelties that dedicated soldier perpetrated. Congressman Charles Carroll of Carrollton complained of Washington, "He is so humane and delicate that I fear the common cause will suffer. . . . The man cannot be too much admired and lamented."[3]

While the true military mind is most concerned with the exertion of force, Washington considered force secondary in winning the war to gentleness, justice, forbearance. This was because the un-

---

[2] Eugene Parker Chase, *Our Revolutionary Forefathers: The Letters of Francois Marquis de Barbé-Marbois* (New York, 1929), p. 113; John C. Fitzpatrick, ed., *The Writings of George Washington*, 39 vols. (Washington, 1931–1944), XXIX, 485 (hereafter cited as *Writings of Washington*).

[3] Charles Carroll of Carrollton to Charles Carroll (October 23, 1777), *Writings of Washington*, VI, 222; XV, 388, 399.

reconstructed civilian was, as he stated again and again, infinitely less afraid of military defeat than of doubt and disunity within the patriot cause.

Although he never abandoned the hope of a sledgehammer blow that would end the war overnight, from week to week and year to year such a quick solution remained a seductive will-o'-the-wisp. In the long reaches, Washington used the army as a propaganda instrument. "Popular expectations," he wrote, "should always be complied with where injury in the execution is not too apparent, especially in such a contest as the one we are engaged in, where the spirit and willingness of the people must in a great measure take place of coercion."[4]

What the public believed had happened, Washington wrote, "might almost as well be so."[5] This opened a way to retrieve defeats: claim at the very least that the enemy casualties had been greater than your own. He also created on paper, for the consumption of the home front as well as the enemy, imaginary legions.

Washington's propaganda activities did not involve infringement of the freedom of the press, a principle which he often stated was essential to a free nation. Since no war correspondents existed, the newspapers relied on letters written from the front by private or public individuals. There is no evidence that Washington ever tried to influence the writers except by controlling the information they in the first place received. He on one occasion asked Congress for "a small traveling press to follow headquarters" and "an ingenious man to accompany this press and be employed wholly in writing for it. . . . If the people had a channel of intelligence that from its usual authenticity they could look up to with confidence," that would frustrate false rumors, undermine despondency and the propaganda of the enemy.[6] Congress did not fall in with this suggestion, and Washington remained his own principal disseminator of information, broadcasting in personal letters to officials his approved version of events.

The hindsight of the historian can only reinforce Washington's

[4] *Ibid.*, XI, 194.
[5] *Ibid.*, XIII, 465.
[6] *Ibid.*, VIII, 443; XXIV, 225.

conviction that the crucial battles of the war were in the arenas of public opinion. Had the British been able to bring even a large minority of the Americans back into active support of the Crown, all opposing military efforts would have been unavailing. Their intelligence would have sprung up like the grass of midsummer, hampering Washington's every move. Guerrillas would have met guerrillas in the glades and under the rocks until everyone would have cried for peace. And the British, as they marched at will from state to state, would have needed to leave behind no more than small detachments to help the local Tories keep the captured communities loyal. They could thus have pinned down the rebellion bit by bit.

Convinced that the uprising had been forced on the population by a small group of agitators and terrorists, the British alternated a withering carrot with an unwieldy stick. Their propaganda opportunities were, indeed, great. Not only had the Revolution started with no unanimity of opinion even among its supporters, but the cause had moved so rapidly that a patriot who moored his boat to any fixed political doctrine was soon left behind. It was not enough to persuade a man once: he had to be persuaded again and again. And the war seemed endlessly long. Mounting discouragement, confusion, and apathy caused serious shrinkage in Washington's army. But whenever a British advance forced the inhabitants of a neighborhood to take sides, it became clear that all the unhappiness had not created renewed allegiance to the Crown. Although some males did join loyalist corps, more became American guerrillas; and when stay-at-homes saw columns moving in the night, they sent word not to the British marchers but the patriot skulkers. There can be no doubt that the British were totally outclassed in the warfare for the minds of men.

It was in those mental arenas that the civilian-soldier George Washington shone the brightest. He kept forever in mind, as more radical statesmen of either the right or the left could not do, that the fundamental objective was not to foster division but to increase unity.

Every man imprisoned or driven to the British was a loss; every man who hesitated in a way not immediately and actively dangerous to the cause should be regarded not as an enemy but as a

potential convert. And conversion was best achieved not by political arguments—Washington was never much of a political arguer
—but by visible virtue: an army less destructive than that of the
enemy; broad tolerance which promised happiness to the widest
possible segment of humanity. Washington reversed the usual role
of a commander-in-chief by urging on rampant civilian authorities
greater respect for civilian rights.

Although Washington often phrased his arguments for tolerance
in terms of expediency, his sentiments stemmed from deep moral
principles. While sadly recognizing the necessity for curbing inimical behavior that was a danger to the cause, he did not believe that
a man should be persecuted as a result of any opinions he held that
had not exploded into action. As he put it in explaining a conception that has been echoed down the years by Jefferson and other
liberals, "Our actions, depending upon ourselves, may be controlled, whilst the powers of thinking, originating in higher causes,
cannot always be molded to our wishes."[7]

In military matters, Washington was much less sure of himself. His
previous experience had been limited to leading untrained and
unconventional Indian-fighters mostly against savages and always
in the wilderness. His contact with professional soldiers had only
been close enough to make it clear to him how much he had to
learn. Even on his own wild terrain, the regulars had captured Fort
Duquesne in a manner that he did not comprehend. As he rode to
Cambridge to assume his new command, George Washington
knew he was as green as grass.

His British opponents sailed across the ocean with an exactly
opposite attitude: they intended to exert proven skills on comical
amateurs. However, the doctrines of the great European commanders like Frederick the Great were in reality no more applicable to the American war than were the naïvetés of a wilderness fighter. The crucial military difference (apart from levels of
innate ability) between Washington and the commanders who
opposed him was that they were sure they knew all the answers,
while Washington tried every day and every hour to learn.

The objective of the type of warfare to which the British had been trained was to drive the enemy backward from position to position with as little loss as possible to your side. But, however successfully this was carried through, it failed to achieve victory on the vast and disorganized American continent, where there were no crucial cities to capture and the unworthy rebels, living like beetles off a leaf, depended on no magazines that could be destroyed, no supply lines that could be cut. A more daring British strategy was needed—but everything in their situation inhibited British daring. The normal pressure on the commanders of expensive professional armies not to endanger them rashly was redoubled by the fact that this one would have to be resupplied and reinforced across three thousand miles of ocean. Furthermore, it is axiomatic that the convinced practitioners of accepted skills are inclined, when their rules fail to work, not to question the rules but to become more and more cautious in situations which seem to them inexplicable.

A recognition, it is true, that this strange war could not be won until Washington's force was destroyed rather than just pushed back, had, as the 1776 campaign unrolled, entered the minds of Howe and his officers. However, this consideration was so far from the established doctrines of the war of position that it was hard to take seriously. And insofar as they did take it seriously, the British lacked the means. Not only were techniques of destructive pursuit lacking in the military copybooks of that time (they were to be worked out later), but the American situation presented particular obstacles. Cavalry could not mop up effectively where walls and trees interposed, and European infantrymen could not hope to catch up with the Americans, who, with their strong legs and shoulders unburdened by equipment, got off as fast as rabbits. And so much of the country over which the regulars had to fight was seamed with stone walls, bumpy with hills, obscured with vegetation: untidily suited to the guerrilla activity of a peasantry familiar with firearms. Guerrilla reprisal was almost impossible to a force in which individual soldiers had been trained not to think for themselves, and from which the men—cavalry, as well as infantry—might desert if they got out of sight of their officers.

The British made various sporadic efforts to break out of the established molds. Despite flocks of difficulties which occurred to well-trained minds, they did make some use of Tory irregulars to counteract the patriot guerrillas. Although it was an established principle that troops in mercenary armies, who were fighting only to earn their livelihoods, would desert if made too uncomfortable, the British command sometimes took the risk of leaving some baggage behind in order to achieve speed. They flirted, albeit in a most gingerly manner, with a scorched-earth policy which (despite its unfortunate propaganda effect) would have enabled their army to leave an impression on the countryside through which they marched. However, the British generals never carried any innovations far enough to achieve solid results.

Although he was at first pushed around like the most ignorant beginner, Washington finally stymied the well-trained and able regulars opposing him. This does not mean that what he taught himself would have been effective against Frederick at Prague or Napoleon at Montenotte. His strategy was a Darwinian achievement of adaptation to environment; it was evolved to overcome the specific problems with which he was faced. It was the triumph of a man who knows how to learn, not in the narrow sense of studying other people's conceptions, but in the transcendent sense of making a synthesis out of the totality of experience.

Poised at the break between the age of reason and the age of empirical knowledge, Washington drew strength from both outlooks. He discarded outworn paraphernalia left over from the past without abandoning himself to the pure expediency of the experimental method. His doctrine was "Good judgment and experimental knowledge properly exerted, never can, when accompanied with integrity and zeal, go wrong."[8]

As a young man, Washington had been interested in his ancestry and had ordered the coat of arms he claimed emblazoned on all amenable articles. After the Revolution, he no longer exhibited any interest in his forebears, answering the queries of genealogists with bored courtesy. He stated that precedents are dangerous things, as they impose on the present the dead hand of the past. In thanking an admirer for his "politeness" in sending him a "piece of

[8] *Ibid.,* XXXIII, 429–430.

antiquity," Washington wrote wryly that its age "and having once been the property of so remarkable a character as Oliver Cromwell, would undoubtedly render it pleasant to almost anyone, and to an antiquary perhaps invaluable."[9]

The Virginian who had found his manhood in a wilderness unknown to literature and had achieved economic independence by discarding the established trade patterns of his neighbors, who was fighting his king and advancing into uncharted political seas, preferred to find things out for himself. As an old man, he was to write sadly, "I must now benefit from the studies and experience of others, but a remnant of it [his life] being left to essay either myself."[10]

But experience is not an instantaneous teacher. To escape from what he considered the "infant state" of his knowledge, he read, on his assuming the Revolutionary command, military manuals imported from abroad and questioned men he considered knowing. In particular, he sat at the feet of the former British regulars Gates and Lee.[11]

Congress had instructed Washington to consult with his officers, and this he gladly did in Councils of War which he ran like miniature legislative assemblies. He took votes. If he were in the minority, he might complain but he gave in. This was not the soul of forceful generalship, but certainly the councils he held in Cambridge were useful as brakes on the commander-in-chief's impetuosity. For Washington, despite the reputation for caution which later experience taught him to earn, was by natural inclination both a rash and overoptimistic fighter.

As Washington, mounting from grade to grade in his college of experience, became surer of himself, he less and less often called his officers together in conferences. Instead (as he was to do when President), he asked for written advice on specific questions. The answers became part of the evidence he weighed. "In all matters of great national moment," he wrote, "the only true line of conduct in my opinion is dispassionately to compare the advantages and dis-

9 *Ibid.,* XXIX, 34–35, 148; Rupert Hughes, *George Washington,* 3 vols. (New York, 1926–1930), I, 6–7.
10 *Writings of Washington,* XXXIV, 406.
11 *Ibid.,* IX, 163.

advantages of the measure proposed, and decide from the balance. The lesser evil, where there is a choice of them, should yield to the greater."

His method of classifying, in his mind and also sometimes on paper, the facts of a situation as opposites, of "collecting" (as he put it) his decision, forced emphasis not on the "speculative" but on the "practical"—i.e., the problem exactly as it existed. However, although he became increasingly uninterested in military theory, he kept always before him general philosophic considerations: "that great line of duty which, though hid under a cloud for some time from a peculiarity of circumstances, may nevertheless bear scrutiny." Because he conceived of men as moral beings and recognized that the major function of his efforts was to sway the minds of men, he labored to merge the moral and the practical. "Nothing in life," he wrote, "can afford a liberal mind more rational and exquisite satisfaction than the approbation of those both wise and virtuous."[12]

Washington's method of weighing evidence blocked his tendency toward rashness, but the method took time, especially when the balance refused to tip one way or the other. Resulting delays sometimes proved unfortunate—obviously at Fort Washington, perhaps in the hesitations that led up to Monmouth—and were the basis of the charges of "indecision" made by Reed and others. However, another possible disadvantage of the method did not develop.

To examine all alternatives and accept the one which seemed, however slightly, the least objectionable, would in ordinary minds induce continuing doubts and halfhearted execution. Once Washington had reached a decision, his hesitations were—as Gouverneur Morris wrote—over: "He could, at the dictate of reason, control his will and command himself to act. Others may have acquired a portion of the same authority. But who could, like Washington, command the energies of his mind to cheerful execution?"[13]

When irritated, his intimates could attribute this, as Lafayette once did, to "his invincible repugnance to retract." However, that

[12] *Ibid.*, XI, 476; XXIX, 35.
[13] Gouverneur Morris to John Marshall, June 26, 1807, Library of Congress.

combination described by Brissot de Warville of "great diffidence in himself" with "an unshakable firmness of character once he had made a decision" was a major secret of Washington's effectiveness.[14]

It also tinged much of Washington's behavior with the appearance of inconsistency. Only in situations which deeply involved what he recognized as his "great line of duty"[15] can one foresee how he is going to act. He was no Byronic hero whose emotional obsessions always thrust him down dictated paths. Operating in a more classical manner, his mind seemed to swing like a pendulum from a stable center. He could move out, as pushed by the momentary summation of forces, in any direction, even if it were opposite to that which had been made expedient by other circumstances the day before. Add to the resulting variety those occasions when his passions overwhelmed his judgment, and others when he hid his true opinions in order to present persuasive arguments to men whose differences of prejudice he recognized, and you get that appearance of random multiplicity which often seems to characterize his day-to-day routine.

As Washington's self-education carried him ever further away from accepted military ideas, he turned from imported books and his original advisers to discussions with new men whom he had personally guided through the same school of experience where he himself still studied. One reason for the successes of the French Revolutionary armies was that, the old hierarchical officer corps having been shattered, naturally brilliant soldiers were able to rise to leadership apart from birth, wealth, and precedent.[16] The same was true in Washington's army. Of the leading generals who opened the war, none except Washington remained till the end influential. Indeed, only Gates and Washington were still in active service.

---

[14] Marquis de Lafayette, *Memoirs . . . Published by his Family* (New York, 1837), I, 20; Jacques Pierre Brissot de Warville, *New Travels in the United States* (London, 1797), I, 370.

[15] *Writings of Washington*, IV, 240.

[16] In aristocratic armies, only a tiny proportion of the population was eligible for the officer corps, and within this group promotion was less based on ability than family position.

Washington encouraged to rise around him Arnold, a disreputable apothecary and trader who (before he turned traitor) became the greatest combat general of the war; Knox, the overweight bookseller who taught himself the fine art of artillery; Greene, the ironmonger with a stiff knee whom those who deny the honor to Washington consider the conflict's ablest all-round general; Lafayette, the twenty-year-old spoiled darling of the French Court who, for all his wildly romantic and egotistical talk, became a cautiously effective general; Hamilton, another twenty-year-old, this one a bastard from the Indies, in whom Washington found the ideal staff officer; the brilliant John Laurens, who might, had it not been for his untimely death, have been one of the greatest of the younger Founding Fathers.[17] Of Washington's final inner team only Steuben had come to the army with accepted military knowledge, and the bogus baron was in European terms a fraud: his contribution was to make drill over again, under American advice, in a manner that suited the American army.

When Washington went increasingly his own way, he was plagued by his former dependences. Reed and Mifflin could not believe that the man whose early palpitations they had witnessed could ever become a brilliant commander. Gates and Lee became convinced that Washington had fallen into the hands of incompetent sycophants, all the more because, after consulting with new men, he was heretical to his old advisers' teachings. The idea that Washington was sinking into military ineptitude was further encouraged by high-ranking European volunteers, men like Conway who had come from abroad as convinced as were the British regulars that they were bringing with them the ultimate answers. All this contributed, during 1777 and 1778, to fracases.

Washington, the usually mild, struck out with his gigantic limbs, and the older order went down. Since the new order remained on the whole loyal to the man who had created and trained them, Washington became, in his control of the American military, unrivaled. This unique position contributed, in itself, toward the

---

[17] Characterized by "intrepidity bordering on rashness," Laurens was killed in August 1782, after all serious fighting was over, in what Washington called bitterly "a trifling skirmish." He was the only member of Washington's inner military circle to succumb, during the entire war, either to bullets or to sickness. *Writings of Washington,* XXV, 281; XXVIII, 97.

eventual victory. Throughout the war, the British high command had been weakened by perpetual inner feuds: Clinton against Howe; Cornwallis against Clinton; the generals against the admirals; etc., etc. Cornwallis' plight at Yorktown was due as much to his disagreements with Clinton as to anything else.

However, Washington often asked of his men more than ordinary persons could achieve: desertions were high and many short-term recruits refused to re-enlist. By their hearths, the returned soldiers told tales that frightened their neighbors from enlisting. Although this contributed to the progressive shrinking of the Continental Army, it did not—most amazingly—have a negative effect on the support for the cause or the national image of Washington. He remained so widely revered that one of the major problems of the party which arose after the war under the leaderhip of Jefferson was that Washington, whom they considered a political mossback, was more popular with the common people than the Jeffersonians themselves.

As he had felt when a leading landowner in Fairfax County, Virginia, Washington did not regard his military eminence as an excuse for self-indulgence, but rather as the opposite. In this, he was very different from the highborn British generals with their mistresses, their hangovers and gaming tables.[18] Washington asked nothing of his men that he was unwilling to do himself. Probably not another soldier in the entire army served so unrelentingly as did the commander-in-chief, who year after year did not allow himself a single day's furlough. And, although he kept up enough dignity at headquarters so that the men did not have to be ashamed of meanness, he shared their shortages and physical hardships whenever crisis made that reasonable.

That Washington was seeking no direct personal gain from his

---

[18] Washington could handle sex and liquor like a well-adjusted man: he seems never to have suffered from great temptations to overindulgence in either. But gambling was another matter: it had been so greatly the favorite sport of his young manhood that his encouragement of it in his regiment during the French and Indian War had got him into trouble. Now he denounced gambling in his general orders with a vehemence that seemed to reflect a continued personal yearning for his old, exciting vice. *Writings of Washington*, XI, 431–432.

service had been dramatized at the start of his command by his refusal of any salary. Although (as we have seen) he did try to buy in for his plantation some depleted cavalry horses, he never took the least personal advantage of his great powers in the control of supply. This made him a paragon in the eighteenth century, when it was standard practice for military officers (like government officials) to further their personal fortunes by collecting what was then considered not dishonest graft but the rightful perquisites of place and rank. Very revolutionary too, because contrary to the whole system of aristocratic preferment by which great families took care of their own, was Washington's utter refusal to practice or countenance nepotism in the appointment of officers. As far as the Continental Congress and the state governments would permit, he followed seniority or rewarded merit.

Men in danger, men conscious of their own inadequacy, do not want a general who might be their equal, who could easily be as bewildered and frightened as they. Yet they do not wish to feel that the commander moves in another orbit, indifferent to their affairs. Washington, so Abigail Adams noticed, "has a dignity which forbids familiarity, mixed with an easy affability which creates love and reverence." A French officer found Washington's face "something grave and serious, but it is never stern, and, on the contrary, becomes softened by the most gracious and amiable smile. He is affable and converses with his officers familiarly and gaily." He could play a wicket with the young men of his staff without having them feel that he was cheapening himself. He would chat with a lonely sentry.[19]

Washington's quality that has been most rubbed away by the fingers of the years and the historians is the charm he exerted on his contemporaries and which contributed much to his riding the wild horses of the times. This was grounded on characteristics which legend no longer allows him: on vulnerability, on the sensitivity of his own feelings which enabled him to be exquisitely

[19] Stewart Mitchell, ed., *New Letters of Abigail Adams, 1788–1801* (Boston, 1947), p. 15; Claude Blanchard, *The Journal of Claude Blanchard . . . 1780–1783* (Albany, N.Y. 1876), p. 117; Thomas Ewing, *George Ewing, Gentleman, a Soldier of Valley Forge* (Yonkers, N.Y., 1928), p. 47.

responsive to the feelings of others. If he sometimes did wear the cold face of a marble bust, it was because he had to protect his sensibilities from an ever-present prying, tearing, demanding world.

Although Washington was by no means an equalitarian who slapped his social inferiors on the back, he responded to all men who came into his focus—however lowly their rank—as individuals whose personal interests should be considered, who had rights as well as duties. In the conventional sense Washington was not a reformer, because when intolerance of human weakness emerged among his emotions, he did not make it a basis of action but did his best to suppress it. He expected men to be weak and fallible, regarding this condition, like the infertile soil at Mount Vernon, as the essential ground on which fine effects would have to be achieved.

He could be corrosive in irritation and terrible in rage, yet he twice allowed himself to be walked over by younger men he admired—first by Reed and then by Hamilton. In each case, not only did he forgive, but he pled humbly for the continued assistance of the friend who had turned on him. When he finally accepted suspicion he reacted with passion, but Washington hated to distrust any man.

"I might," he wrote good-humoredly in answering a gossipy letter from an old friend, "entrench myself behind the parade of great business with as much propriety as most men"[20]—but this was contrary to his nature. Some historians have accused him of being a poor executive who wasted his time on small details. But very often those small details would be lack of food, of supplies, of medicines in a regiment; and then he would ride there, at full speed as always,[21] to see what could be done. Even if he could do nothing, that he had come was a poultice to hurt minds and even added warmth to a dying fire. His face would darken to see his men suffer. That he suffered too, the cast of his features revealed. . . .[22]

[20] *Writings of Washington*, IV, 432.
[21] Marquis de Chastellux, *Travels in North America in the Years 1780, 1781 and 1782*, Howard C. Rice, Jr., ed., 2 vols. (Chapel Hill, N.C., 1963), I, 111.
[22] *Writings of Washington*, XII, 278, 343, 431.

In those years when soldiers were supposed to practice their profession as ordered, without personal concern for the matters about which they were fighting, the greatest innovation of the Continental Army was the conception that men could be successfully called on to make great sacrifices if they believed that they were serving their own welfare as civilians and also the truth. This military invention, as it came to be practiced in Europe by the armies of the French Revolution and moved onward to sweep the world, was entirely to recast warfare. It was an outgrowth of the rise of nationalism, unusable by international aristocracies, since a man taught to fight for himself might end up fighting an alien (or an unpopular) king. However, a sense of dedication to freedom was natural to the American air. Washington believed with all his heart in its military importance, and worked out how to harness by strategy this strange new force of popular enthusiasm.

Washington labored to inspire his soldiery with confidence in the value and the nobility of the cause. . . .

Since (so Washington believed) man was naturally good, a release from aristocratic restraints would permit the emergence of virtue: the result would be the creation of free, democratic, and peaceful states.[23] As Washington put it when the forming of the United States seemed to be foundering in a sea of confusion and selfishness, everything would eventually work out for the best as there was "virtue at the bottom."[24]

Since Washington foresaw that the establishment of political liberty would create a better world, the cause of American freedom became, by extension, the cause of all mankind. It also took on religious significance.

---

[23] Napoleon, the first great user of mass armies, is supposed to have commented to Lafayette that during the American Revolution the future of the world was decided by forces no larger than corporals' guards. In 1812, Napoleon's army was almost twenty times the Continental Army at its very largest. This was because American nationalism had not so far overcome individualism as to make feasible a general draft. The *levée en masse* was first enacted by the French in 1793. Edward Meade Earle, *Makers of Modern Strategy* (Princeton, N.J., 1943), p. 77; Arnold Whitridge, *Rochambeau* (New York, 1965), p. 145.

[24] *Writings of Washington*, XXVII, 58.

Long before the conflict with England exploded, Washington had felt that some supernatural force—he liked to call it, in the manner of Stoic philosophers, "Providence"—moved actively in the affairs of men. He was sure that it was a virtuous force, furthering the welfare of mankind. Lacking the specific contexts supplied by dogma or (despite his polite adherence to his ancestral Church of England) sectarianism, his religious convictions merged naturally and completely with his philosophical and political conceptions. He could not doubt that, since national political liberty would establish international peace and happiness, fighting the American Revolution was worship to the "Great Governor of the Universe," who would protect and reward his servants.[25]

This confidence in celestial assistance seemed doubly important to him when he first assumed the command because he was very conscious of his own inadequacy for the task ahead, and also of the imperfections of his army. He was inclined to conclude that faith by itself must and would do wonders. Believing that soldiers adequately inspired could overcome any inferiority in numbers, equipment, military know-how, he several times during 1776—at Kip's Bay, Fort Washington and elsewhere—put his men in impossible positions.

Indeed, 1776 was Washington's most educational year. Sir William Howe, proving himself the very model of a British major general, triumphed again and again in the struggle for positions to which he had been trained: the Americans were driven from Long Island, from New York City, from Manhattan, up the Hudson to White Plains, and across the Hudson and out of New Jersey. But in the process Washington came to appreciate a great advantage his army had over the enemy: superior mobility. On one aspect of this, the ability of his troops to think for themselves and take off without waiting for orders when in impossible positions, Washington never commented upon favorably—he could not do so and keep an army capable of obeying orders—but he may well have learned to include it in his calculations as a safety hatch. The more

[25] James Thomas Flexner, *George Washington: The Forge of Experience, 1732–1775* (Boston, 1965), pp. 243–245; *Writings of Washington*, XXVIII, 66; XXX, 11.

unequivocally favorable aspects of the American mobility were based not only on self-reliance but also on morale.

Because the men were willing to suffer great hardships for a cause which they believed involved all that made life worth living, they did not need to drag behind them slow trains of wagons, were not encumbered by quantities of equipment, were willing to march in any weather for any number of hours that the human frame, strained to its utmost, could stand. This opened to Washington the possibility of the kind of action which he had seen the Indians carry off in the wilderness: raiding parties that struck the enemy unexpectedly, completed their victory in a few hours, and vanished before any superior force could reach them. The first fruits of this strategy were the battles of Trenton and Princeton, which were, in turn, triumphant proofs of how effective a hit-and-run technique could be in this war. Not only was the propaganda impact sensational, but the British were frightened into abandoning their effort to hold New Jersey down with a network of small garrisons. Sudden raids—or the threat of them—would keep the enemy from setting up and protecting Tory enclaves with anything short of major power.

European strategy involved face-to-face confrontations of the opposing armies as each tried to push the other back. Since both armies moved ponderously, battles were foreseeable: this had been the situation in most of the American action during 1776. After that, Washington tried to function differently. Although he was in 1777 maneuvered into a battle of positions at Brandywine, and he tried in 1778 to take advantage of obvious strategic possibilities at Monmouth, he had become convinced that formal battles did not suit the American genius. His first military mentor, the Iroquois chief known as the Half-King, would have been pleased to see how greatly Washington came to rely on the conception of surprise.

However, if the British were not to march at will wherever they pleased, Washington needed to find some method of stopping them that did not involve drawing up his army in their path. He discovered how to keep the British in New York with completely conventional strategy which was geared to the conventional organization of their army. Since they could not advance if their supply lines were seriously menaced, he could prevent their marching overland to Philadelphia by merely sitting on the heights near Morristown that overhung the road. A similar strategic post in the hills behind White Plains could be used to block any overland incursion into New England. Moving past unconquered forts (as the Indians did) seemed to Washington a reasonable maneuver,[26] but he knew that the British would never go up the Hudson Valley leaving West Point in their rear, all the more because they were dependent for supply on shipping that could not circumnavigate the fort. The British were thus, as far as overland movement was concerned, trapped in New York unless they were willing to attack one of his strongpoints at great disadvantage.

Although not averse to a plum that could easily be shaken off a bough, the British were not, as a matter of policy, perpetually probing the American position for small advantages. They thought primarily in terms of operating with large units and when superiority of force tended largely to their side. Washington, on the other hand, was forever alert. He forever sought to make a strike, large or small, if only for the propaganda effect. Increasingly, he aimed his spy network at searching out any place where any group of the enemy had got off base—and he seemed Argus-eyed, since the inhabitants who watched the British from their windows were usually patriot sympathizers. The skillful enemy commanders did not give Washington many opportunities, but the ever-present danger urged them to keep their forces concentrated and contributed to the conservatism to which they had, in any case, been trained.

Washington developed what were, in effect, three striking forces graduated in strength. Although the continual threat that hordes of militia would arise like mists from the fields was a deterrent to enemy enterprise—the British could never confidently foresee what numbers a thrust would have to overcome—Washington had little faith in the militia as a mass force. He did his best to keep those spreaders of confusion quarantined from his main army. Taking advantage of the special gifts of the individual American farmer, he kept the militia, in units that could be as small as a single soldier, forever on the prowl. They were particularly useful

[26] *Writings of Washington*, IV, 47.

as lookouts, in harassing small British foraging parties, and in turning back incursions by Tory irregulars.[27]

Next in impact after the militia were small, elite units of the Continental Army—the riflemen earlier in the war, light infantry detachments at a later date—who could retard, although not stop, a major British march and could be sent out secretly at night (as in the action against Stony Point) to beat up important British outposts. And then there was the Continental Army in its entirety, which Washington was perpetually trying to enlarge and train so that it could deliver the knockout punch which would be necessary if the war were to be ended by military action.

In the war's earlier campaigns, the British only needed to fear the fighting power of the Continental Army under special circumstances: when Washington was defending some extremely strong terrain or when he could (as at Trenton and Princeton) surprise an outpost. However, Germantown presaged a new era, since the main encampment of the British force was, if only temporarily, overrun. Then came the reorganization of the Continental Army at Valley Forge. How effective this had been was demonstrated at Monmouth, which was not by any means a surprise attack, as Germantown had been, but such a foreseeable engagement on a conventional battlefield as had formerly brought easy British triumphs. Monmouth demonstrated to the enemy command the frightening fact that the Continental Army was now so improved that it was capable of meeting the British and German regulars on their own terms.

The British high command never dared challenge Washington again in any major way. Rather than come out from behind his fortifications in New York, Clinton sent detachments to the south, where the population was less concentrated and there was the possibility of a slave revolt; where there was no Continental Army and no Washington. Since the British held on to their New York base, their southern operations forced them to divide their army in a way which Washington recognized at once offered the chance of

---

[27] The militia operated in larger units and on a more important scale where Washington and the Continental Army were not, particularly in South Carolina.

subduing them piecemeal.[28] Although the march to Yorktown was not specifically his idea, his strategy had set the stage.[29]

However, the years in military service which trained Washington to be an expert soldier did not in the least incline him to visualize his role in the future as that of a veteran looking backward. This was dramatically demonstrated by his decision, at the moment of parting, to accept injustice to the demobilizing soldiers in preference to action that would endanger the development of the free civilian institutions to which they would now return. And the fact that his opposition stopped the antidemocratic movement not only in the army but among the financiers and politicians makes it plain that he was playing a role much wider than that of commander-in-chief.

Even as during the war all the generals who were Washington's rivals faded away, he increasingly overtopped all civilian leaders active on the continent. John Adams, having beaten somewhat vainly against the great Virginian rock, went off to France. Franklin was coming to the end of his great career and also labored abroad. Jefferson, after writing the Declaration of Independence, went back to Virginia where he proved not very effective as the governor of a war-torn state. Robert Morris, who for a time wielded great power, continued to be distrusted outside the financial community; Thomas Paine was distrusted by almost everyone. John Hancock was a windbag with a large signature, and Patrick Henry was a windbag with a large voice. Samuel Adams was shrinking. Hamilton and Madison were too young to show their full stature.

[28] *Writings of Washington,* XIII, 15–16; XVIII, 510–511.

[29] The arrival of the French had, until the inauguration of the Yorktown campaign, amazingly little effect on the strategic situation. The admirals, like their British counterparts, totaled up the relative weights of armament and, usually finding themselves outclassed, made no effort to meet the enemy. And compared to Rochambeau's usual stance, Howe and Cornwallis were wild radicals. From Rochambeau's arrival in July 1780 to June 1781, the French lent hardly any further assistance to Washington than that supplied by the menace to the British army and navy of their mere presence at Newport. (They did not even assign to Washington an artillaryman or an engineer.) Then, as cautious men can suddenly be goaded into throwing discretion to the winds, Rochambeau forced the Virginia campaign which even Washington considered foolhardy.

Historians have not adequately stressed the all-important fact that Washington did not (like Grant and Eisenhower) pass through two semi-independent careers, one as soldier and the other as President. In many and in continually augmenting respects, he became in 1775, twelve years before his official inauguration as President of the United States, the chief executive of the emerging nation. Except for the loop created by his temporary return to Mount Vernon, Washington moved, from his acceptance of the Revolutionary command to his Farewell Address, in one single straight line.

From the first, Washington could have put on the portable desk he carried around with the army, the sign sported in the White House by Harry Truman: "The buck stops here." This was a situation far from pleasant to Washington. The hard matters, the issues that courted unpopularity, moved with the most alacrity to his door. Whenever possible, he would send them scurrying back to Congress, accompanied by impassioned missives saying that if the matters were not instantly solved, the war effort would surely collapse. The executiveless Congress would refer the matter to a standing committee, debate the committee's report, and then, perhaps, appoint a special committee. As inaction followed in-action, the issue would appear in a more urgent form at head-quarters. If he could see no other way out, Washington would make the necessary decision. Otherwise, he would send the orphaned issue back again to Congress with an even more emo-tional letter in which he might point out that he was always willing to take his share of responsibility, but this time it was too much: this was altogether Congress' problem. The legislators, who were capable of criticizing their general for presumption when he settled matters, might now formally censure him for irresolution. Or they might let the matter sink, as far as Washington could see, into utter obscurity. Then he would ask how he was expected to lead the army when no one would tell him what was happening.

This continuing activity forced Washington to face almost every type of problem he would eventually have to face as President. He found himself involved in naval matters, in foreign affairs, in the use of rivers and highways, in politics, in commerce, in manu-facturing. The Virginia agrarian was even driven into racking his planter's brain in searches for the solutions to problems of currency and finance. His wartime experiences, which demonstrated that a nation could not be powerful without a strong and fluid economy, undoubtedly made Washington, when President, so much more receptive than was his fellow agrarian Jefferson to Hamilton's advanced, nonagrarian economic conceptions.

Writers who equate the Continental Congress with the long-established governments of stable nations, and who assume that Washington penned on all occasions everything he thought, have deduced from his endlessly iterated complaints that the Congress frustrated their commander-in-chief out of incompetence both willful and malignant. Actually, although he often tried, by ignoring excuses, to stir the legislature into overriding difficulties, Washington realized that the congressmen struggled, even as he himself did, with woefully inadequate means. Despite his verbal protests, he was in action extremely tolerant of such confusion and inefficiency as could be remedied—if at all—only by revolutionary changes within the cause. Having been wildly insubordinate in fighting his king, he was respectful and subordinate to Congress in a way that seemed pusillanimous to radicals like Charles Lee.

As a farmer, as a tamer of wildernesses, as a plantation owner rebuilding his estate, Washington had learned that the best results cannot be achieved overnight. And he had served long enough in the Virginia Burgesses to realize that slow maturing also characterizes legislatures. He did not expect matters to proceed in an orderly manner, nor, though he often expressed despair, did he ever really repine. However black were his military prospects during the Revolution, he was never as helpless as he had been when entrusted with turning back savage raids during the French and Indian War. Improvisation had always been his way of life. Having needed to import so many of his plantation tools from across the ocean through the lame cooperation of venal and indifferent factors, he was used to not receiving what he expected and was entitled to receive. Yet he had always got by somehow. He was not one of those forceful executives who argue that you invite worse trouble by postponing problems. He believed that if you could by temporary expedients keep a leaky ship afloat and on the right course for long enough, some unforeseeable dawn would reveal opening before you the friendly harbor of your dreams.

Had Washington been less accommodating at the start of his command, he would surely never have been allowed to reach the unrivaled power he eventually attained. Yet men have come up modestly before in history only to have modesty vanish: it is an axiom that power corrupts. Surely a man endowed with such gifts for leadership as Washington possessed must have desired, in some part of his complicated nature, to indulge his genius to the hilt. As we have seen, he thanked "the Greatest and Best of Beings" for leading him to "detest the folly and madness of unbounded ambition."[30]

But he felt temptations in the opposite direction too. The American farmer often dreamed of resigning so that he could go home: homesickness was a continuing aspect of Washington's military moods. How he longed for the mail that would bring him news of Mount Vernon: how he repined when the letters were lost or delayed! The arrival in camp every winter of that living symbol of a peaceful hearth, his wife, helped to keep him from being overwhelmed by that despair which on her arrival he poured into her ears, filling her with sorrow for his unhappiness.

Although he carried it out so well, Washington found his military task in many ways a painful one. He was by nature not a destroyer but a builder: he was an appreciater not a hater. There were, of course, chained in his nature, wolves of violence which could be released to make him an effective fighter, yet this fierceness, too closely allied to the other passions which he made it a lifetime effort to control, was not among the aspects of his personality with which his intellect was most congenial. In practicing cruelty and inducing pain, he tore himself as well as the enemy.

And, although he was a transcendent improviser, the labor of carrying on the war was almost more than his strength could bear. He could not, like an English general, rise from his wine, give an order, and return to his bottle, sure that the order would be carried out. As commander of a hand-to-mouth army, he was, so he complained, "a perfect slave." How he yearned for "that ease and

[30] *Writings of Washington,* XXVII, 269.

tranquillity to which, for more than eight years, I have been an entire stranger, and for which a mind, which has been constantly on the stretch during that period and perplexed with a thousand embarrassing circumstances, oftentimes without a ray of light to guide it, stands much in need." Oh, to be a man "free from the load of public cares and subject to no other control than that of his own judgment and a proper conduct for the walk of private life!"[31]

Many another man would have thought that the way to escape from outside control was to make his word a law through the land which no one would dare contravene. This conception was utterly foreign to Washington. To take responsibility, he wrote, "must make me responsible to the public" for any failure.[32]

Washington welcomed criticism from people he trusted if it were given directly to him and in private. As he wrote Reed, "I can bear to hear of imputed or real errors. The man who wishes to stand well in the opinion of others must do this, because he is thereby enabled to correct his faults or remove prejudices which are imbibed against him." As he explained to Rochambeau, "Our popular government imposes a necessity of great circumspection." This was because the voice of criticism could not be silenced. "Error is the portion of humanity, and to censure it, whether committed by this or that public character, is the prerogative of freemen."[33]

However, Washington resented and feared public criticism which might alienate from him the affections of the people. This dread of censure lay behind many of his most obvious faults. We have seen him shove blame off on others which his own shoulders should have more largely borne, and it is reasonable to suspect that his tendency to muddy the record in order to present his defeats as victories was motivated by personal reasons in addition to a desire to keep up the national morale. And, as he defended himself from even the implication of error, Washington could assume a disturbingly self-righteous tone. Yet his uneasiness under public criticism was more than a meanness: It was the reverse side of his great political virtue.

31 *Ibid.,* XXVII, 12, 89.
32 *Ibid.,* III, 422, 466.
33 *Ibid.,* IV, 240; XI, 160; XIX, 422.

He sought power not for its own sake but in order to earn love and praise. Washington still subscribed to the principle of Stoic philosophy he had embraced as a young man: the conviction that "the approbation and affections of a free people" was "the greatest of earthly rewards." Power imposed by fear, inspiring hate, could have brought him nothing but acute unhappiness. "How pitiful in the eyes of reason and ambition," he wrote, "is that false ambition which desolates the world with fire and sword for the purposes of conquest and fame, when compared to the milder virtues of making our neighbors and our fellow men as happy as their frail conditions and perishable natures permit *them to be.*"[34]

Washington wished to act in a manner satisfactory to his fellow citizens, but his yearning to be loved did not urge him to cater to popular whim. "The wishes of the people," he wrote, "seldom founded in deep disquisitions or resulting from other reasonings than their present feeling, may not entirely accord with our true policy and interest." And again: "It is on *great* occasions *only,* and after time has been given for cool and deliberate reflection, that the *real* voice of the people can be known."[35]

Washington's formative years had been spent among those patriarchal leaders of a semi-aristocratic agrarian society whose ranks he had eventually joined. Although Virginia voters had a right to get drunk at the expense of the candidates on election day, the leaders did not normally kowtow to the electorate. They did not wander the fields taking public opinion polls. They gained ascendancy by being willing and able to bring their intelligence and property to bear in effectively helping their less powerful and less informed neighbors to achieve ends which they persuaded their followers were for the common good. Nothing in Washington's Virginia training urged him to seek popularity by shaking hands and grinning. And his elevation to leadership in the Revolution had not resulted from electioneering—quite the reverse. He had sought to evade the responsibility which had been forced upon him.

Rising as if in answer to some scientific law, Washington took to leadership like a balloon taking to the air. When, as in the case of

[34] *Ibid.,* XXX, 5.
[35] *Ibid.,* XI, 289; XXXV, 32.

the Conway Cabal, rivals tried to shoot him down, he defended himself with both rancor and brilliant skill; but from day to day he accepted his pre-eminence as naturally as a man accepts his right hand. He did not even seem conscious of how powerful he was, how grievously he outdazzled those around him. All the more because it was so effortless, this dominance made enemies of men who considered themselves as good as he was, or better—or who disapproved of his opinions. And some historians, more used to contemporary patterns, have assumed that because he did not struggle for office, Washington was a clodlike puppet lifted by brute chance.

Since he did not have to stoop to conquer, no important outside pressure impeded Washington's efforts to steer by the highest stars. He could wholeheartedly pursue his conviction that he could serve his fellowmen best by serving the great principles.

It was in his ability to recognize the great principles that Washington's most fundamental greatness lay. He was not an effervescent thinker throwing off those plumes of inspiration which delight the inventive intellectual mind. His mind, indeed, was not inventive in the sense of defining conceptions for the first time. He selected rather among the alternatives that were presented to him by the possibilities of his place and generation.

Washington undertook his lifelong course in self-education and self-discipline at a time of major transition, when the old order, having not yet been conquered by the new, existed simultaneously with it. Although he took a leading part in the warfare that arose between the two systems, he was far from being, on a philosophical plane, a blind partisan. He had, indeed, a foot planted firmly on both sides of the divide. In a lesser man, this would have made for shilly-shally. In Washington, it made for double strength. He blended the romantic and the republican with the classical and the aristocratic into a synthesis that embraced much of the best in both orders.

As a leader, Washington brought to elective office the highest aristocratic ideals. His creativity was in the classical manner: the gift of seeing clearly, judging comprehensively and deeply. Yet he belonged to the romantic era in his disdain for precedent, his eagerness to think all matters out anew. He was no more inclined to travel history's long-built highways than to cut his way along lightly blazed trails into that blind wilderness the future.

Again and again to discover, when immersed in the welter of troubled times, the best routes ahead is a towering intellectual achievement. Gathering up complexity, he transmuted it into simplicity. His gift was to grasp so profoundly the heart of the matter that he could resolve what others endlessly argued about in a few clear sentences which, however radical their substance, carried the conviction of the obvious.

And typically, the obvious that he discovered was inspiring. "It should be the highest ambition of every American," Washington wrote, "to extend his views beyond himself, and to bear in mind that his conduct will not only affect himself, his country, and his immediate posterity; but that its influence may be co-extensive with the world, and stamp political happiness or misery on ages yet unborn."[36]

[36] *Ibid.*, XXX, 395 n.

✪

To Avert "Some Awful Crisis": Washington at the Constitutional Convention

He arrived on the 13th [of May, 1787], after encountering weather more threatening than bad, and was given a welcome that lacked nothing the affection of the people could bestow. Senior officers of his old army met him at Chester and dined with him; at Gray's Ferry, the City Light Horse and many mounted citizens fell in as escort; the artillery fired a salute when he entered the town; the bells of Christ Church were rung; at the boarding establishment of Mrs. House a crowd was awaiting him.[1] Although that lady operated what was regarded as "one of the most genteel" places of entertainment in the city,[2] the General was not permitted to remain there. Robert Morris and Mrs. Morris, whose invitation Washington gratefully had declined before he left Mount Vernon,[3]

[1] John C. Fitzpatrick, ed., *The Diaries of George Washington, 1748–1799*, 4 vols. (Boston, 1925), III, 216 (hereafter cited as *Diaries*); *Independent Gazetteer* (Philadelphia), May 14, p. 3; *Pennsylvania Packet* (Philadelphia), May 14, p. 3; *Pennsylvania Gazette* (Philadelphia), May 16, p. 3.

[2] *Independent Gazetteer, loc. cit.*

[3] John C. Fitzpatrick, ed., *The Writings of George Washington*, XXIX, 210–211 (hereafter cited as *Writings of Washington*).

now urged him so warmly to lodge with them that he accepted and forthwith had his luggage removed to the financier's famous home.[4] Before he ended the day, Washington paid his first call— an official visit to Benjamin Franklin, now President of the Executive Council of Pennsylvania, whom Washington had not seen since 1776. The meeting of course was cordial, because each respected and admired the other, and it held out, also, the promise of close relations in the weeks ahead: Franklin had accepted appointment as one of Pennsylvania's delegates to the Convention and, feeble though he admitted himself to be, he intended to take his seat. The diplomatist was philosophical and at the same time optimistic with respect to the meeting. ". . . if it does not do good," he wrote Jefferson, "it must do harm, as it will show we have not wisdom enough among us to govern ourselves . . ."[5]

With this visit to crown it, Washington's first day in Philadelphia could not be described with a lesser adjective than triumphant. He carefully recorded all the public occurrences of his entry, even to "on my arrival, the bells were chimed"[6] and he would have been justified in adding that, after three years and a half, there appeared to be no wane in the affection of the people for him, not a hint that he was "in the swallowing gulf of blind forgetfulness." Philadelphia had not welcomed him more eagerly when he arrived from Yorktown. The cordiality of the reception was all the more impressive because, in a sense, it was national. Five conventions, meeting simultaneously, had brought to the town representatives from nearly all the states.[7]

To the chagrin of the General, the most important of these conventions, the one to revise the Articles of Confederation, was the slowest in assembling. On the 14th, the date set for the opening, Pennsylvania and Virginia alone were represented. The next

[4] *Diaries,* III, 216.

[5] Letter of April 19, 1787, to Jefferson; A. H. Smyth, ed., *Writings of Benjamin Franklin,* 10 vols. (1905–1907), IX, 574.

[6] *Diaries,* III, 216.

[7] Besides the Federal Convention and the general meeting of the Cincinnati, the eleventh General Assembly of the Pennsylvania Society for the Abolition of Slavery, the Presbyterian Synod and a convention of Baptists, not identified, met in Philadelphia at the same time during May (*Pennsylvania Packet,* May 18, p. 2; *Pennsylvania Mercury,* May 25, 1787, p. 3).

day, individual members from New Jersey, Delaware and North Carolina reported, but not in sufficient numbers to organize the delegations from those states. One delegate only arrived on the 16th. While this was deplorable, James Madison cheerfully attributed members' tardiness to a long spell of bad weather that must have made every road a muddy mirror for the verdure of spring.[8] Washington apparently felt much the same disgust he had expressed over the tardiness of delegates in going to Annapolis for the commercial convention, but he believed that sooner or later a sufficient number of representatives would arrive to speak for a majority of the states and to organize the Convention. In this good hope he met daily with the other Virginians, who talked of the work to be done, and, no doubt, acquainted him with constitutional questions he had not considered in the quiet of Mount Vernon.[9] As the able, vigorous men of the Virginia delegation proceeded with their discussions, they developed a "plan" of government, a paper based chiefly on proposals that James Madison and Edmund Randolph had brought with them.[10] Washington probably did not make any specific contribution of form or of subtance to this plan, though his common sense and his experience doubtless were employed in determining what was necessary and what was practicable.

In addition to participating in these daily conferences, Washington visited friends, drew up a chair at their table, and perhaps not unwillingly changed his role of host for that of guest. His first dinner was *en famille* with the Morrises, his next was with the members of the Society of the Cincinnati,[11] a thin platoon of not more than a score of former officers, half of them distinguished

8 Max Farrand, ed., *The Records of the Federal Convention of 1787*, 4 vols. (1937), III, 20.
9 Cf. George Mason in George Bancroft, *History of the Formation of the Constitution of the United States*, 2 vols. (1882), II, 421–422, May 20, 1787.
10 *Madison Papers*, VII, 66, LC; Edmund Randolph to Madison, March 27, 1787, *Madison Papers*, VII, 56, LC, and frequently printed; Irving Brant's *James Madison*, cited hereafter as *Brant*, III, 11–12; Moncure Conway, *Omitted Chapters of History Disclosed in the Life and Papers of Edmund Randolph, Governor of Virginia; First Attorney-General United States, Secretary of State*, cited hereafter as *Conway, Randolph*, pp. 71 ff.
11 *Diaries*, III, 216, 217.

and the other half little known.[12] These gentlemen understood readily why their President-General had come to Philadelphia when he had said he could not do so and they gave him as a matter of course their unhesitating and complete vote of confidence by re-electing him,[13] with the understanding that the active duties of the office were to be discharged by the Vice President, Thomas Mifflin.[14] This removed Washington's main ground of apprehension and doubtless was one consideration in reconciling him to delay that dragged on, day after day, to the wrathful disgust of his colleague George Mason, who was bored by "the etiquette and nonsense so fashionable" in Philadelphia.[15] Washington enjoyed, in his dignified manner, the social affairs that Mason detested, and in contrast to his youthful diffidence, he found no distress in drinking tea at the home of Benjamin Chew, "in a very large circle of ladies," who were guests at a wedding.[16] Perhaps the General's kindly impulses were tested on one occasion, at least, during this period of waiting. That was when Mrs. Morris "and some other ladies," in his helpless phrase, took him to a "charity affair," at which still another lady, one "in reduced circumstances," presented a reading. All that he could bring himself to say of it was, "Her performance was tolerable at the College Hall."[17]

Washington, the critic of elocutionary art, became Washington the planter, a more familiar part to play, in several visits to country places around Philadelphia; but when he wrote of these estates he never failed to mention in his diary the main business of the day—that Delaware "was represented" on Monday the 21st of May, that "the representation from North Carolina was completed" the next day, and that when the impatient delegates assembled as usual on the 23rd and the 24th, "no more States" had spokesmen on the floor.[18]

[12] The largest number of listed delegates was twenty, as of May 16. See Society of the Cincinnati, *Proceedings,* I, 26.

[13] *Ibid.,* 34. Henry Knox, Alexander Hamilton and Elias Boudinot constituted the committee that waited on him (*ibid.*).

[14] Mifflin succeeded Horatio Gates (*ibid.*).

[15] Kate Mason Rowland, *Life of George Mason,* 2 vols., (1892), II, 103.

[16] *Diaries,* III, 218.

[17] *Ibid.,* 217; *Independent Gazetteer,* May 29, 1787, p. 2.

[18] *Diaries,* III, 218.

At last, upon the arrival of another member from New Jersey, a qualified number of delegates from seven states were counted on the 25th of May; and as seven were a majority of the states, men who had been waiting almost two weeks proceeded to organize the Convention. Most considerately and graciously, Robert Morris, a member from Pennsylvania, the hostess state, arose to perform a service Benjamin Franklin would have discharged if he had not been detained at home that day by weakness and bad weather.[19] In a few words, the financier said that on instructions from the Pennsylvania delegation and on its behalf, he proposed Washington as President of the Convention. John Rutledge of South Carolina seconded and expressed the hope that the choice would be unanimous. It was. Morris and Rutledge conducted the General to the chair, from which, briefly and modestly, he expressed his thanks for the honor done him, and asked the indulgence of members for the unintentional mistakes into which his ignorance of the requirements of the position might lead him.[20]

The other details of organization were completed quickly, a committee on rules was named, adjournment was voted to Monday the 28th.[21] Members lingered after that motion passed, to shake hands and to bow to the new presiding officer, or else they streamed out-of-doors into another bad day of the city's long period of unkind weather. It had been in a chamber not far distant, almost twelve years previously, that Washington had heard his name mentioned for another honor, and, in embarrassment, had hurried from the room. The Virginia planter and retired colonial field-officer had not wanted to be commander-in-chief in 1775, and the same planter from the Potomac, former head of the army, did not desire this new post;[22] but there was a similarity of a sort between the two elections and a difference of some interest. Both were calls in a day of danger to America. Selection to lead the army had put

---

[19] *Farrand* (Madison), I, 4. In these references to *Farrand*, the parentheses will include the authority cited by that admirable editor. The page reference follows. A parenthetical "Journal" will contain reference to the formal record of the Convention, with Farrand's pagination.

[20] *Ibid.* (Madison), 3–4 and (Yates) 5–6. *Pennsylvania Packet*, May 28, 1787, p. 3.

[21] *Farrand* (Journal), I, 2.

[22] *Writings of Washington*, XXIX, 216, 225.

Washington in the tent where the decisions had to be made; designation as President of the Convention would take him off the floor for part of his time, away from the contention of rival advocates. He was committed to the work of the Convention by accepting membership in it; he was lifted above partisanship by the very nature of the duty he had to discharge. At the same time, having no speeches to prepare or committee meetings to attend, he could lend both ears to all spokesmen and thereby doubtless learn much that he had not acquired previously in camp or on his plantation. Presidency of the Convention was education and preparation.

The Convention itself was that and vastly more—if not in its seeding, then in its fruiting. Dull-eared delegates, participants in the organization of many legislative bodies, might hear only the repetition of the old formulas of an initial meeting. Eyes dimmed by the reading of scrawled resolutions and ill-printed Journals might see little that was new in this assembly. Where memory ran back to vain appeals to stubborn states for the ratification of the feeble Articles of Confederation, or to the disregarded pleas of a penniless Congress for the right to levy an impost, delegates might shake their heads and sigh as they walked from the convention hall that 26th of May. Their task might be hopeless—jealous states never would consent to create a government greater than their own. Every self-esteemed little Caesar had rather be first in an Atlantic village than second at a western Rome. If, by circumstance, experience were reversed—if shame or danger or calculation induced politicians to lay down powers a stronger union might take up—what splendor the future would hold. Wisdom and righteousness would be America's! Washington did not have the eloquence of delegate Rufus King to describe the nation's tomorrow, nor did he possess the skill of his young friend James Madison in arraying arguments as if they were a flawless line of battle; but he had glimpsed the edge of the great valley of America, which students might not see over the top of their law books, and he had followed the routes by which the restless and the landless could enter and occupy that bountiful empire. He believed that if America had power to maintain the law, and revenue with which to pay her public debts, she could prosper, could assure a larger life for her sons and daughters and could recover the place she had in the good opinion of the world when she was struggling for independence. A government strong enough to enforce the will of a free people would not be a tyrant. It would be a protector. America's shores would be unassailable; but her ports would be open as an asylum, in Washington's own words, for "the oppressed and needy of the earth."[23] Where so much might be gained, or lost when almost in the people's grasp, who could begrudge the days of waiting, the weeks of debate, that agreement in the Convention would require?

Monday and part of Tuesday, May 28 and 29, were spent in adopting rules of procedure.[24] Later in the transactions of the 29th, speaking for the Virginia delegation, Edmund Randolph, in the stiff language of the Journal, "laid before the House, for their consideration, sundry propositions, in writing, concerning the American confederation and the establishment of a national government."[25] These "propositions," which Randolph explained in a long, formal speech, embodied the "Virginia Plan" that had been developed in the daily meetings Washington had attended. A government of three branches, legislative, executive and judicial, was to be created. The Legislature was to consist of two chambers, one elected by the people of the several states, the other chosen by the elected branch from a list of nominees submitted by the individual state legislatures. This central bicameral law-making body was to have all the relevant powers vested in Congress by the Articles of Confederation and, in addition, the power to pass laws where the states were unable to act or were not in harmony. All state laws that contravened the terms of union could be "negatived" by the "National Legislature" which likewise could "call forth the force of the Union against any member of the Union failing to fulfill its duty under the articles thereof." A "National Executive" would have the powers suggested by the title, insofar as the Articles of Confederation conferred authority of this type on Congress. "A general authority to execute the national laws" was added. The

[23] Letter of March 30, 1785, to Lucretia Wilhemina van Winter, *Writings of Washington,* XXVIII, 119–120.

[24] *Farrand,* I, 7–16.

[25] *Farrand* (Journal), I, 16. The text of the "Virginia Plan" was believed by Farrand (III, 594), to have been copied correctly by Madison in *ibid.,* 20 ff. No original is known to exist.

"National Judiciary" was to have particular regard to "questions which may involve the national peace and harmony."[26] Again and again that word "national" recurred, without specific definition.

These proposals and another plan of government prepared by Charles Pinckney[27] were referred that same Tuesday afternoon to the Committee of the Whole. When the committee began its sittings on the 30th with Nathaniel Gorham of Massachusetts as its chairman, Washington could take a seat temporarily with the other members. Nine states now were represented by thirty-seven members.[28] No less than seven of them had served along with Washington in the Continental Congress of 1774 or 1775 or both;[29] four had been on his personal staff during the Revolutionary War—Thomas Mifflin, Edmund Randolph, Alexander Hamilton and James McHenry. At least thirteen others, besides Washington himself, had been officers in the Continental Army;[30] an additional thirteen had been officers of the militia. A total of twenty-one members were college graduates,[31] twenty-nine were or had been lawyers or judges; nearly all had held political office or had served on Revolutionary committees. The average age of members

[26] *Farrand* (Madison), I, 20–23, based on an abstract supplied by Randolph.

[27] For the confusion of Pinckney's original plan with one apparently drawn up at a later time, see *Farrand,* III, Appendix D, 595 ff.

[28] Rhode Island, New Hampshire and Maryland had no spokesmen on the floor. Doctor Franklin, who would have been the thirty-eighth member, apparently had not attended as of this date. The total number who participated in the Convention as members, according to *Farrand* (III, 387–390), was fifty-five. In the textual summary, those who attended after May 25 are included along with those who were present when deliberations began.

[29] These were Benjamin Franklin, John Langdon, William Livingston, George Read, John Rutledge, Roger Sherman and James Wilson. Members who came to Congress in 1775, after Washington left Philadelphia to assume army command, are not counted among the seven.

[30] Including commissioned members of Washington's staff, this brought the total of ex-officers to eighteen, or almost exactly one-third of the total attending membership.

[31] Included is James Wilson who, on application, received his honorary M.A. from the College of Philadelphia. Princeton (College of New Jersey) had graduated nine, Yale four, and Harvard and Pennsylvania (College of Philadelphia) three each. Samuel Johnson is credited to Yale, at which he won his Bachelor's degree, and not to Harvard, where he later became a Master of Arts.

was forty-four, but four were under thirty or approaching that age.[32] While a considerable part of the membership was unknown personally to Washington when the Convention assembled, he soon had ample proof of what had been written him previously about the men elected in the different states: they represented high ability and at the outset impressed George Mason, who was somewhat suspicious, as men "of the purest intentions."[33] Madison wrote: ". . . [the Convention] in general may be said to be the best contribution of talents the States could make for the occasion."[34] It was pleasant to sit among these men during the day and, in the evening, to meet them socially.[35] Conversation had to be casual and guarded because the Convention voted on the 29th that "members only be permitted to inspect the journal" and that "nothing spoken in the house be printed, or otherwise published, or communicated without leave." Although this rule occasionally was violated,[36] most members were conscientious and close-mouthed. They would not talk of the one subject every guest at a

[32] Jonathan Dayton, 27; John Francis Mercer, 28; Richard Spaight and Charles Pinckney in their thirtieth year. Hamilton already had reached 30 in January, 1787. As the exact date of Gunning Bedford's birth in 1747 is not known, there is a possibility he had attained 40 by the time the Convention met. William Houstoun of Georgia was about 41; his birth date is given in *Dictionary of American Biography* as c. 1746.

[33] Letter to George Mason, Jr., June 1, 1787, George Bancroft, *History of the Formation of the Constitution* (1882), II, 425.

[34] Letter of June 6, 1787, to William Short, *Papers of William Short*, II, 354, LC.

[35] Washington's diary records most of these gatherings. The morning after the Convention opened, he returned all his calls (*Diaries,* III, 219), including one on Noah Webster (Ford, *Notes on Life of Noah Webster,* I, 215); on Sunday, May 27, he went to high mass at "The Romish Church" (*Diaries,* III, 219; *Pennsylvania Herald,* May 30, 1787, p. 3); Monday he dined at Robert Morris' and drank tea "in a large circle at [Tench] Francis's"; Tuesday he dined "at home" and went to a concert; the remaining days of the week were spent in the same whirl (*Diaries,* III, 220). On June 4, he reviewed the City Troop and the infantry militiamen, but the people were so anxious to see him that they did not leave room enough for maneuvers (*Pennsylvania Mercury,* June 8, p. 3; *Independent Gazetteer,* June 8, 1787, p. 3). After that, for a few days, Washington's social activities diminished and his time alone at the Morris home increased. The General needed early morning and evening hours, because he went as far as he could in managing his plantations by letter from Philadelphia.

[36] *Farrand,* III, 48–49, 54, 66, 80.

tea and every frequenter of taverns wished to discuss. Washington himself exercised so much care that he made no notes even in his diary of what happened behind the doors of the convention hall.[37]

The General could have written much that was optimistic had he felt free to confide to his journal an outline of the first ten days' deliberations. Everything went well. Washington would take the chair each morning and, after the usual preliminaries would turn over the gavel to Judge Nathaniel Gorham, who acted as Chairman of the Committee of the Whole. For nearly the entire day's sitting, the members would debate the successive items of the Virginia Plan, which they approved in broad outline with disarming alacrity. Progress was rapid and in accordance with the proposals the delegates of the Old Dominion had made initially.[38] After one or another of the involved principles was discussed on a given day for three hours or more, the committee would rise, Washington would resume the chair, and Judge Gorham would report progress, with a request for leave to sit again in committee. Adjournment usually followed at once. Among nearly all members, the disposition was to find the largest basis of agreement and to defer the issues on which there was wide disagreement. The spirit of accommodation seemed so pervasive that echoes of accord were audible in the newspapers, along with rumbling criticism of Rhode Island for ignoring the Convention.[39] Much of the hope that newspapers voiced for its success was founded on the presence and influence of Washington. "Ye men of America," shouted the *Massachusetts Centinel*, "banish from your bosoms those daemons *suspicion* and *distrust*. . . . Be assured the men you have delegated . . . are men in whom ye may confide. . . . Consider, they have at their head a Washington," the mention of whose name tempted the editor to trail off into verse.[40]

Men of differing political background in dissimilar states could not hope to continue in accord. By the second week in June,

[37] Cf. *Diaries*, III, 220.

[38] *Farrand* (Journal), I, 30–31, 46–47; *ibid.* (Madison), 64; *ibid.*, 35, 54.

[39] *Pennsylvania Herald*, June 9, p. 3, June 20, 1787, p. 3. *Newport Herald* (R.I.), June 7, 1787, p. 2.

[40] Issue of June 13, 1787, p. 3. Cf. *Independent Chronicle* (Boston), June 14, 1787, p. 3.

members were divided on the question, Should the first branch of the National Legislature[41] be elected by the people or by the legislatures of the several states? Other issues of wider import were shaping themselves: Should the equality of state representation that had prevailed in the Continental Congress be continued —one state, one vote, whether Rhode Island or Virginia? If the first branch of the new lawmaking body was to be elected by the people, should slaves be counted in determining the basis of representation? To maintain the authority of the national government, must its Congress of necessity be vested with power to coerce the states or to "negative" their laws? Indeed, why should the new government be national? Could it not remain federal, with the largest freedom to the states, great and small?

After the Virginia Plan was reported, in substance, by the Committee of the Whole on the 13th of June, these questions, one after another, became the spearheads of attack on the plan. Debate on the floor of the Convention was as searching and detailed as if the Committee of the Whole had not discussed the "propositions" at all. Delegates from the smaller states immediately found a rallying post in resolutions introduced on the 15th of June by William Paterson, a New Jersey delegate. He proposed the amendment of the Articles of Confederation in such a manner as to increase substantially the powers of Congress while preserving federal, as distinguished from national government, except in two particulars: With the consent of an unspecified number of states, a delinquent member of the Union might be forced to meet its obligations; second, the acts of Congress and all ratified treaties were to be the "supreme law of the respective States"[42]—a new doctrine, admirably phrased, that probably made an instant appeal to some of the ablest intellects in the Convention. The Committee of the Whole proceeded to debate this plan and to listen to an excursus by Alexander Hamilton on proposals of his own that commanded

[41] In all these discussions, the body that subsequently became the House of Representatives consistently was termed the "first branch," and the Senate the "second branch."

[42] *Farrand* (Madison), I, 244–245. Differences between the Virginia and the New Jersey Plans were given succinctly by James Wilson in a speech of June 16. *Ibid.* (Madison), 260.

little following.[43] Powerful speeches by Edmund Randolph,[44] James Wilson[45] and James Madison[46] led to the rejection, June 19, of Paterson's outline, seven states to three,[47] and put the Virginia Plan before the Convention again.

This procedure returned Washington to duty as presiding officer after he had sat as a silent member from the 30th of May onward, except for the time spent during that period in opening and in closing the sittings. He voted with the majority of the Virginia delegation in most of the divisions,[48] but on the embarrassing question of vesting the federal government with power to negative all state laws, his colleagues most thoughtfully did not call on him to commit himself.[49] As for speeches, he felt that in his capacity as President he should not express opinions on matters pending in the Convention,[50] though his previous record as a lawmaker would indicate that he probably would have spoken seldom and briefly, if at all, had he been under no restraint. His only remarks to the house, during this period of the Convention, were a warning to members not to be careless with papers that concerned their work, an admonition he thought he should voice after Thomas Mifflin stumbled upon a copy of some of the secret "propositions" a delegate carelessly had dropped.[51]

Washington had been pleased, at the beginning of the Convention, to find members more in accord than he had expected,[52] but when the basic differences developed during the second week in June, he wrote home for additional clothing because, he said almost glumly, "I see no end to my staying here."[53] Work was as hard, too, as the task was long. He had motions to put and points

[43] *Farrand* (Madison and others), I, 282 ff.
[44] *Ibid.* (Madison), 255.
[45] *Ibid.* (Yates), 260.
[46] *Ibid.* (Madison), 314.
[47] *Ibid.* (Journal), 313. Maryland was divided.
[48] *Farrand* (Madison), I, 97; *ibid.,* II, 121.
[49] *Ibid.* (Madison), 168. Madison specifically noted, "Genl. W. not consulted."
[50] *Ibid.* (Madison), II, 644.
[51] Hunt's Madison, III, 56 n. with the quotation from A.H.R., III, 324–325, reprinted in *Farrand,* III, 86–87.
[52] *Writings of Washington*, XXIX, 228.
[53] *Ibid.,* 233. A few days later he sent for his umbrella (*ibid.,* 235).

of order to settle during a fortnight of close and vigorous discussion that had to be followed attentively. Social activities, for some reason, were increasingly frequent also,[54] and added to the weariness he felt at the end of the day's sitting. Debate was becoming ill-tempered and tedious, particularly on the question of state representation in the proposed legislative branch of government. By the 28th the frowning factions were caparisoned for battle in a mood that made Doctor Franklin appeal unsuccessfully for prayers at the opening of each day's session.[55] On the 29th, fighting to the last, the spokesmen of the small states were outvoted, six to four, with Maryland divided, on a resolution that established an "equitable" instead of the "equal" basis of representation they sought in the first chamber.[56] In the analogy of their own legislatures, this meant to members that the House of Representatives of a new Congress would be elected, by methods as yet undetermined, in proportion to population.

The men who spoke for the less populous areas continued to argue for equal representation in both chambers, but naturally they mustered their forces anew to win in the second chamber what they had failed to procure in the first. Washington stood with the other Virginia delegates who favored representation on the basis of population for both houses of the National Legislature, but he did not lose his sense of reality. He was as convinced as ever that the stubborn selfishness of some of the state governments was responsible both for the weakness of the Union and for resistance to making it stronger. His counsel was simple: "To please all is impossible, and to attempt it would be vain. The only way, therefore, is . . . to form such a government as will bear the scrutinizing eye of criticism, and trust it to the good sense and patriotism of the people to carry it into effect."[57] In discussing this once with

[54] He described them briefly when he explained to Mrs. Richard Stockton why he had been delayed for a few days in acknowledging a "poetic performance" of hers. See *ibid.,* 236.

[55] *Farrand* (Madison), I, 450–452. The account of this incident credited by William Steele in 1825 to Jonathan Dayton (*ibid.,* III, 467–473) was denied by Madison (*ibid.,* 531) and is apocryphal beyond all possible defense.

[56] *Ibid.* (Journal), 460.

[57] Letter of July 1, 1787, to David Stuart, *Writings of Washington,* XXIX, 239.

members of the Convention, "his countenance," said Gouverneur Morris, "had more than usual solemnity; his eye was fixed and seemed to look into futurity." His words were firm: "It is too probable that no plan we propose will be adopted. Perhaps another dreadful conflict is to be sustained. If, to please the people, we offer what we ourselves disapprove, how can we afterwards defend our work? Let us raise a standard to which the wise and the honest can repair. The event is in the hand of God."[58]

It looked the very next day, July 2, as if the time had come to raise the standard. Prolongation of the debate over representation in the Legislature of the new government had served only to array small states against large more stubbornly than ever. In the absence of several members, five state votes were mustered for a resolution to equalize representation in the second chamber. Defeat of the small states in the contest over the composition of the first chamber thus was offset, but at the price of a threatened impasse. When neither side would yield, Charles Cotesworth Pinckney proposed and nearly all the delegations agreed that a "grand committee" of one member from each state be appointed to fashion a compromise. Hugh Williamson of North Carolina spoke for the cool-headed element when he said, "If we do not concede on both sides, our business must soon be at an end."[59] As the committee would require many hours for its deliberations, the Convention adjourned over the 3rd and 4th of July.

Washington took no part in the debate, but as Pinckney's motion accorded precisely with what he had written Doctor Stuart, he almost certainly voted for the South Carolinian's recommendation, even though Madison opposed.[60] During the adjournment

---

[58] Morris, *An Oration, Upon the Death of General Washington*, 21, quoted at length in *Farrand*, III, 381–382. As related by Morris in 1800, this incident may have occurred before the Convention began its work, but his language is not positive. To record it in connection with the similar though less rhetorical statement to Stuart manifestly is justified and chronologically may be correct. There is no good reason for questioning the substantial accuracy of the remarks quoted by Morris whenever made. Washington employed the same metaphor, in reverse, when he spoke, September 22, 1788, of the circular of the New York Convention "as a standard to which the disaffected might resort." *Writings of Washington*, XXX, 96.

[59] See the debate in *Farrand* (Madison), I, 511 ff.

[60] *Ibid.*, 515.

for the festivities of the 4th, the General shared in patriotic services at the Reformed Calvinist Church, and dined with the Pennsylvania Cincinnati at the State House. That afternoon he "drank tea" with Mr. and Mrs. Samuel Powel, whose intelligent and considerate company he enjoyed often in Philadelphia;[61] but good food and even better company had not relieved his apprehension when, on the morning of the 5th, he returned to the Convention hall. He found that Doctor Franklin with much difficulty[62] had prevailed on the "grand committee" to recommend this compromise: representation in the first chamber was to be on the basis of one member for each 40,000 population of each state, with one member for any state that counted fewer than 40,000 heads; the chamber elected on this principle was to have exclusive authority to originate bills levying taxes, appropriating money and fixing salaries; the second chamber should not be empowered to amend these bills, but with respect to no other legislation was it to be subordinate; finally—this was the core of the compromise—in this second branch, each state was to have "an equal vote."[63]

These proposals were regarded by the small states as a victory[64] and they forthwith were attacked by two of the most powerful debaters in the Convention, James Madison and Gouverneur Morris,[65] who employed experienced parliamentary maneuver along with skillful argument. Some phases of the compromise were turned over on the 6th of July to a special committee for review;[66] when this group reported, its findings were referred to

---

[61] Next only to Robert and Mrs. Morris, his host and hostess, the Powels were apparently his closest friends in the city. For the ceremonies of the 4th, see *Independent Gazetteer,* July 6, p. 3 (the most comprehensive account), copied in *Pennsylvania Journal* (Philadelphia), July 7, p. 3. See also, *Pennsylvania Journal,* July 4, p. 3 and *Pennsylvania Packet,* July 6, 1787, p. 3. In his journal entry, *Diaries,* III, 226, Washington gave the name of the orator of the day as "a Mr. Mitchell, a student of law." Newspapers referred to him as "James Campbell, Esq." Before attending the exercises at the church, Washington visited the anatomical display of Dr. Abraham Chovet or Chavet. See *Diaries,* III, 226 n.

[62] *Farrand* (Yates), I, 523; *ibid.* (Madison), 526 n.

[63] *Farrand* (Journal), I, 524.

[64] *Ibid.* (Madison), 526 n.

[65] *Ibid.* (Madison), 527.

[66] *Ibid.* (Journal), 538.

another "grand committee."[67] Even the patient and innately optimistic Washington became gloomy. Affairs, he wrote Alexander Hamilton, were "in a worse train than ever; you will find but little ground on which the hope of a good establishment can be formed." Then he added, in a tone of depression he scarcely had employed since the gloomiest days of his most disastrous military campaigns: ". . . I almost despair of seeing a favorable issue to the proceedings of our Convention, and do therefore repent having had any agency in the business."[68]

Most of the occurrences of the next week were of a sort to deepen Washington's disgust with those he described as "narrow-minded politicians or under the influence of local views."[69] He witnessed a seesaw of advantage between the spokesmen of the large states and the champions of the small, in the matter of representation in the Federal Legislature,[70] until, on July 16, there was a balance of five to five that apparently could not be shifted.[71] Some of the members were for adjournment and for immediate report to the country on the differences that had arisen; others still pleaded for a compromise; a few stated frankly their belief that equality of representation in the second chamber had to be conceded if the Convention was to avoid failure.[72] Discussion was renewed at an informal conference held before the house was called to order the next morning, July 17, but so much diversity of opinion was expressed that Madison thought the listening members from the smaller states would conclude they had no reason to fear

[67] *Ibid.* (Journal), 558.

[68] Letter of July 10, 1787, *Writings of Washington*, XXIX, 245. Hamilton had left the Convention in the belief that it would do little and that he personally was powerless because he was opposed consistently in his own delegation by the other members in attendance, John Lansing and Judge Robert Yates. Although Hamilton declared himself willing to return to the Convention if service there would not be a waste of time (*A. Hamilton*, IX, 418), he apparently realized that the influence of George Clinton and of the Governor's strong following was to be thrown against any recommendation to increase the federal prerogative. See *Pennsylvania Journal*, July 21, p. 3; *Daily Advertiser* (New York), July 21, p. 2; *Pennsylvania Packet*, July 26, 1787, p. 2.

[69] *Writings of Washington*, XXIX, 245–246.

[70] *Farrand* (Journal), I, 538, 549, 557, 558, 563, 565; *ibid.*, II, 1, 13.

[71] *Ibid.* (Madison), 17.

[72] *Ibid.* (Madison), 17–20.

their opponents could agree on any plan of opposition to equality in the second chamber.[73]

From that very day, as if in acceptance of the inevitable, a spirit of reconciliation began to show itself even though there was irony in the report of a Philadelphia paper that men were saying the room in which the Convention held its meetings appropriately could be called "Unanimity Hall."[74] On July 17–21, more progress was made in framing a constitution than in any previous period of five days. Final decision on representation in the second branch was deferred; the motion to give the new Congress power to "negative" state laws was abandoned in favor of the clause first sketched in the "Jersey Plan"—that the acts of the Federal Legislature should be the "supreme law of the respective States."[75] Fundamental agreement was reached on the form and function of the judiciary, on the admission of new states, on the guarantee to the states of a republican form of government,[76] on a complicated scheme for the election of the Executive,[77] and, unanimously, on the grant to the Executive of power to negative all laws of the National Legislature.[78]

Washington must have been pleased with this and perhaps was refreshed for his daily ordeal in the chair by a brisk round of social activities.[79] After a Sabbath in the country, he enjoyed on the 23rd of July perhaps the most satisfying day he had spent, to that date, in the Convention. Members still had under consideration the powers and term of the National Executive and they wished to conclude this discussion and to reach a meeting of minds. Everything else that had been decided on the floor—a surprising range

[73] *Ibid.* (Madison), 20. While there is no record, one way or the other, of Washington's attendance at this conference, it is improbable that he was present.

[74] *Pennsylvania Journal,* July 21, 1787, p. 3.

[75] *Farrand* (Journal), II, 22. This supremacy was to apply, also, to "all treaties made and ratified under the authority of the United States" (*ibid.*).

[76] *Ibid.* (Journal), 37–39.

[77] *Ibid.* (Journal), 50, 60.

[78] *Ibid.* (Journal), 71. When the Executive did this, the challenged legislation could not be made effective otherwise than with the concurrence of two-thirds of the members of both legislative chambers.

[79] All of them, including a visit to Spring Mill and to General Mifflin's estate, July 22, are listed in *Diaries,* III, 227–228.

of accord—was referred to a committee of five "for the purpose of reporting a constitution conformably to the proceedings aforesaid." The unimaginative language could not conceal the shining fact: a constitution, complete in all its parts, was to be put on paper! Three more days, July 24–26, sufficed to effect agreement on the Executive; the accepted resolutions on that branch were given the new "Committee on Detail," as it was termed; and the Convention itself adjourned to the 6th of August, in order to allow the committee ample time for its difficult work.[80]

During this ten-day intermission, while the committee labored,[81] Washington played many parts—guest, traveler, veteran, planter, fisherman, patron of industry. Two days were given to rest and correspondence.[82] Then on the 30th of July, in Gouverneur Morris's phaeton, to which his own horses were hitched,[83] the General rode out to Mrs. Jane Moore's property, a part of which had been within the Valley Forge encampment. On Trout Creek, which Mrs. Moore's farm adjoined, Morris wished to try his hand at the shrewd act of casting[84] for the fish that gave their name to the creek. While his companion stumped along the bank of the stream on the 31st of July,[85] Washington rode over the whole of

[80] *Farrand* (Journal), II, 118. Washington mistakenly dated adjournment July 27. See *Diaries*, III, 229.

[81] Its members were Nathaniel Gorham, Oliver Ellsworth, James Wilson, Edmund Randolph and John Rutledge. *Farrand*, IV, 72.

[82] *Diaries*, III, 229.

[83] Washington's carriage was being painted and relined. See Washington to Samuel Powel, July 25, 1787, *Powel Papers*, Mount Vernon.

[84] *Diaries*, III, 230.

[85] The presence of Gouverneur Morris with Washington on this excursion is an almost conclusive refutation of the story that Morris, on a dare, slapped Washington on the back during the Convention and, for his presumption, received "for several minutes . . . an angry frown" until he "retreated abashed and sought refuge in the crowd" (*Parton*, as below). Had Morris received this treatment prior to July 31, even he would not have had the temerity to go on a journey with Washington. If the alleged incident had occurred later in the Convention, it is improbable that Morris would have been on the cordial footing shown in the letters that passed between him and Washington that autumn and later. See *Sparks's Morris*, I, 288 ff. and *Writings of Washington*, XXIX, 490. Morris, besides, was a welcome guest at Mount Vernon in November, 1787 (*Writings of Washington*, XXIX, 322; *Diaries*, III, 269–270). It should be added that the back-slapping story, of which there are two versions, never appeared in print, so far as is known, until 1870, and then as a second-generation old man's tale (see *Farrand*, III,

the cantonment of 1777–1778, which he never had seen in summer's green. He looked at the mouldering fortifications and at the camps in the woods, near fields that still had not been brought back to duty under the disciplinary plow. Cheerful or gloomy as his reflections may have been, Washington did not set them down in his diary, but as he was riding back to Mrs. Moore's, he saw some farmers at work and he asked them about the growing of buckwheat, with which he had been experimenting at Mount Vernon. Their observations he wrote out fully as soon as he could, in space more than four times as great as that which he gave to the scene of some of his blackest misery.[86] From the vicinity of Valley Forge, Washington returned to Philadelphia and, on the 3rd of August, went up to Trenton with a party to see whether the perch in the Delaware were interested in bait. This time the General himself used a rod with little luck one day and more success the next. He dined with Col. Samuel Ogden at the Trenton Iron Works,[87] and on the 4th at Gen. Philemon Dickinson's "Hermitage" which had been a Jäger picket post that thrilling "day after Christmas," 1776, when Sullivan's men had stumbled or slid past it in the surprise attack on Trenton.[88] Not a reminiscent word of this did Washington put in his diary. As always, tomorrow interested him vastly more than did yesterday.[89] He was back in Philadelphia, late in the evening of August 5, to be certain he did not miss the proceedings of the 6th, when the Committee on Detail was expected to report.[90]

Printed copies of the draft constitution were ready for members when John Rutledge rose to speak on behalf of the committee. Washington and all the other members listened and some followed the type across the page, line after line, as the Secretary read the entire text. With little argument, the Convention adjourned till the next day and, individually or as delegations, praised the committee

---

85 and 85–86 n., with quotations from W. T. Read's *Life and Correspondence of George Read* . . . , 441n., and James Parton's *Life of Jefferson* . . . , 369).
[86] *Diaries*, III, 230.
[87] *Ibid.*, 231.
[88] See Freeman, *Washington*, IV, 316 ff.
[89] Cf. *Diaries*, III, 231.
[90] *Ibid.*

or pointed to the sections they disapproved.[91] Washington himself spent the evening at Robert Morris'[92] and no doubt studied the committee's proposals. The next day, August 7, rejection of a motion to go into Committee of the Whole for consideration of the text[93] gave Washington the hard assignment of presiding during a floor debate that might be more tangled and retarded than ever, because of endless motions to amend.

Members now began with vigor and with some impatience a detailed scrutiny, day after day, of the suggested text, though some of them realized that the completion of their task still would be a work of weeks.[94] Progress was steady, if not swift. Washington, rising early, walked daily from Morris' home to the State House alone and by this time was a familiar if still an awesome figure—in a blue coat and a cocked hat, with his hair in a queue, crossed and powdered. He was composed but, said an observer, he "seemed pressed down in thought."[95] In the chair, he presided with what was termed "his usual dignity,"[96] and, as he had the respect and consideration of all members, he was saved from the pitfalls of parliamentary law. Almost hourly, during the early days of August, he listened as voices from the floor reached the "aye" or "no" of decision that went far beyond the time and the vision of the participants. From the 7th through the 11th, the Convention plodded toward agreement. The pace was slower the next week because members were critically of two minds over the admission of foreign-born citizens to the National Legislature, and over the origin of appropriation bills.[97] During the days of this verbose

[91] *Farrand* (Madison), II, 177, 189; cf. *ibid.* (McHenry), 190–192.
[92] *Diaries,* III, 232.
[93] *Farrand* (Madison), II, 196.
[94] James Madison to his father, July 28, August 12, 1787 (*Madison Papers,* VII, 105, 117, LC; *Writings of Washington,* XXIX, 258). It was known generally that the Convention was debating a constitution, paragraph by paragraph (*Pennsylvania Herald,* August 8, 1787, p. 3). Correspondents reported the public impatient for news. Rumbles of possible disunion and of the organization of separate confederacies circulated. See, as typical, Rev. James Madison, Sr., to his cousin, August 1, and James McClurg to Madison, August 5, 1787; *Madison Papers,* VII, 106, 112, LC.
[95] Memoir of Maj. Samuel S. Forman by L. C. Draper in Forman's *Narrative of a Journey down the Ohio and Mississippi in 1789–90,* p. 15.
[96] *Newport Herald,* August 16, 1787, p. 3.
[97] *Farrand* (Journal), II, 265–267, 294–296.

debate, Washington conserved his strength, going out seldom in the evening, and he did not miss an hour from his duties.[98] He accorded emphatically, no doubt, in a resolution of August 18 that fixed the hours of the daily sittings from ten to four o'clock and ruled out all motions to adjourn before the scheduled hour.[99]

That Saturday, August 18, an armful of proposals to give specific powers to Congress was turned over to the Committee on Detail, and the involved question of federal assumption of state debts was referred to a special committee.[100] Then the Convention discussed the relation of the new government to the defense of America.[101] On adjournment that afternoon to Monday, the 20th, it was to the credit of Washington's endurance that he still had energy for an excursion on Sunday. With his friend Samuel Powel, he rode out to White Marsh, went over his old encampment there, proceeded to Germantown and probably visited the Chew House, scarred with bullet marks and reeking still in memory with the burned powder of British muskets and American six-pounders.[102] The entire day was somber—even if its shadows were of yesterday. Either the special circumstances of the journey or the analogy of the struggle for a better government prompted Washington to reflect "on the dangers which threatened the American Army" at White Marsh.[103] That camp site and Germantown exemplified the cruel vigils and the tortured hours of Washington during the dreadful months between the landing of Howe at Head of Elk, late in August, 1777, and the debouch of the lean American forces from Valley Forge when Howe evacuated Philadelphia in May, 1778. Those days of defeat and of hunger had been preceded by anxious, futile and wasteful campaigns and they had been followed by long waiting, by sinister cheating in the market places, and by every form of sloth and evasion in the seats of government. Independence had

---

98 Cf. *Diaries*, III, 232–233.

99 *Farrand* (Journal), II, 322–323.

100 *Ibid.* (Journal), 321–322.

101 *Ibid.* (Journal), 323.

102 See *ibid.*, 508. The supposition that Washington went to the Chew House is based on the statement in his diary that he "visited Mr. Blair McClenegan" [McClenacham], owner of the property. See *Diaries*, III, 233.

103 *Ibid.*

been won in woe; the dark forces that had prolonged the contest still lived. ". . . there are seeds of discontent in every part of the Union," Washington warned, "ready to produce other disorders if the wisdom of the present Convention should not be able to devise, and the good sense of the people be found ready to adopt a more vigorous and energetic government . . ."[104]

In that spirit he returned from Germantown to Philadelphia and, the next day, Monday, August 20, began another hard week as presiding officer of the Convention. Members apparently had lost none of their positiveness and they divided readily on the detail of the constitution, but few of them wasted the time of their colleagues in long orations. They would argue, object, defend, vote—and take up the next section of the draft constitution. On the 22nd, they paused for a time to debate the ethics and economy of the slave trade and, in so doing, disclosed more clearly the differences between North and South, between commercial and plantation states, between those that found slave owning uneconomical and those that thought it profitable. The cleavage was as deep as that between large states and small and was vehemently outspoken. At the moment, the Convention agreed to accept the proposal of Gouverneur Morris to refer the question of the slave trade and other disputed clauses to a committee. "These things," said Morris, "may form a bargain among the Northern and Southern States."[105]

Then, on Thursday the 23rd, in discussing the draft, the Convention reached the seventh article,[106] which made the legislative acts and existing and future treaties of the United States "the supreme law of the several States." After scrutinizing and simplifying the language, the Convention adopted this article unanimously, perhaps to the surprise and certainly to the relief of the old soldier in the chair, who during the war had pleaded often and vainly with unheeding states. Simultaneously with this decisive and inclusive action, the Convention, by a majority of one state, rejected the much discussed alternative, the amendment that would have em-

[104] Letter of August 17, 1787, to Lafayette, *Writings of Washington,* XXIX, 260.

[105] *Farrand* (Madison), II, 374.

[106] Text in *Farrand* (Journal), II, 381–382. See also *ibid.* (Madison), 389, and *ibid.* (Journal), 409. These provisions became the second section of the article finally numbered VI.

powered the National Legislature to negative any state law if two-thirds of the members of both branches so voted.[107]

An awkward obstacle was out of the way! The road was getting better. On the 25th, a busy day for Washington, the members accepted another major compromise, one that forbade Congress to prohibit the importation of slaves prior to 1808.[108] When Washington put this motion and not long afterward announced adjournment, the day being Saturday, he could have told himself that the week's labor had been as productive as any of the Convention's life. He had much reason for satisfaction and for rekindled hope when he rode out into the country eight or ten miles on Sunday.[109] Most of the remaining hours of his day of rest were given to the composition of a long letter of instruction for George Augustine Washington on the farm at home.[110]

Briskly on Monday, the 27th of August, the members began discussion of the committee's draft provisions regarding the judiciary. Despite the presentation of a theme on which every one of the twenty-nine lawyers in the Convention had opinions, the debate was mild and agreement was not difficult.[111] By the last day of the month, consideration of the draft had reached the stage where it seemed desirable to name a committee to review all postponed questions and to report them for final action.[112] An even better augury of the early completion of the text was the drafting of clauses on the ratification of the constitution by the states. The Articles of Confederation provided that amendment had to be by the unanimous consent of the states, but it so manifestly was impossible to prevail on all of them, Rhode Island, in particular, to approve any strong central government that few members, if any, favored adherence to this requirement. Washington himself had encountered again and again the indifference and procrastination of the states in days when delay seemed a death sentence to America, and he was willing to make the constitution effective when a majority, a bare seven of the states, approved.

---

[107] *Ibid.* (Madison), 390.
[108] *Farrand* (Journal), II, 408–409.
[109] *Diaries*, III, 234.
[110] *Writings of Washington*, XXIX, 263–266.
[111] *Farrand* (Journal), II, 423–425, 434.
[112] *Ibid.* (Journal), 473.

The Convention voted, more conservatively, to require the assent of nine states.[113]

The last major article of the draft constitution awaiting decision was that which set forth the method by which the Executive was to be elected and was to be vested with power.[114] Discussion of this had become so involved that final action had been deferred. Now, in the week of September 3, the Convention resumed the debate and in four days reached agreement.[115] On Saturday the 8th of September, Washington and his companions had the satisfaction of referring their document to a committee of five "to revise the style of and arrange the articles agreed to by the House." The delegates selected for this task were most admirably equipped for it—William Samuel Johnson, Alexander Hamilton, Gouverneur Morris, James Madison and Rufus King, men of clear heads and precise pens.[116] A happy description of their larger assignment appeared fortuitously, and at almost this very time, in the *Pennsylvania Packet:* "The year 1776 is celebrated," says a correspondent, "for a revolution in favor of Liberty. The year 1787, it is expected, will be celebrated with equal joy, for a revolution in favor of Government."[117]

Unaware of the scope of this new "revolution," the Spanish Minister, Don Diego de Gardoqui, arrived in Philadelphia from New York, about September 8, primarily to meet Washington,[118] who, of course, welcomed the representative of a government with which delicate negotiations over the free navigation of the Mississippi were being conducted. Philadelphians of station shared this sense of responsibility toward Gardoqui and they entertained him

---

[113] *Farrand* (McHenry), II, 482; *ibid.* (Journal), 472.

[114] Originally Article X on the report of the Committee on Detail; *ibid.* (Madison), 185.

[115] *Farrand* (Journal), II, 493–496, 505–508, 517–521, 532–534.

[116] *Farrand* (Journal), II, 547. The text, as referred to the committee, was reconstructed with much care by Professor Farrand and was printed in *ibid.,* 565 ff. Some doubt exists concerning the action that immediately followed the appointment of the Committee on Style. A motion to reopen the question of Congressional representation may have been voted down, six states to five, though this maneuver may have been on the 10th. See *ibid.,* 580 n.

[117] Issue of September 6, 1787, p. 3.

[118] *Diaries,* III, 235.

sumptuously. Washington attended these affairs, September 13–15, and a dinner given in his own honor by the City Light Horse,[119] but he did not permit anything to interrupt materially the final labors of the Convention. Monday, the 10th, was given to debate on amendment and ratification;[120] on the 11th, the Committee on Style[121] not being ready to report, the Convention merely assembled and adjourned.[122]

Waiting was rewarded: an admirable text was presented on the 12th by the chairman, Judge William Samuel Johnson,[123] and, once read, was sent to the printer so that every member might familiarize himself with the precise letter of the text and with titles and terms.[124] The "first branch of the Legislature" was, for example, to be styled the House of Representatives; the second was to be known as the Senate. "President" was the designation recommended for the Chief Executive; the court of last resort was to be called the Supreme Court of the United States. While the compositors set the type that recorded these changes, the Convention debated various issues concerning which there was no basic disagreement between North and South, or large states and small. On one such question, Washington differed from the majority and voted unsuccessfully against an amendment that reduced from three-fourths to two-thirds the majority required to pass a law over the President's veto.[125] Then, as always, he favored a strong

119 *Ibid.*, 235–236.

120 *Farrand* (Journal), II, 555–557.

121 Madison termed it the Committee on Style and Arrangement; the Journal mentioned it as the Committee on Revision; in American constitutional history it usually is known as the Committee on Style.

122 *Ibid.* (Journal), 581.

123 It was, needless to say, primarily the work of Gouverneur Morris (*ibid.*, III, 170, 420). "A better choice could not have been made," said Madison long afterwards, "as the performance of the task proved" (*ibid.*, 499). Morris himself never was satisfied with his language in part of the article (III) on the Judiciary (*ibid.*, 420).

124 *Ibid.* (Journal), II, 582. It should be noted that for the last few days of the Convention the surviving records are so confused and fragmentary that Farrand wrote (*ibid.*, n.) it was "impossible to reach any satisfactory conclusion with regard to the various questions and votes."

125 *Farrand* (Madison), II, 587. It will be remembered that the word "veto" does not appear in the Constitution. The Journal and Madison's Notes usually employ the term power or right "to negative."

Executive. He probably believed that a President would not withhold approval in other than the most extreme cases, and that when laws were so defective or so vicious that they had to be disapproved, three-fourths of the members were not a larger part of the whole than should be required to override the President.

Several close votes followed on numerous sections, some of them long contested, but in no instance did the majority fall below the minimum of six.[126] The balance at last had been stabilized and was not to be shaken. On his own copy of the printed text, Washington inserted changes made through section 10 of Article I in the debate of September 14.[127] The next day, September 15, Washington noted various other verbal amendments and, as presiding officer, he put no less than twenty-five motions.[128] Before the last and most fateful of these was reached, Edmund Randolph took the floor and announced to the distress if not to the surprise of the General that he would not sign the constitution unless it included a provision, which he thereupon submitted, for another general convention to pass on amendments that might be proposed by the states to the text now ready for final action.[129] Washington's neighbor, George Mason, made a similar statement;[130] Elbridge Gerry, who had pursued an erratic course throughout the Convention, gave a number of reasons why he would not subscribe.[131] Nothing could be done to satisfy these men otherwise than by jeopardizing far more than was risked as a result of their opposition. All the states unflinchingly voted "No" on Randolph's motion for a second convention.[132]

It was now almost six o'clock, nearly two hours beyond the usual time of adjournment. The last proposal from the floor for change in the text had been made. Washington waited quietly and

[126] See, for example, Hugh Williamson's proposal on the 14th to increase by 50 per cent the membership of the House of Representatives [*ibid.* (Madison), 612].

[127] *Farrand* (Journal), II, 610. A sheet of Washington's amended copy appears as an illustration in this volume.

[128] There may have been others not covered by the table in *ibid.* (Journal), 622.

[129] *Ibid.* (Madison), 631.

[130] *Ibid.* (Madison), 632.

[131] *Ibid.* (Madison), 632–633.

[132] *Ibid.* (Madison), 633.

without visible emotion for the great moment. When it came, he arose: the motion is to agree to the constitution as amended;[133] the Secretary will call the roll of the states. From every delegation the answer of the majority was "Aye."[134] Engrossment of the text was ordered; the gavel fell.[135] The first stage of the battle for sound, strong American government had ended, more wisely and more easily than had seemed possible. From the Convention floor the issue must be carried to the thirteen states, in a wide, charging and decisive campaign.

Sunday, the 16th of September, was given by Washington to letter writing[136] and to a ride with Robert and Mrs. Morris to their country home for dinner.[137] Monday, the 17th, found Washington in the chair for the final ceremonies of signing the engrossed Constitution and, perhaps, for one proposal that was much on his mind. He found, if he did not already know, that a last-minute effort was to be made to persuade the three dissenters to join the majority in signing the Constitution. Doctor Franklin was present and, though too feeble to make a speech, he had written one which James Wilson read for him with the permission of the house. It was a wise and spirited appeal for the subordination of individual opinion to the nation's good, and it contained both an admission of Franklin's dislike of some articles and the cheerful declaration of his faith in the document as a whole. "It . . . astonished me, sir," he said, "to find this system approaching so near to perfection as it does; and I think it will astonish our enemies, who are waiting with confidence to hear that our councils are confounded like those of the builders of Babel; and that our States are on the point of separation, only to meet hereafter for the purpose of cutting one another's throats." The old philosopher ended with a motion which Gouverneur Morris had drafted in the hope it would satisfy

133 It is much to be regretted that neither the name of the mover nor the exact form of the motion is known.
134 *Farrand* (Madison), II, 633. Madison's entry was: "On the question to agree to the Constitution, as amended, All the States ay."
135 *Ibid.* Washington walked back to Robert Morris' and spent the evening there (*Diaries*, III, 236).
136 Six are represented by copies in Washington's Letter Book. Three of these had to do with his business affairs; three were notes introducing Charles Pinckney to friends in France.
137 *Diaries*, III, 236.

Gerry, Mason and Randolph—that the enacting clause be: "Done in Convention, by the unanimous consent of the States present the 17th of September, &c, in witness whereof we have hereunto subscribed our names."[138]

Before this motion was put, Judge Gorham proposed that, even though the final text was engrossed, one line be scratched and the basis of representation in the House be reduced from 40,000 to 30,000. Rufus King and Daniel Carroll supported Gorham and urged the members to make the concession. This was what Washington had been waiting for. When he rose to put the motion, he explained that his position as president had kept him from expressing his views and that perhaps it still should impose silence, but he could not forbear voicing his wish that Judge Gorham's motion prevail. Objections to the Constitution should be as few as possible. One of them was involved here. Many members believed the House so small it gave "insufficient security for the rights and interests of the people." A basis as high as 40,000 always had seemed to him among the most objectionable parts of the Constitution. Late as it was in the proceedings of the Convention, he thought amendment would give much satisfaction.[139] With that, he ended the only speech he had delivered during the session,[140] and he had immediate reward. The desired change was made unanimously and without further discussion[141]—not because all members agreed but because all of them wished to do what Washington desired.

This was the last and most gracious *nem. con.* of the meeting. The rest was appeal, explanation, expostulation, assent, then the adoption of Franklin's motion. Although the dissenters and two of the South Carolina members were in opposition,[142] the Constitution was accepted "by the unanimous consent of the States present." A resolution was adopted for the transmission of the finished document to Congress, with the expressed opinion that it should be submitted to popular conventions in the states. Other

[138] *Farrand* (Madison), II, 642–643.
[139] *Ibid.* (Madison), 644. The quotation is from Madison and may not be of Washington's exact words.
[140] Madison's note, as *supra*.
[141] *Farrand* (Madison), II, as *supra*.
[142] *Ibid.* (Madison), 647.

sections of the same resolve set forth the views of the delegates on the manner in which the Constitution should be put into effect after nine states had ratified it.[143] The covering letter was a persuasive appeal for a Constitution that was "liable," the members affirmed, to as few exceptions as could reasonably have been expected. This letter was signed "Your Excellency's most obedient and humble Servants, George Washington, President. By unanimous Order of the Convention."[144]

The rule of secrecy was repealed, and the papers of the Convention were entrusted to Washington for disposition, in accordance with the order of the new Congress "if ever formed under the Constitution."[145] Formal signing of the document followed. It was during this ceremony that Franklin said he was satisfied the sun painted on the back of the President's chair was the rising, not the setting orb. Continued refusal of Mason, Gerry and Randolph to attach their signatures did not dampen the satisfaction with which members completed their difficult labor, adjourned *sine die*,[146] streamed to the City Tavern, had dinner together and said farewell to one another. Washington walked, after that, to Morris' house, where he received the Convention records from the secretary, and at last, in quietness, to quote his words, "retired to meditate on the momentous work which had been executed . . ."[147]

The next day, September 18, after brief visits to the homes of friends, he had an early dinner, and with delegate John Blair as companion in his chariot, he set out for home. Near Head of Elk, on the 19th, he found a ford swollen beyond all possible use, and, as he was in his usual hurry of travel, he decided to cross on an old

[143] *Ibid.*, 666–667.
[144] *Farrand*, II, 667. The letter almost certainly was the work of Gouverneur Morris, in whose autograph is the copy now among the *Papers of G. W.*, LC. Farrand (Journal), II, 583 n; cf. *ibid.*, III, 499. For action of the Convention in directing that the address be prepared, and in declining to make a public appeal in advance of a decision by Congress on the Constitution, see *ibid.* (Journal), II, 556–557, 582; *ibid.* (Madison), 564, 622–623. As neither the Journal nor Madison's Notes mentions the letter in the final proceedings, the precise place of the reading and signing of the document in the day's proceedings is not known.
[145] *Ibid.* (Madison), 648.
[146] *Ibid.* (Madison), 649.
[147] *Diaries*, III, 237.

bridge. He and Blair went over on foot, probably to lighten the load, and they suffered no injury, but one of the horses broke through the weak flooring and almost dragged the other animal and the carriage into the water. By good fortune, abundant aid was at hand promptly, the horse was rescued,[148] the journey proceeded. About sundown, on the 22nd, Washington reached Mount Vernon "after an absence of four months and fourteen days," precisely reckoned and set down in his diary.[149]

They had been days during which his largest contribution was not that of his counsel but that of his presence. His votes, where recorded, were often on the losing side. Although he favored bringing the new government into operation when seven states ratified, the Convention decided to make nine the number. It must have been known that he thought a three-fourths vote should be required to override a Presidential veto, but the majority insisted on two-thirds. Letters from members seldom mentioned him among those at the forge where the Constitution was hammered out, blow on blow. Madison, Gouverneur Morris, James Wilson, Rufus King, Edmund Randolph—these were the men, not Washington, who shaped the Constitution. Oliver Ellsworth[150] may not have been far in error when he said, late in life, that Washington's influence in the Convention was not great.

Outside the Convention, the reverse was true. In giving the body prestige and maintaining public confidence in it while deliberations dragged slowly, Washington had no peer and no second other than Franklin. It had been so from the early days of the Convention, when skeptics were asking whether the assembly would be representative or respectable even. Madison assured Jefferson that Washington's attendance was "proof of the light in which" the General viewed the Constitution;[151] Col. Edward Carrington's

[148] Diaries, III, 237–238. The accident alarmed Washington's admirers. Said the Delaware Gazette (Wilmington), the "fortunate circumstances" of the General's crossing on foot "probably saved a life so dear to the country." Quoted in Pennsylvania Packet, October 3, p. 2 and Pennsylvania Herald, October 4, 1787, p. 3. See also Independent Gazetteer, October 11, 1787, p. 3.
[149] Diaries, III, 238.
[150] Farrand, III, 396–397.
[151] Letter of June 6, 1787; Farrand, III, 36.

opinion was that the participation of Washington disclosed the "deep impression upon his mind of the necessity of some material change."[152] As public curiosity rose, and impatience with it, while the delegates argued, copies of Washington's farewell circular to the states were offered the public;[153] Charles Willson Peale painted a new portrait[154] which soon was reproduced for sale as a mezzotint.[155] Again and again, the General was presented as the man to be trusted. "A Washington," the New York *Daily Advertiser* asserted, "surely will never stoop to tarnish the lustre of his former actions, by having an agency in anything capable of reflecting dishonor on himself or his countrymen . . ."[156] Said a correspondent of the *Pennsylvania Packet:* "In 1775, we beheld [Washington] at the head of the armies of America, arresting the progress of British tyranny. In the year 1787, we behold him at the head of a chosen band of patriots and heroes, arresting the progress of American anarchy, and taking the lead in laying a deep foundation for preserving that liberty by a good government, which he had acquired for his country by his sword."[157] In Washington's own state, a Petersburg journal printed a correspondent's sketch of what he believed the powers of Congress should be: ". . . the grand federal convention it is hoped will act wisely, for on their determination alone, and our acquiescence, depends our future happiness and prosperity, and if there lives a man equal to so arduous a task, it is a Washington."[158]

152 Letter of June 9, 1787, to Jefferson, *ibid.*, 38. Cf. Louis Otto, Chargé d'Affaires, to Comte de Montmorin, June 10, 1787, *ibid.*, 45.

153 *Evening Chronicle* (Philadelphia), June 12, 1787, p. 1 and several times later.

154 *Diaries,* III, 226, 227.

155 *Pennsylvania Herald,* September 20, 1787, p. 3.

156 Issue of July 26, 1787, p. 2.

157 Issue of August 23, p. 3; reprinted in *Pennsylvania Mercury,* August 24, 1787, p. 3.

158 This undoubtedly was from the *Virginia Gazette* (Petersburg), and was quoted in *Newport Mercury* (R.I.), August 27, 1787, p. 2.

HAROLD W. BRADLEY

✪

The Political Thinking of
George Washington

It has become an axiom among historians that the period of the
establishment of national government in the United States was one
in which the Republic was blessed with a remarkable group of
political leaders, among whom were a few men with unusual insight into the problems and institutions of government. Foremost
among these political giants were Alexander Hamilton and
Thomas Jefferson, who not only founded and led political parties
but who succeeded in impressing upon those parties their own
views upon the nature and function of government and the appropriate relationship between government and the citizen. Second
to Hamilton and Jefferson in the quality of leadership, but equal to
them in the realm of political thinking, were John Adams and
James Madison. These four men constituted a quartet which has
not been surpassed and perhaps has not been equaled in the
history of political thought in the United States. The enduring
quality of their contributions to political practice and theory has
led historians to dismiss with little consideration the ideas of the
man who more than any other was at the center of political activity
during the early years of the Republic. All too often, President

Reprinted from Harold W. Bradley, "The Political Thinking of George
Washington," *The Journal of Southern History*, XI (November 1945), pp.
469–486. Copyright 1945 by the Southern Historical Association. Reprinted
by permission of the Managing Editor.

Washington appears in history only as a dignified and colorless figure moving mysteriously in the political background, supporting the program of Hamilton, succumbing to the influence of his Secretary of the Treasury, and associated in the popular mind with the Hamiltonian concepts of government.

There is historical justification for thus subordinating the role of Washington in his own administration. He may have been "first in war, first in peace, and first in the hearts of his countrymen," but quite conspicuously he was not first in politics. He did not wish to be a politician and he did not seek to become a molder of political forces. His warning in the Farewell Address against "the baneful effects of the spirit of party generally" was doubtless the heartfelt expression of his own disillusionment after nearly eight years of active political life. But it was a warning which he might have uttered with as much sincerity at the opening of his Presidency as at its close. If Washington deliberately avoided the role of political leader, he would seem equally miscast as a political philosopher. He was neither a phrase maker nor an original thinker. His public papers and his private correspondence are filled with pleasant platitudes reflecting the accepted virtues of his day. Thus, when about to assume the Presidency, he assured Lafayette that nothing more than "harmony, honesty, industry and frugality" were needed "to make us a great and happy people";[1] and in his First Inaugural he declared that "there is no truth more thoroughly established than that there exists . . . an indissoluble union between virtue and happiness; between duty and advantage."[2] Six years later, while bitter political strife swirled about him, he informed a correspondent that "in politics, as in religion" the principles upon which he acted were "few and simple," and of these the most important was "to be honest and just . . . and to exact it from others."[3]

[1] Washington to Marquis de Lafayette, January 29, 1789, John C. Fitzpatrick, ed., *The Writings of George Washington*, 37 vols. (Washington, 1931–1940), XXX, 186. This collection is cited hereinafter as *Writings of Washington*.

[2] James D. Richardson (comp.), *A Compilation of the Messages and Papers of the Presidents, 1789–1897*, 10 vols. (Washington, 1896–1899), I, 53.

[3] Washington to Dr. James Anderson, December 24, 1795, *Writings of Washington*, XXXIV, 407.

One may search the public papers of Washington without finding a concise statement of political philosophy. The greater part of the eight annual messages to Congress were devoted to matter-of-fact descriptions of the state of the Union. Among the topics discussed in those messages, foreign relations and Indian affairs received the most attention. Of the great issues of domestic policy which divided the nation during his first administration, only the enforcement of the excise laws was given more than perfunctory notice in the reports to Congress. These messages contain frequent references to the economic conditions of the day. In his recommendations to Congress, agriculture, commerce, and manufactures were almost invariably linked together, as indeed they had come to be in his thinking. He urged Congress and his fellow countrymen to support religion, morality, education, and science, and he suggested the establishment of a national university with the observation that existing institutions lacked the funds necessary to command "the ablest professors in the different departments of liberal knowledge."[4] It is also evident from his public papers that Washington, as President, favored a strong constitutional government which would be responsive ultimately to the public will but which would not be subject to the whims or caprice of a temporary majority. These were cautious statements of a conservative philosophy; under close scrutiny they do not appear to have been Hamiltonian. They were, instead, the guarded public expressions of political ideas which Washington had stated freely to his friends in private correspondence during the years of relative leisure at Mount Vernon from 1783 to 1789.

The practical figure of the first President seems curiously remote from the realm of abstract ideas. Washington, however, appears to have fancied himself as something of an amateur philosopher—at least in the field of political thought. His private correspondence is filled with allusions to the delights of the philosophically minded— a category in which obviously he included himself. Perhaps a better clue to his self-analysis is his description of himself, in a letter to Lafayette, as "a Philanthropist by character, and . . . a

[4] Richardson, *Messages and Papers of the Presidents,* I, 202.

Citizen of the great republic of humanity at large."[5] This self-portrait of the prosaic Virginia farmer sitting in his home above the Potomac and passing philosophical judgments upon the policies and aspirations of men on both sides of the Atlantic is one which may amaze the historian. It suggests, however, a mind which had thought carefully if not profoundly upon the fundamental political issues of his day. The product of this thought may be found scattered through hundreds of letters to intimate friends or even to casual correspondents.

A survey of this correspondence and of his official career indicates that the dominant note in the political thinking of Washington, both before and after 1789, was his unwavering belief that only a strong central government, able to determine and enforce national policies, would enable the United States to assume its appropriate position among the nations of the world. This conviction was the product of experience rather than of meditation. As commander of the army, Washington felt a natural sympathy for the plight of his unpaid men, and while counseling them against rash measures he urged Congress and the states to recognize the services of the army by making provision for the payment of the money due the soldiers.[6] It was the states, he believed, which were delinquent in this matter rather than Congress, and he felt for the states the same distrust that he felt for private debtors who refused to honor their obligations. Furthermore, Washington by his very position as commander of the army had been compelled to transcend local interests to become a national figure concerned with national aspirations and national policies. The members of Congress were the representatives of the states, but he had been the repository of national hope and of such national power as could be created. The inevitable conflict between a civilian Congress responsible to local feeling and the commander of an army in the

[5] Washington to Lafayette, August 15, 1786, *Writings of Washington,* XXVIII, 520.
[6] Washington to Alexander Hamilton, March 4, 1783, *ibid.,* XXVI, 186–187; Washington to John A. Washington, June 15, 1783, *ibid.,* XXVII, 13. To Hamilton, Washington wrote that the "predicament" in which he found himself as both citizen and soldier had been "the Subject of many contemplative hours."

field had confirmed him in his suspicion of too much local autonomy. With reason, and probably with some emotion, he informed Hamilton, in March, 1783, that no man in the country could be "more deeply impressed" with the necessity of strengthening the federal government because no man had felt more keenly "the bad effects" of a diffusion of authority.[7] Three months later, in a circular letter addressed to the individual states, he asserted that he could prove "to every mind open to conviction" that the war might have been won in less time and with less expense had Congress possessed greater energy and greater power.[8] He suggested the remedy in a letter to a prospective historian of the Revolution, the Reverend William Gordon. The people, Washington complained, were content to know only that the war had been fought and won and they had failed to inquire why the victory had been so long delayed or the cost so great. These difficulties, he explained, had been caused in large measure by a "want of energy in the Federal Constitution"; the remedy for this political disease was "a Convention of the People" which would confer the necessary power upon the central government.[9] At the close of the year, he sounded a more ominous note in his final orders to the army, asserting that "unless the principles of the federal government were properly supported and the powers of the union increased, the honor, dignity, and justice of the nation would be lost forever."[10]

Washington was candid in his hope that the Articles of Confederation would be amended or superseded by a constitution which would provide the federal government with increased power and which would free it from a slavish dependence upon the whims and local concerns of the states. In this matter, however, he was not an extremist. In urging a redistribution of powers he employed vague language, being content merely to suggest that Congress be granted "sufficient powers" to give "consistency, stability and dignity" to the federal government, or—as he more often ex-

[7] Washington to Hamilton, March 31, 1783, *ibid.*, XXVI, 277.
[8] The circular, dated Newburgh, June 8, 1783, is in *ibid.*, XXVI, 483–496. The statement cited is on p. 495.
[9] Washington to William Gordon, July 8, 1783, *ibid.*, XXVII, 49.
[10] "Farewell Orders to the Armies of the United States," November 2, 1783, *ibid.*, XXVII, 226.

pressed it—the powers necessary for "general purposes."[11] What those powers should be was left to the imagination of his correspondents and of the historian, but his satisfaction with the Constitution of 1787 seems to offer a clue to his views as to the proper spheres of state and federal authority.

Washington returned to Mount Vernon at the close of 1783, content with the prospect of ending his career as a gentleman farmer and amateur philosopher. He retired to private life with foreboding that the eight years of struggle might yet prove to have been futile, but these gloomy thoughts were balanced by the conviction that with "a little political wisdom" the United States might become as "populous and happy" as its territory was extensive.[12] Although he traveled little in the next three years, he did not lose contact with the outside world. Scarcely a week passed that invited or uninvited guests did not come to Mount Vernon to share his hospitality, for which they paid with idle gossip or news of events on either side of the ocean. More important among his sources of information was an extensive correspondence with men of prominence in this country and in Europe. To a privileged few of these correspondents he freely confessed his growing fear that the potential greatness of the new republic was being sacrificed on the altar of pride and jealousy of thirteen quarreling states.[13] When the delicate problem of national and state finances led to a demand for the issuance of paper money and then to the threat of civil war in some of the states, the residue of optimism with which he had returned to Mount Vernon disappeared. As he read reports of Shays's Rebellion and of the paper money struggle in Rhode Island, his faith in the wisdom and rectitude of the people was severely

[11] Washington to Lafayette, April 5, 1783, *ibid.*, XXVI, 298; Washington to Tench Tilghman, April 24, 1783, *ibid.*, XXVI, 359; Washington to John A. Washington, June 15, 1783, *ibid.*, XXVII, 12.

At a dinner given in his honor at Annapolis on December 22, 1783, Washington offered the toast, "Competent powers to Congress for general purposes." James Tilton to Gunning Bedford, December 25, 1783, *ibid.*, XXVII, 285–286 n.

[12] Washington to Sir Edward Newenham, June 10, 1784, *ibid.*, XXVII, 417.

[13] See, for example, Washington to Benjamin Harrison, January 18, 1784, *ibid.*, XXVII, 305–306; Washington to James Madison, November 30, 1785, *ibid.*, XXVIII, 336; Washington to Bushrod Washington, November 15, 1786, *ibid.*, XXIX, 68.

shaken. To correspondents who turned to him for counsel, he indicated his own wish that the powers of the central government should be greatly strengthened, though he thought that proposals which would virtually eliminate the powers of the individual states were too radical to be acceptable to the majority of the people.[14] He noted that "even respectable characters" contemplated the establishment of a monarchy "without horror."[15] He would not approve so drastic a step until all other measures failed; but in a letter to Madison, written at the close of March, 1787, he indicated a tacit acquiescence in this remedy if the proposed increase in the powers of Congress should fail to produce an efficient government which could command the respect of the people.[16]

Recent historical studies have suggested that the years from 1781 to 1787 were less critical than John Fiske supposed. Washington, however, would have subscribed without reservation to the statement that they were indeed the "critical period." Alarmed by what he regarded as painful evidence that the nation was on the verge of disintegrating in disorder and dishonor, he welcomed the call for the Philadelphia Convention and he accepted the new Constitution with unfeigned satisfaction as the only alternative to anarchy.[17] He did not regard the proposed Constitution as perfect, frankly confessing that it contained much which did not meet his "*cordial* approbation."[18] There is no clue as to what provisions he would have altered, nor is there any clear evidence as to whether he agreed with those who regretted that even greater power had not been granted to the federal government. It is apparent, however, that he did not favor conferring unlimited power upon any political authority, including presumably the central government. He assured his nephew, Bushrod Washington, that no man was "a warmer advocate" of "proper restraints and wholesome checks in

[14] Washington to Henry Knox, February 3, 1787, *ibid.*, XXIX, 153; Washington to David Humphreys, March 8, 1787, *ibid.*, XXIX, 172–173; Washington to the Secretary for Foreign Affairs (John Jay), March 10, 1787, *ibid.*, XXIX, 176.

[15] Washington to Jay, August 1, 1786, *ibid.*, XXVIII, 503.

[16] Washington to Madison, March 31, 1787, *ibid.*, XXIX, 190.

[17] Washington to Charles Carter, December 14, 1787, *ibid.*, XXIX, 339.

[18] Washington to Governor Edmund Randolph, January 8, 1788, *ibid.*, XXIX, 358.

every department of government";[19] and in writing to Lafayette he defended the Constitution as one which contained "more checks and barriers against the introduction of Tyranny" than any yet devised by men.[20] Eight years later, in the Farewell Address, he asserted that "the efficient management" of public business required "a government of as much vigor as is consistent with the perfect security of liberty."[21] In view of the political situation in 1796, it is probable that this rather vague statement of principle was intended as a warning against any weakening of the federal authority rather than as a plea for an increase in its powers.

Washington's views on other great issues of his day were generally less emphatic and occasionally reflected inconsistencies. This is particularly true of his judgments as to the validity of the democratic processes. During his last year in the army and the first year of his retirement at Mount Vernon he avoided a direct commitment upon this delicate problem. He did indeed assert, in 1783, that Congress was "in fact . . . the People,"[22] and he argued that it could not be dangerous to increase the powers of Congress, for its members were "the creatures of the people," to whose wishes they were completely amenable.[23] More significant, perhaps, was his advocacy of short sessions of Congress which would permit the delegates to return to their homes and mingle with their constituents. Such a procedure would be reciprocally beneficial, for the Congressmen could explain national problems to their fellow citizens and in turn they would become "better acquainted" with the sentiments of the people whom they represented.[24] In 1786, he modified this theme somewhat in a letter to his nephew, Bushrod Washington. He declared that he did not question the

[19] Washington to Bushrod Washington, November 10, 1787, ibid., XXIX, 312.
[20] Washington to Lafayette, February 7, 1788, ibid., XXIX, 410–411.
[21] Richardson, Messages and Papers of the Presidents, I, 218.
[22] Washington to Harrison, March 4, 1783, in Writings of Washington, XXVI, 184.
[23] Washington to Gordon, July 8, 1783, ibid., XXVII, 51; Washington to Harrison, January 18, 1784, ibid., XXVII, 306. In view of the fact that Congress was then the sole repository of central authority, these statements may be regarded as more of a defense of the central government than an expression of sympathy with a democratically controlled legislature.
[24] Washington to Thomas Jefferson, March 29, 1784, ibid., XXVII, 377.

thesis that representatives "ought to be the mouth of their Constituents," nor would he deny the right of the latter to give instructions to their delegates in the legislature. He contrasted, however,
the position of representatives in state legislatures with those in
Congress. The latter were compelled to deal with national issues
upon which the people were often poorly informed, and they must
consider the welfare of the entire nation rather than the interests of
a single locality. If Congressmen, therefore, were bound by instructions from their constituents, great national issues would be
decided on the basis of local interests and insufficient knowledge.[25] This was a middle-of-the-road doctrine. It fell far short of
the views of the democratically inclined Antifederalists, but it
reflected none of the indifference to the wishes of the public commonly attributed to the Federalists.

By the summer of 1785, Washington's faith in the wisdom of
the people was being shaken by the refusal of individual states to
cooperate with Congress in forming a national policy. The people,
he several times complained, "must feel" before they would see or
act.[26] The news of the insurrection in western Massachusetts
drove him still farther along the road of disillusionment, and in
apparent despair he wrote to John Jay that "we have probably had
too good an opinion of human nature in forming our confederation," and added that experience taught that men would not
"adopt and carry into execution measures . . . calculated for
their own good, without the intervention of coercive power."[27] In
a similar mood, he addressed to David Humphreys the rhetorical

[25] Washington to Bushrod Washington, September 30, November 15,
1786, ibid., XXIX, 22–23, 67.
[26] Washington to G. W. Fairfax, June 30, 1785, ibid., XXVIII, 183–184;
Washington to Lafayette, July 25, 1785, ibid., XXVIII, 208; Washington to
David Humphreys, March 8, 1787, ibid., XXIX, 173. To Lafayette he added
that "the people will be right at last."
[27] Washington to the Secretary of State for Foreign Affairs (John Jay),
August 1, 1786, ibid., XXVIII, 502. See also, Washington to Madison,
March 31, 1787, ibid., XXIX, 190–191. Washington's skepticism was shared
by Jay, who already had reached the conclusion that the "wise and good
never form the majority of any large society." Jay to Dr. Richard Price,
September 27, 1785, Henry P. Johnson (ed.), The Correspondence and
Public Papers of John Jay, 4 vols. (New York, 1890–1893), III, 168.

inquiry, "What, gracious God, is man! that there should be such inconsistency and perfidiousness in his conduct?"[28]

The state of the nation in 1786 had temporarily destroyed Washington's belief in the ultimate wisdom of the people, but his disillusionment was not permanent, and the events of 1787 and 1788 largely restored his faith. He returned to Mount Vernon from the Philadelphia Convention still fearing that "the multitude are often deceived by externals,"[29] but when by August, 1788, eleven states had ratified the Constitution, Washington became confident that "the People when rightly informed will decide in a proper manner."[30] His recent skepticism was conveniently forgotten, and he proudly informed Lafayette that he had never believed that the United States would become "an awful monument" to the doctrine that "Mankind, under the most favourable circumstances . . . are unequal to the task of Governing themselves."[31] In March, 1789, he believed that it would be "necessary . . . to conciliate the good will of the People" inasmuch as it would be impossible "to build the edifice of public happiness, but upon their affections."[32] He had returned to a qualified belief in democracy, and with this belief he entered the Presidency. Apparently he held similar views after eight months in that office, for in January, 1790, he declared that he had always believed that "an unequivocally free and equal Representation of the People in the Legislature, together with an efficient and responsable [*sic*] Executive, were the great Pillars on which the preservation of American Freedom must depend."[33] As he approached the period of conflict within the Cabinet between Hamilton and Jefferson, he stood midway between the two antagonists in his views on democracy.

The vicissitudes of the Presidency provided a serious test of Washington's wavering views concerning democracy. The unex-

---

[28] Washington to David Humphreys, December 26, 1786, in *Writings of Washington*, XXIX, 125–126.
[29] Washington to Madison, October 10, 1787, *ibid.*, XXIX, 285.
[30] Washington to Charles Pettit, August 16, 1788, *ibid.*, XXX, 41.
[31] Washington to Lafayette, June 19, 1788, *ibid.*, XXIX, 526.
[32] Washington to Samuel Vaughan, March 21, 1789, *ibid.*, XXX, 240.
[33] Washington to Catherine Macaulay Graham, January 9, 1790, *ibid.*, XXX, 496.

pected bitterness of the opposition to the policies of his administration, the disillusioning breach with Jefferson, and his growing dependence upon Hamilton were factors which might have shaken a stronger faith than his in the efficacy of democratic institutions. It is clear that he was distressed by that inescapable adjunct of democratic government, the rise of partisan opposition to the government in power. When this political division invaded his Cabinet, he urged both Hamilton and Jefferson to cultivate a tolerance of opposing views and to accept in good faith the decisions of Congress and the executive. He reluctantly admitted that differences in political opinion were unavoidable, but he declared that it would be difficult if not impossible "to manage the Reins of Government" unless there were "mutual forbearances, and temporising yieldings *on all sides.*"[34] The appearance of so-called "Democratic Societies" as centers of opposition to the policies of the national government aroused mingled apprehension and indignation in his mind. He attributed the resistance to the excise laws to the machinations of those societies and asserted that their influence, if not counteracted, "would shake the government to its foundation."[35] By 1795, Washington's patience with partisan opposition had reached the vanishing point. He seems to have been both surprised and annoyed by the hostility to the treaty with Great Britain, and when both the treaty and its friends were denounced in public gatherings he took the extreme position that "meetings in opposition to the constituted authorities" were "*at all times,* improper and dangerous."[36] There is no evidence, however, that Washington realized that his thinking had come dangerously close to a negation of the democratic spirit. Nor did he yet regard himself as a partisan. In writing to one of the most partisan of his supporters, Timothy Pickering, Washington described himself as a man "of no party . . . whose sole wish is to pursue, with undeviating steps a path which would lead this Country to respect-

[34] Washington to Jefferson, August 23, 1792, *ibid.,* XXXII, 130–131; Washington to Hamilton, August 26, 1792, *ibid.,* XXXII, 132–133.
[35] Washington to Henry Lee, August 26, 1794, *ibid.,* XXXIII, 475–476; Washington to Burges Ball, September 25, 1794, *ibid.,* XXXIII, 506–507; Washington to John Jay, November 1, 1794, *ibid.,* XXXIV, 17.
[36] Washington to John Adams, August 20, 1795, *ibid.,* XXXIV, 280.

ability, wealth and happiness."[37] One year later, in the Farewell Address, he devoted much attention to the danger of partisanship, declaring that it was indeed the "worst enemy" of popular government.[38]

To the end of his life, Washington failed to recognize the close relationship between partisan politics and the practical expression of the views of the majority. There was no conscious inconsistency, therefore, between his hostility to parties and his continued confidence in the wisdom of the people. During the closing year of his Presidency and thereafter, he several times asserted that the mass of the citizens needed only to understand a question to decide it properly,[39] and as the crisis with France approached a climax he declared that the sentiments of the majority *"ought* to be unequivocally known," as it was "the right of the People" that their will should be put into effect.[40] He declared that, as President, it had always been his "earnest desire to learn, and to comply, as far as is consistent, with the public sentiment," but this was modified by his belief that such an expression of popular will could be valid "on *great* occasions *only"* and after there had been opportunity for "cool and deliberate reflection" on the part of the public.[41] After nine months in the relative calm of Mount Vernon he reiterated this general opinion. During periods of crisis, he believed, reason abdicated and men were ruled by passions, but when these passions subsided

[37] Washington to Timothy Pickering, July 27, 1795, *ibid.,* XXXIV, 251.

[38] Richardson, *Messages and Papers of the Presidents,* I, 218. A year in retirement did not modify Washington's views on this vital issue. In March, 1798, at a time when his successor was beset with opposition similar to that experienced by Washington, he asserted that "misrepresentation and party feuds have arisen to such a height, as to distort truth and to become portentous of the most serious consequences, . . . whether they can end at any point short of confusion and anarchy is *now* in my opinion more problematical than ever." Washington to Alexander White, March 1, 1798, *Writings of Washington,* XXXVI, 175–176. [For Washington's later views on this subject, see Marshall Smelser, "George Washington and the Alien and Sedition Acts," *The American Historical Review,* LIX (1954), 322–334 (ed.).]

[39] Washington to Jay, May 8, 1796, *ibid.,* XXXV, 37; Washington to John Marshall, December 4, 1797, *ibid.,* XXXVI, 93; Washington to Alexander Addison, June 3, 1798, *ibid.,* XXXVI, 280; Washington to James Lloyd, February 11, 1799, *ibid.,* XXXVII, 129.

[40] Washington to Thomas Pinckney, May 28, 1797, *ibid.,* XXXV, 453.

[41] Washington to Edward Carrington, May 1, 1796, *ibid.,* XXXV, 32.

and the "empire" of reason was restored those public servants who pursued "the paths of truth, moderation and justice" would regain the public confidence and their just influence.[42] This was a comforting hope, and to Washington it appeared to justify a basic confidence in the wisdom of the people. In principle, it appears to place him closer to Jefferson and Madison than to the Federalist leadership with which he had been associated during the latter part of his Presidency.

The moderate conservatism which prompted Washington to accept a qualified democracy was reflected more clearly in his belief in a balanced economy. Washington was a farmer with the true farmer's love of the land, believing that "the life of a Husbandman" was of all vocations "the most delectable."[43] Agriculture, he asserted, was "the proper source of American wealth and happiness";[44] and he predicted that Americans would continue to be "an agricultural people . . . for ages to come."[45] Holding these views, he could assure Jefferson, in 1788, that "the introduction of any thing" which might divert the attention of the people from agricultural pursuits "must be extremely prejudicial, if not ruinous to us."[46]

Gradually, however, Washington became convinced of the value of commerce and manufacturing in the life of a nation. In 1784 he had admitted to Jefferson that commerce had "its advantages and disadvantages"; and a year later he observed that it was a question debated "among Philosophers and wise men" as to whether foreign commerce was "of real advantage" to a nation.[47] By 1786, his hitherto uncertain views appeared to be taking more definite shape, for he informed Lafayette that he reflected "with pleasure" that

[42] Washington to John Luzac, December 2, 1797, ibid., XXXVI, 84.

[43] Washington to Alexander Spotswood, February 13, 1788, ibid., XXIX, 414. In writing to Arthur Young, he described agriculture as "a subject, which may be more conducive than almost any other to the happiness of mankind." Washington to Young, December 4, 1788, ibid., XXX, 153.

[44] Washington to Theodorick Bland, August 15, 1786, ibid., XXVIII, 517; Washington to Samuel Chamberline, April 3, 1788, ibid., XXIX, 455.

[45] Washington to Lafayette, August 15, 1786, ibid., XXVIII, 519.

[46] Washington to Jefferson, January 1, 1788, ibid., XXIX, 351.

[47] Washington to Jefferson, March 29, 1784, ibid., XXVII, 376; Washington to James Warren, October 7, 1785, ibid., XXVIII, 290.

commerce would have a beneficial effect upon "human manners
and society," uniting mankind "like one great family in fraternal
ties."[48] He was not prepared to comment on the economic consequences of commerce, but in March, 1789, on the eve of assuming the Presidency, he informed a correspondent in Ireland that
although American prosperity "must depend essentially" upon
agriculture, the "useful arts and commerce ought not . . . to be
altogether neglected."[49] Among the "useful arts" to which he referred was manufacturing. He did not wish to "force the introduction of manufactures, by extravagant encouragements, and to the
prejudice of agriculture," but he suggested, in January, 1789, that
much might be accomplished in manufacturing through the labor
of women and children "without taking one really necessary hand
from tilling the earth."[50] A year later, in his first annual message
to Congress, he declared that the "safety and interest" of the
nation required the development of such manufactures as would
render it independent of other nations for essential goods and
particularly for military supplies.[51] The policies of his administration have generally been regarded as more conducive to the expansion of manufacturing than to the encouragement of the farmers. This was not, on his part, a deliberate slighting of the agricultural population. Near the close of his administration he reaffirmed
his personal loyalty to agriculture as a way of life, asserting that it
was the occupation most congenial to his "nature and gratifica-
tions";[52] and in the last of the annual messages to Congress he
reasserted his conviction that "with reference either to individual
or national welfare agriculture is of primary importance."[53] His

[48] Washington to Lafayette, August 15, 1786, *ibid.,* XXVIII, 520–521. In
December, 1786, Washington wrote to Governor Edmund Randolph of
Virginia that the encouragement of manufacturing was "certainly consistent
with that sound policy which ought to actuate every State." Washington to
Randolph, December 25, 1786, *ibid.,* XXIX, 120.
[49] Washington to Sir Edward Newenham, March 2, 1789, *ibid.,* XXX,
217–218.
[50] Washington to Lafayette, January 29, 1789, *ibid.,* XXX, 186–187.
[51] Richardson, *Messages and Papers of the Presidents,* I, 65.
[52] Washington to James Anderson, December 24, 1795, *Writings of Washington,* XXXIV, 406.
[53] Richardson, *Messages and Papers of the Presidents,* I, 202.

willingness to admit industry and commerce to a vital though subordinate role in the national economy placed him again somewhere between Jefferson and Hamilton. In one respect his views presented a striking parallel to those of his fellow Virginian, for like Jefferson he was suspicious of great cities, whose "tumultuous populace" he declared were "ever to be dreaded."[54]

Like so many of the great men of his day, Washington accepted the idea of progress and hoped that improvements in society might indeed be realized. He distrusted precedents, which he once described as "the arm which first arrests the liberties and happiness of a Country."[55] To Lafayette he wrote, in 1788, that he loved "to indulge the contemplation of human nature in a progressive state of improvement and melioration";[56] and a year later he described himself as indulging in "innocent Reveries, that mankind will, one day, grow happier and better."[57] Perfection, he confessed, was not to be expected in this world;[58] and after hearing the news from France, early in 1790, he warned a French correspondent against too great an acceleration along the road of improvement.[59] The same idealism that rejoiced in the probability of progress influenced his thinking upon the problems of war and of peace. On at least one occasion, in 1785, he went so far as to assert that it was his "first wish" that the plague of war should be "banished from off the Earth."[60] Three years later he expressed interest in a proposal for a universal language, hoping that such a project, if successful, might "one day remove many of the causes of hostility from amongst mankind."[61] Washington was no paci-

[54] Washington to Lafayette, July 28, 1791, *Writings of Washington,* XXXI, 324.

[55] Washington to Sir Edward Newenham, November 25, 1785, *ibid.,* XXVIII, 322–323.

[56] Washington to Lafayette, January 10, 1788, *ibid.,* XXIX, 375.

[57] Washington to Count Rochambeau, January 29, 1789, *ibid.,* XXX, 189.

[58] Washington to Lafayette, February 7, 1788, *ibid.,* XXXI, 40–41.

[59] Washington to Marquis de la Luzerne, April 29, 1790, *ibid.* XXXI, 40–41.

[60] Washington to David Humphreys, July 25, 1785, *ibid.,* XXVIII, 202–203; Washington to Lafayette, July 25, 1785, *ibid.,* XXVIII, 206.

[61] Washington to Lafayette, January 10, 1788, *ibid.,* XXIX, 375.

fist; he favored a small peacetime army and he more than once expressed surprise and displeasure that the great maritime powers had not crushed the piratical states on the North African coast. His antipathy to war, however, appears to have been genuine, and presumably it explains in part his later anxiety that this country should avoid a participation in the quarrels of the Old World.

The same cautious humanitarianism which led Washington to deplore the cruelties of war was reflected in his thinking upon some of the other problems of his day. Several times he expressed the hope that the United States would provide "a safe and agreeable Asylum to the virtuous and persecuted part of mankind."[62] He likewise indicated his general disapproval of the institution of slavery though he did not favor rash or extra-legal measures to accomplish this desirable end.[63] His interest in education is well known, and probably no project was closer to his heart in the closing years of his life than his oft-repeated proposal that a national university should be established in the new capital city.[64] Such a university, he suggested to Hamilton, should be one in which the young men from all sections of the country would mingle to "receive the polish of Erudition in the Arts, Sciences, and Belles Lettres." The value of a liberal education, however, apparently occupied a secondary place in his thinking. He was disturbed by the danger that young Americans who were educated in Europe might return to their native land with their faith in republican institutions impaired. A national university located in the national capital would provide an appropriate setting for instilling a love of country and an understanding of "the Interests and poli-

[62] Washington to Lucretia van Winter, March 30, 1785, *ibid.*, XXVIII, 120; Washington to the Rev. F. A. Vanderkemp. May 28, 1788, *ibid.*, XXIX, 504.

[63] Washington to Robert Morris, April 12, 1786, *ibid.*, XXVIII, 408; Washington to Lafayette, April 5, 1783, *ibid.*, XXVI, 300; Washington to Lawrence Lewis, August 4, 1797, *ibid.*, XXXVI, 2.

[64] Washington to John Adams, November 15, 1794, *ibid.*, XXXIV, 23; Washington to the Commissioners of the District of Columbia, January 28, 1795, *ibid.*, XXXIV, 106–107; Washington to Jefferson, March 15, 1795, *ibid.*, XXXIV, 146–147; Washington to Governor Robert Brooke, March 16, 1795, *ibid.*, XXXIV, 149–150; Extract from Washington's Will, July 9, 1799, *ibid.*, XXXVII, 279–280; Eighth Annual Message to Congress, Richardson, *Messages and Papers of the Presidents,* I, 202.

tics of the Nation." More important, it would serve as a meeting ground for students from every part of the United States, and Washington hoped that these young men would return to their homes convinced that there "was not that cause for those jealousies and prejudices" which then existed in the several sections.[65] In education as in politics, Washington's thinking was dominated by his intense nationalism and his fear of sectional rivalries.

It was fitting that a thoughtful man intimately concerned with the problems of public life should give some consideration to the purpose of government. A landowner and a creditor, he accepted without question the obligation of government to protect property.[66] But other considerations influenced his speculations upon this subject. In 1788, he expressed surprise that there was a single king in Europe who failed to recognize that his own reputation rested on "the prosperity and happiness of his People."[67] In more specific terms, he declared in 1790 that the "aggregate happiness of society . . . is, or ought to be, the end of all government."[68] This is not to be confused with the inalienable right to "the pursuit of happiness" proclaimed in the Declaration of Independence, for Jefferson referred to the individual while Washington was thinking in terms of society, but "the aggregate happiness of society" was a democratic rather than a Hamiltonian ideal.

In the academic sense of the term, Washington was not a political philosopher. He prepared no treatise on government or politics, and he failed to contribute directly to the extensive pamphlet debates on political issues during the years of his retirement from 1783 to 1789. Yet it is apparent that Washington had given more than casual thought to the fundamental issues of political principle which divided the American people in the years preceding and following the framing of the Constitution. On some issues, such as the competence of the people in political affairs, Washington's

[65] Washington to Hamilton, September 1, 1796, in *Writings of Washington,* XXXV, 199–200.
[66] Washington to Henry Lee, October 31, 1786, *ibid.,* XXIX, 34.
[67] Washington to Lafayette, June 19, 1788, *ibid.,* XXIX, 524.
[68] Washington to Comte de Moustier, November 1, 1790, *ibid.,* XXXI, 142.

views fluctuated with the course of events; on other matters, such as the most desirable basis of the national economy, there was a steady development away from a sole reliance upon agriculture to a recognition of commerce and manufacturing. But through all of his thinking upon political principles ran the major conviction that government must be strong or it is no government worthy of the name. In many respects his views in 1789 appear to have been close to those of Madison, who likewise favored a strong government, and at the beginning of his administration he seems to have had as much respect for and confidence in the political views of Madison as he had for the ideas of any other important public figure.

The memory of an old man is a notoriously treacherous guide for the historian. It provides, however, a brief postscript to this study. In 1813, Jefferson recalled the political conflicts of Washington's administration, but exonerated Washington of the charge that he had held Federalist views. On the contrary, declared Jefferson, "General Washington did not harbor one principle of federalism." The "only point on which he and I ever differed in opinion," continued Jefferson, "was, that I had more confidence than he had in the natural integrity and discretion of the people, and in the safety and extent to which they might trust themselves with a control over their government."[69] Jefferson's recollections appear to have been more interesting than accurate. Washington did hold at least one principle of federalism—belief in strong government—and it was on that point that his thinking had been clear and consistent for many years. The growing breach between Washington and Jefferson, after 1790, apparently developed primarily because Washington was persuaded to place the strengthening of the central government above all other considerations and only incidentally because of differences of opinion as to the wisdom and virtue of the people. Whether the ease with which Washington was persuaded to accept a program for increasing the power of the central government was the result of the "fatal . . . influence" of

[69] Jefferson to John Melish, January 13, 1813, *The Writings of Thomas Jefferson* (Monticello ed.), 20 vols. (Washington, 1904), XIII, 212.

Hamilton over Washington, as John Adams suggested,[70] or whether it arose primarily from the strength of the convictions which Washington had developed during and after the Revolution must be left to the speculation of any who may wish to make a more intensive study of this question.

[70] Adams to Jefferson, July, 1813, and July 22, 1813, *ibid.*, XIII, 301, 323.

✪

George Washington and Religious Liberty

In the fight against bigotry in America, George Washington played a role second to none. Both as commander-in-chief of the Continental Army and as President, he used his immense prestige and influence to encourage mutual tolerance and good will among American Protestants, Catholics, and Jews and to create a climate of opinion in which every citizen shall, as he phrased it, "sit in safety under his own vine and fig tree and there shall be none to make him afraid."[1] In private letters and in public statements the first President voiced his utter detestation of intolerance, prejudice, and "every species of religious persecution" and often expressed the hope that "bigotry and superstition" would be overcome by "truth and reason" in the United States.[2]

The fact is that Washington was firmly committed to religious liberty and freedom of conscience. Like Jefferson and Madison, he looked upon the new nation as a pluralistic society in which people with varied religious persuasions and national backgrounds learned to live peacefully and rationally together instead of resorting to force and violence. What was unique about the United States, in addition to "cheapness of land," was the existence of "civil and religious liberty," which "stand perhaps unrivalled by any civilized

[1] Papers of George Washington, CCCXXXV, 20, Library of Congress, Washington, D.C.

[2] *Ibid.*, p. 110, XCXXXIV, 84.

Reprinted from Paul F. ▉▉▉er, Jr., "George Washington and Religious Liberty," *William and Mary ▉▉▉terly,* Series 3, 17 (1960), pp. 486–506, by permission of the author.

nation of earth."[3] In his general orders for April 18, 1783, announcing the cessation of hostilities with Great Britain, he congratulated his soldiers, "of whatever condition they may be," for having "assisted in protecting the rights of human nature and establishing an Asylum for the poor and oppressed of all nations and religions. . . ."[4] The "bosom of America," Washington declared a few months later, was "open to receive . . . the oppressed and persecuted of all Nations and Religions; whom we shall wellcome to a participation of all our rights and privileges."[5] When asking Tench Tilghman to secure a carpenter and a bricklayer for his Mount Vernon estate in 1784, he remarked: "If they are good workmen, they may be of Asia, Africa, or Europe. They may be Mohometans, Jews or Christians of any Sect, or they may be Atheists."[6] He was, as John Bell pointed out in 1779, "a total stranger to religious prejudices, which have so often excited Christians of one denomination to cut the throats of those of another."[7]

When and by what process Washington became "a total stranger to religious prejudices" is difficult to determine. In colonial Virginia, the Anglican Church was established by law and and occupied a preferential position. This was Washington's church, and he served for many years as vestryman and churchwarden for Truro Parish. The Virginian establishment was considerably liberalized during the eighteenth century, but dissenting groups were subjected to a variety of legal disabilities and on occasion experienced open persecution. Baptist historians, in fact, sometimes explain Washington's deep-seated devotion to religious freedom as a revulsion against the wave of Baptist mobbings and jailings that took place in Virginia on the eve of the Revolution.[8] This played some part

[3] Washington to Robert Sinclair, May 6, 1792, John C. Fitzpatrick, ed., *The Writings of George Washington . . . 1745–1799* (Washington, D.C., 1931–1944), XXXII, 37.

[4] *Ibid.*, XXVI, 335–336.

[5] To Members of the Volunteer Association and Other Inhabitants of the Kingdom of Ireland Who Have lately Arrived in the City of New York, New York, December 2, 1783, *ibid.*, XXVII, 254.

[6] Washington to Tilghman, March 24, 1784, *ibid.*, p. 367.

[7] William Spohn Baker, *Character Portraits of Washington* (Philadelphia, 1887), p. 77.

[8] Joseph Martin Dawson, *Baptists and the American Republic* (Nashville, 1956), p. 90.

in the development of Madison's views on religious liberty; but as for Washington, no evidence exists to prove the assertion.[9]

There is evidence, however, that Washington learned at an early age the economic disadvantages that frequently accompany legal restrictions on religious freedom. When he was about eighteen, his elder half-brother, Lawrence, became deeply involved as a member of the Ohio Company in negotiations for the sale of fifty thousand acres of land beyond the Alleghenies to a group of Pennsylvania Germans. The Germans wanted to purchase the land but as dissenters they were unwilling to pay taxes to support the Anglican Church, and Lawrence attempted to persuade the Virginia Assembly to exempt them from the parish levies. "I am well assured," he wrote in April, 1751, to John Hanbury, the Ohio Company's English partner, that "we shall never obtain it by a law here." He went on to say:

It has been my opinion, and I hope ever will be, that restraints on conscience are cruel, in regard to those on whom they are imposed, and injurious to the country imposing them. England, Holland, and Prussia I may quote as examples, and much more Pennsylvania, which has flourished under that delightful liberty, so as to become the admiration of every man, who considers the short time it has been settled. . . . This colony [Virginia] was greatly settled in the latter part of Charles the First's time, and during the usurpation, by the zealous churchmen; and that spirit, which was then brought in, has ever since continued, so that except a few Quakers we have no dissenters. But what has been the consequence? We have increased by slow degrees . . . whilst our neighbouring colonies, whose natural advantages are greatly inferior to ours, have become populous.[10]

The conviction that "restraints on conscience" are "cruel" to the victims and "injurious" to those imposing them Washington may well have learned from his older brother. Biographers are generally agreed that Lawrence was a major influence on the young Washington. Many years later, when Washington was attempting to secure immigrants from the Palatinate to settle on his western lands, he emphasized that he saw "no prospect of these people

[9] Gaillard Hunt, *The Life of James Madison* (New York, 1902), p. 12.

[10] Jared Sparks, ed., *The Writings of George Washington* (Boston, 1834), II, 481.

being restrained in the smallest degree, either in their civil or religious principles; which I take notice of, because these are privileges, which mankind are solicitous to enjoy, and emigrants must be anxious to know."[11]

Washington's personal views on the entire question of belief in religion—never formally stated—are also relevant to an understanding of his attitude toward religious liberty. He was a lifelong member of the Episcopal Church and was firmly convinced that organized religion was an indispensable basis for both morality and social order. He was, however, completely lacking in creedal commitment of any kind. He was never, as Benjamin Tallmadge wrote Manasseh Cutler regretfully in January, 1800, "explicit in his profession of *faith in,* and *dependence on* the finished Atonement of our glorious Redeemer. . . ."[12] Although his letters abound in references to God, Providence, heaven, and divine favor, especially in his later years, there is no mention of Jesus Christ anywhere in his extensive correspondence, nor are his infrequent references to Christianity anything but formal in nature. At times, in fact, Washington wrote as if he considered himself an outsider. Commenting hopefully on the Marquis de Lafayette's "plan of toleration in religious matters" for France, he wrote: "Being no bigot myself to any mode of worship, I am disposed to indulge the professors of Christianity in the church, that road to Heaven which to them shall seem the most direct plainest easiest and least liable to exception."[13] This sense of detachment, tinged with irony, appears even more clearly in a letter discussing the controversies between Protestants and Catholics in Ireland: "Of all the animosities which have existed among mankind, those which are caused by a difference of sentiments in religion appear to me to be the most inveterate and distressing, and ought most to be deprecated. I was in hopes, that the enlightened and liberal policy, which has marked the present age, would at least have reconciled *Christians* of every denomina-

[11] Washington to Henry Riddell, February 22, 1774, *Writings of Washington* (Fitzpatrick ed.), III, 481.

[12] Charles Swain Hall, *Benjamin Tallmadge, Revolutionary Soldier and American Businessman* (New York, 1943), p. 167.

[13] To Lafayette, August 15, 1787, *Writings of Washington* (Fitzpatrick ed.), XXIX, 259.

tion so far, that we should never again see their religious disputes carried to such a pitch as to endanger the peace of Society."[14]

Washington was a typical eighteenth-century deist—his writings are sprinkled with such catch phrases as "Grand Architect," "Director of Human Events," "Author of the Universe," and "Invisible Hand"—and he had the characteristic unconcern of the deist for the forms and creeds of institutional religion. He had, moreover, the upper-class deist's strong aversion for sectarian quarrels that threatened to upset the "peace of Society." No doubt Washington's deist indifference was an important factor in producing the broad-minded tolerance in matters of religion that he displayed throughout his life.

Like most American deists (and unlike many European deists), Washington had little or no anticlerical spirit. In addition to attending his own church with a fair degree of regularity, he visited others, including the Roman Catholic, and he contributed money to the building funds of various denominations. At first he had no objections to the proposal of the Virginia legislature to levy a general tax for the support of the churches of the state, following the disestablishment of the Anglican Church after the Revolution. "Altho. no man's sentiments are more opposed to *any kind* of restraint upon religious principles than mine are," he told George Mason, "yet I must confess, that I am not amongst the number of those who are so much alarmed at the thoughts of making people pay towards the support of that which they profess, if of the denomination of Christians; or declare themselves Jews, Mahomitans or otherwise, and thereby obtain proper relief." Having learned, however, of the "disquiet of a respectable minority" over the assessment plan and fearing that its adoption would "rankle and perhaps convulse, the State," he expressed his regret that the issue had been raised and hoped that "the Bill could die an easy death."[15] This experience seems to have convinced him, once and for all, of the impracticality of all proposals of this kind for state support of religion.

[14] Washington to Sir Edward Newenham, October 20, 1792, *ibid.*, XXXII, 190.
[15] Washington to George Mason, October 3, 1785, *ibid.*, XXVIII, 285.

But it would be wrong to assume that Washington's views were shaped solely by social expediency and theological indifference. Though he was not given much to philosophical reflection, he did try on one occasion to work out a more fundamental basis for his views on liberty. In a fragmentary passage apparently intended for use in his Inaugural Address or in his First Annual Message to Congress, Washington asked: "[Shall I] set up my judgment as the standard of perfection? And shall I arrogantly pronounce that whosoever differs from me, must discern the subject through a distorting medium, or be influenced by some nefarious scheme? The mind is so formed in different persons as to contemplate the same objects in different points of view. Hence originates the difference on questions of the greatest import, human and divine."[16] Without reading too much into this isolated passage, one may note that Washington's attempt to find a basis for liberty in a pluralistic view of human perceptions is very Jeffersonian in spirit. Differences of opinion, Jefferson always insisted, "like differences of face, are a law of our own nature, and should be viewed with the same tolerance"; such differences lead to inquiry and "inquiry to truth."[17] Perhaps, then, Washington's association with Jefferson had something to do with his clear-cut pronouncements on religious liberty during his Presidency. Intolerance in any form—religious or secular—was as foreign to Washington's mind as it was to Jefferson's.

Washington had little occasion during the Revolution to make formal pronouncements on the subject of religious freedom, but he made it clear, as commander-in-chief of the Continental Army, that he was firmly opposed to all expressions of religious bigotry among his soldiers. Roman Catholic historians frequently single out the fourteenth item of his instructions of September 14, 1775, to Colonel Benedict Arnold on the eve of the Canada expedition to show that the American commander was "one of the very few men of the Revolution who had . . . outgrown or overcome all reli-

[16] *Ibid.*, XXX, 299.
[17] Jefferson to Col. William Duane, July 25, 1811, Albert Ellery Bergh, ed., *The Writings of Thomas Jefferson* (Washington, 1905), XIII, 67; Jefferson to P. H. Wendover, March 13, 1815, *ibid.*, XIV, 279.

gious prejudices in political matters."[18] Washington's instructions were these: "As the Contempt of the Religion of a Country by ridiculing any of its Ceremonies or affronting its Ministers or Votaries has ever been deeply resented, you are to be particularly careful to restrain every Officer and Soldier from such Imprudence and Folly and to punish every Instance of it. On the other Hand, as far as lays in your power, you are to protect and support the free Exercise of the Religion of the Country and the undisturbed Enjoyment of the rights of Conscience in religious Matters, with your utmost Influence and Authority." In a letter to Arnold accompanying the instructions, Washington added: "I also give it in Charge to you to avoid all Disrespect to or Contempt of the Religion of the Country and its Ceremonies. Prudence, Policy, and a true Christian Spirit, will lead us to look with Compassion upon their Errors without insulting them. While we are contending for our own Liberty, we should be very cautious of violating the Rights of Conscience in others, ever considering that God alone is the Judge of the Hearts of Men, and to him only in this Case, they are answerable."[19]

Obviously, the hope of winning Canadian Catholics to the American cause shaped Washington's orders as much as the "Rights of Conscience in others." Even the Continental Congress, which had made strongly anti-Catholic public statements regarding the Quebec Act in 1774, had learned to be solicitous of the welfare of Canadian Catholics by the fall of 1775. But though the note of condescension in Washington's reference to Catholic "Errors" is unmistakable, there is no evidence that Washington ever shared in the deep-seated anti-Catholic prejudice that existed in the colonies on the eve of the Revolution. He had, it is true, criticized the Quebec Act, but at no time did he join Alexander Hamilton and other patriot leaders in charging that its purpose was to establish "Popery" in the colonies. If his orders to Arnold were not exactly "a model of the statesmanlike tolerance in religious matters which

18 John C. Fitzpatrick, *George Washington Himself* (Indianapolis, 1933), p. 182.
19 Instructions to Arnold, September 14, 1775, *Writings of Washington* (Fitzpatrick ed.), III, 495–496; Washington to Arnold, September 14, 1775, *ibid.,* p. 492.

set Washington apart from so many of his contemporaries,"[20] they probably do show that he was "impatient of religious intolerance."[21]

A similar combination of policy and principle led Washington on November 5, 1775, to issue strict orders forbidding the celebration of Pope's Day (the colonial equivalent of Guy Fawkes Day in England and especially popular in New England) among the troops at Cambridge: "As the Commander in Chief has been apprized of a design form'd for the observance of that *ridiculous and childish custom* of burning the Effigy of the pope—He cannot help expressing his surprise that there should be Officers and Soldiers in this army so void of common sense, as not to see the impropriety of such a step at this Juncture; at a Time when we are solliciting . . . the friendship and alliance of the people of Canada, whom we ought to consider as Brethren embarked in the same Cause. The defense of the general Liberty of America: At such a juncture, and in such Circumstances, to be insulting their Religion, is so monstrous, as not to be suffered or excused. . . ."[22]

Catholic writers have generally looked upon Washington's orders as those of "a brave and tolerant mind." "Every Catholic heart in the colonies," declared Peter Guilday, "must have taken courage" at his action.[23] "The insult to the Catholic religion was distasteful to his more liberal mind," according to John Gilmary Shea.[24] And, indeed, the observance of Pope's Day may have "received its death blow," as James Haltigan put it, "at the hands of the noble Washington,"[25] for there are no records of its cele-

[20] Robert C. Hartnett, "The Religion of the Founding Father," *Wellsprings of the American Spirit*, F. Ernest Johnson, ed. (New York, 1948), p. 53.

[21] Rupert Hughes, *George Washington* (New York, 1927), II, 343.

[22] November 5, 1775, *Writings of Washington* (Fitzpatrick ed.), IV, 65; italics mine.

[23] Peter Guilday, *The Life and Times of John Carroll, Archbishop of Baltimore, 1735–1815* (New York, 1922), I, 83; and his Foreword to John Carroll, *Eulogy on George Washington Delivered in St. Peter's Church, Baltimore, February 22, 1800* . . . (New York, 1932), p. xi.

[24] John Gilmary Shea, *History of the Catholic Church in the United States* . . . (New York, 1886–1892), II, 147.

[25] James Haltigan, *The Irish in the American Revolution* (Washington, 1908), p. 348.

bration in America after 1775.[26] No doubt the decline in anti-Catholic feeling (resulting from the loyal support which American Catholics gave the Revolutionary cause and from the alliance with France) during the Revolutionary period accounts for the disappearance of the custom. Yet, Washington was the first to put an end to such anti-Catholic demonstrations, and his example undoubtedly carried great weight. For this he won the profound gratitude of American Catholics; so much so that during the nineteenth century a legend developed that Washington had joined the Catholic Church, or at least was thinking of doing so, shortly before he died.[27]

American Universalists have also claimed Washington because he upheld the right of John Murray, the founder of American Universalism, to officiate as chaplain in the Continental Army. The doctrine of universal salvation that Murray brought from England to America in 1770 had aroused bitter hostility among orthodox clergymen. By eliminating the fear of hell, Murray's teaching, it was charged, undermined morality and led to atheism. In spite of these slanders, Murray won the admiration and friendship of influential laymen in New England before the Revolution, and in May, 1775, leading officers in the Rhode Island brigade, including Nathanael Greene and James Varnum, invited him to become their chaplain. Several weeks after Washington arrived in Cambridge to take command, the rest of the chaplains petitioned for Murray's removal.[28] In his general orders for September 17, however, Washington announced tersely: "The Revd. Mr. John Murray is appointed Chaplain to the Rhode-Island Regiments and is to be respected as such."[29] For this, the Universalists have looked upon Washington as "noble-minded" and "immortal."[30] "History," said one writer of Washington's order regarding Chaplain Murray, "furnished no more signal instance of a rebuke of bigoted intoler-

[26] Ray Allen Billington, *The Protestant Crusade, 1800–1860* (New York, 1938), p. 19.

[27] Thomas O'Gorman, *A History of the Roman Catholic Church in the United States* (New York, 1895), p. 289.

[28] *The Life of the Rev. John Murray . . . Written by Himself . . .*, new ed. (Boston, 1869), p. 317.

[29] *Writings of Washington* (Fitzpatrick ed.), III, 497.

[30] *Life of Murray*, pp. 316–317.

ance."[31] Others, while acknowledging that "the immortal chief"
was "not a professed Universalist," have suggested that his outlook was essentially that of a Universalist.[32]

But the General simply wanted his men to have chaplains of
their own choosing. Moreover, he was anxious to keep religious
controversies out of the Continental Army. When Congress proposed, in 1777, substituting chaplains at the brigade level for the
various regimental chaplains, Washington objected:

> It has . . . a tendency to introduce religious disputes into the Army,
> which above all things should be avoided, and in many instances
> would compel men to a mode of Worship which they do not profess.
> The old Establishment gives every Regiment an Opportunity of having
> a Chaplain of their own religious Sentiments, it is founded on a plan
> of a more generous toleration, and the choice of the Chaplains to
> officiate, has been generally in the Regiments. Supposing one Chaplain
> could do the duties of a Brigade, (which supposition However is in-
> admissable, when we view things in practice) that being composed of
> four or five, perhaps in some instances, Six Regiments, there might be
> so many different modes of Worship. I have mentioned the Opinion of
> the Officers and these hints to Congress upon this Subject; from a
> principle of duty and because I am well assured, it is most foreign to
> their wishes or intention to excite by any act, the smallest uneasiness or
> jealousy among the Troops.[33]

The desire to keep religious friction at a minimum in the army
and the determination to follow a policy of "generous toleration"
was plain common sense. Washington needed every man he could
get and he knew (and others gradually learned) that Catholics and
Universalists could be as good soldiers as anyone else. But what
about men whose religious principles led them to refuse to bear
arms in the cause? When the war moved to Pennsylvania in 1777,
Washington was faced for the first time with the necessity of working out some policy with regard to the pacifist Quakers.

Washington had had some experience with Quakers in Virginia
before the Revolution and he seems to have had no objection to

[31] John Prince, quoted by Clarence R. Skinner and Alfred S. Cole, *Hell's Ramparts Fell: The Life of John Murray* (Boston, 1941), p. 125.

[32] Richard Eddy, *Universalism in America* (Boston, 1884), I, 332.

[33] Washington to President of Congress, June 8, 1777, *Writings of Washington* (Fitzpatrick ed.), VIII, 203–204.

the exemption of the "conscientiously scrupulous" from the draft laws.[34] In the summer of 1777 he ordered the immediate release of a group of western Virginia Quakers who had been drafted into the army and marched two hundred miles, with muskets tied on their backs, to his camp outside Philadelphia.[35] But he had difficulty in understanding the determined neutralism of Pennsylvania's Quakers toward the American Revolution. Their refusal to have anything to do—even in nonmilitary matters—with the revolutionary government of the state mystified him. He seems, in fact, to have believed for a time, as did patriots generally, that the Quakers were Tory in sympathy and were working secretly to help the British. When issuing orders for the impressment of supplies from the countryside during the British occupation of Philadelphia, Washington twice instructed his officers to concentrate particularly on the "unfriendly Quakers and others notoriously disaffected to the cause of American liberty." He also placed severe restrictions on Quaker movements in the Philadelphia area during March, 1778.[36]

Yet on two occasions during this period he reacted with courtesy and consideration in personal encounters with the Quakers. Six delegates from the Philadelphia Yearly Meeting, who visited his headquarters in October, 1777, to present him with a "Testimony against War," were "kindly entertained" by him, listened to with respect, and treated to dinner.[37] A few months later, at Valley Forge, he interceded with Pennsylvania authorities on behalf of four Quakers wishing to send food, clothing, and medical supplies to a group of Philadelphia Quakers exiled by the Pennsylvania government to Winchester, Virginia. "Humanity pleads strongly in their behalf," he told Governor Thomas Wharton.[38]

Washington's treatment of the Quakers during the Revolution has been accorded high praise by Quaker writers. "In all the rela-

[34] *Ibid.*, VII, 35, 79.
[35] "Memoirs of James Pemberton," *Friends' Miscellany*, VII (1835), 65.
[36] *Writings of Washington* (Fitzpatrick ed.), IX, 318; X, 120; XI, 114.
[37] "Minutes of the Yearly Meeting for Pennsylvania and New Jersey Held in Philadelphia . . . [September 26 to October 5] 1778," p. 415, Department of Records, Philadelphia.
[38] *Writings of Washington* (Fitzpatrick ed.), XI, 223–224.

174 PAUL F. BOLLER, JR.

tions of the General with the Friends," concluded Isaac Sharpless, "we find the greatest courtesy on his part, and the most respectful language, whether in minutes of meetings or in private letters on theirs. He understood their scruples and respected them, and they felt the reality of his politeness and sense of justice."[39] Sharpless certainly overstated the case—Washington did suspect the Quakers of "evil intentions" during the Pennsylvania campaign[40]—but he was probably correct in asserting that the American commander "appreciated" the Quakers "far better than did those militant civilians, the Adamses of Massachusetts," and that "many a commander would have treated them with scant forbearance."[41] After the Revolution, when Warner Mifflin called upon him to explain the pacifist views of the Society of Friends, Washington declared: "Mr. Mifflin, I honor your sentiments; there is more in that than mankind have generally considered."[42]

Although Washington's behavior toward the Catholics, Universalists, and Quakers showed his religious toleration, only once during the Revolution did he single out religious liberty, in a formal public statement, as one of the objectives for which the war was being fought. This was on November 16, 1782, in response to a welcoming address made by the ministers, elders, and deacons of the Reformed Protestant Dutch Church of Kingston, New York, on the occasion of his visit to the town. The church leaders declared that "our Religious Rights" were "partly involved in our Civil,"[43] and Washington answered: "Convinced that our Religious Liberties were as essential as our Civil, my endeavors have never been wanting to encourage and promote the one, while I have been contending for the other; and I am highly flattered by finding that my efforts have met the approbation of so respectable a body."[44] No doubt Washington had assumed all along that civil rights included religious freedom. In an address to the United Dutch Re-

---

[39] Isaac Sharpless, *A History of Quaker Government in Pennsylvania, 1682–1783* (Philadelphia, 1902), p. 168.
[40] *Writings of Washington* (Fitzpatrick ed.) VIII, 45.
[41] Sharpless, *Quaker Government*, pp. 169, 220.
[42] *The Friend of Peace* (1820), II, 8.
[43] Papers of Washington, CCX, November 7–22, 1782.
[44] *Writings of Washington* (Fitzpatrick ed.), XXV, 346–347.

formed churches of Hackensack and Schalenburgh, New Jersey, shortly after the close of the war, he mentioned the "protection of our Civil and Religious Liberties" as one of the achievements of the Revolution.[45]

If Washington said little about religious liberty during the war, he had much to say publicly and of an explicit nature on the subject after he became President. In each case what he said grew out of some point raised in a formal address to him. After his inauguration as President on April 30, 1789, Washington received a flood of congratulatory addresses from towns, cities, colleges, state legislatures, fraternal organizations, and religious bodies, to each of which he was expected to make a formal acknowledgment. Wherever he went, there were the inevitable complimentary speeches and polite replies. Among these many exchanges were twenty-two with the major religious bodies of his day. Understandably, there is much in these addresses and in Washington's responses of a ceremonial, platitudinous, and even pompous nature. The addresses were, as the Virginia Baptists put it, largely "shouts of congratulations":[46] praise for Washington's services in war and peace, pledges of loyal support for the new government, expressions of hope for the flourishing of religion and morality in the new nation, and invocations of divine blessings upon the President. Washington's replies were properly modest in regard to himself, expressed gratification at the professions of loyalty to the government, and, as regards religion, frequently consisted of little more than paraphrases of what had been said to him.[47] Nevertheless, there is much that is valuable in these exchanges for the insight which they give into Washington's views on religious freedom and the relationship between Church and State.

Such was the case in his exchange with the Virginia Baptists. This group had not forgotten the discrimination it had suffered before the Revolution and had doubts as to whether the federal Constitution provided adequate safeguards for religious liberty.

[45] *Ibid.*, XXVII, 239.
[46] Papers of Washington, CCCXXXIV, 81.
[47] See, for example, Washington's exchanges with the Methodist, Episcopalian, Dutch Reformed, and Universalist churches, *ibid.*, pp. 25–26, 41–42, 49–50, CCCXXXV, 13–15.

176   PAUL F. BOLLER, JR.

The General Committee of Baptists in Virginia in March, 1788, appointed a committee, headed by John Leland, to prepare an address to Washington on the subject and to secure the cooperation of Baptists in other states in seeking amendments to the Constitution. The address was adopted at the annual meeting of the General Committee at Richmond in May, 1789, and transmitted to Washington.[48] It reads:

When the Constitution first made its apearance in Virginia, we, as a Society, had unusual strugglings of mind; fearing that the *liberty of conscience,* dearer to us than property or life, was not sufficiently secured— Perhaps our jealousies were heightened on account of the usage that we received under the royal government, when Mobs, Bonds, Fines, and Prisons were our frequent attendants.—Convinced on one hand that without an effective national government we should fall into disunion and all the consequent evils; and on the other fearing that we should be accessary to some religious oppression, should any one Society in the Union preponderate over all the rest. But amidst all the inquietudes of mind, our consolation arose from this consideration "The plan must be good for it bears the signature of a tried, trusty friend"—and if religious liberty is rather insecure, "The administration will certainly prevent all oppression for a Washington will preside." . . .[49]

Washington's reply seemed to satisfy the Baptists. He praised them as "firm friends to civil liberty" and "persevering Promoters of our glorious revolution," and tried to quiet their fears about the Constitution. "If I could have entertained the slightest apprehension," he assured them, "that the Constitution . . . might possibly endanger the religious rights of any ecclesiastical Society, certainly I would never have placed my signature to it. . . ." As for the future, "if I could now conceive that the general Government might ever be so administered as to render the liberty of conscience insecure, I beg you will be persuaded that no one would be more zealous than myself to establish effectual barriers against the horrors of spiritual tyranny, and every species of religious persecution—For you, doubtless, remember that I have often expressed my sentiments, that every man, conducting himself as a

[48] Robert B. C. Howell, *The Early Baptists of Virginia* (Philadelphia, 1857), pp. 224–226.
[49] Papers of Washington, CCCXXXIV, 82.

good citizen, and being accountable to God alone for his religious opinions, ought to be protected in worshipping the Deity according to the dictates of his own conscience."[50] Baptist writers, while applauding this message in its entirety, have been especially fond of the phrase, "effectual barriers against the horrors of spiritual tyranny," which some of them look upon as the forerunner of Jefferson's "wall of separation between church and state."[51]

Several months after his exchange with the Virginia Baptists, Washington had occasion to spell out his ideas on liberty of conscience at greater length. Philadelphia Quakers, seeking a "formal reconciliation" with the new government, joined with New York Friends in sending a delegation to New York, in October, 1789, to read a statement to Washington prepared by the Philadelphia Yearly Meeting.[52] They began by assuring Washington of their affection for him personally and of their loyalty to the federal Constitution. Then: "The free toleration which the citizens of these States enjoy in the public worship of the Almighty, agreeable to the dictates of their consciences, we esteem among the choicest of blessings; and as we desire to be filled with fervent charity for those who differ from us in matters of faith or practice . . . so we trust we may justly claim it from others. And on a full persuasion that the divine principles we profess lead into harmony and concord, we can take no part in carrying on war, on any occasion or under any power; but are bound in conscience to lead quiet and peaceable lives in godliness and honesty. . . ." Apparently still rankling from charges of treason that had been

[50] *Ibid.*, p. 84.
[51] Conrad H. Moehlman, *The Wall of Separation between Church and State* (Boston, 1951), p. 87. Baptist historians have also regarded this correspondence as a major event in the campaign for a federal bill of rights and have even suggested that the religious-liberty provisions in the First Amendment "resulted from what might have seemed the extreme sensitiveness of the Virginia Baptist General Committee." Albert H. Newman, *A History of the Baptist Churches in the United States* (New York, 1894), p. 374; Richard B. Cook, *The Story of the Baptists in All Ages and Countries* (Baltimore, 1884), pp. 249–250. There was, of course, no such direct relationship; see Robert A. Rutland, *The Birth of the Bill of Rights, 1776–1791* (Chapel Hill, 1955), *passim*.
[52] Margaret E. Hirst, *The Quakers in Peace and War* (London, 1923), p. 144.

hurled at them during the Revolution, the Quakers went on to assure Washington that they had never been guilty, "from our first establishment as a religious society, with fomenting or countenancing tumults or conspiracies. . . ."[53]

In his friendly response, Washington gently, but frankly, took exception to Quaker pacifism. At the same time he stated his position on the rights of conscience in religious matters with precision and clarity:

Government being, among other purposes, instituted to protect the persons and consciences of men from oppression, it is certainly the duty of Rulers, not only to abstain from it themselves, but according to their stations, to prevent it in others. The liberty enjoyed by the People of these States of worshipping Almighty God agreeable to their consciences is not only among the choicest of their *blessings,* but also of their *rights.* While men perform their social duties faithfully, they do all that Society or the State can with propriety demand or expect, and remain responsible only to their Maker for the religion or mode of faith which they may prefer or profess. Your principles and conduct are well known to me, and it is doing the People called Quakers no more than justice to say, that (except their declining to share with others the burthen of the common defence) there is no denomination among us, who are more exemplary and useful citizens. . . . I assure you very explicitly that in my opinion the conscientious scruples of all men should be treated with great delicacy and tenderness, and it is my wish and desire that the laws may always be as extensively accomodated [*sic*] to them, as a due regard to the Protection and essential interests of the nation may justify and permit.[54]

As pacifists, the Quakers could not fully agree with the balance that Washington struck between the rights of conscience and the "essential interests of the nation." But the delegation "was very much pleased with his behaviour," as Susanna Dilwyn wrote afterwards; "indeed he gains the esteem of everybody—those who agree with few other things all unite in admiring General Washington."[55] Later Quaker writers concur with her judgment, generally agreeing that Washington's "appreciation of Quakers" at

[53] Papers of Washington, CCCXXXIV, 52.
[54] *Ibid.,* p. 52.
[55] "Susanna Dilwyn to Her Father, [Nov.] 4, 1789," *Friends Intelligencer,* CVI (1949), 700.

this time helped to dissolve lingering animosities toward the Society of Friends.[56]

If the Baptists and the Quakers were particularly interested in liberty of conscience under the new Constitution, there were others who deplored the omission of any reference to deity in the document. The members of the Constitutional Convention were by no means hostile to organized religion but they were undoubtedly anxious to avoid embroiling the new government in religious controversies; the clause prohibiting religious tests for office-holding was adopted, as Luther Martin acknowledged, "by a great majority of the convention and without much debate," and it was certainly welcomed by fervent believers in the separation of Church and State like the Baptists.[57] Presbyterians in northern New England, however, were somewhat less enthusiastic about this constitutional aloofness from religion. In October, 1789, as Washington was traveling in New England, the ministers and elders of the First Presbytery of the Eastward (composed of Presbyterian churches in northeastern Massachusetts and New Hampshire) sent him a long welcoming address from Newburyport in which they commented in some detail on the Constitution. They had no objection to "the want of *a religious test,* that grand engine of persecution in every tyrant's hand," and they praised Washington for his benevolent tolerance in religious matters. But, they stated, "We should not have been alone in rejoicing to have seen some explicit acknowledgment of the *only true God and Jesus Christ, whom he hath sent* inserted somewhere in the *Magna Charta* of our country."[58]

Washington's reply was a clear statement of his views on the proper relationship between Church and State. After thanking the Presbytery for its "affectionate welcome," he declared: "And here, I am persuaded, you will permit me to observe that the path of true piety is so plain as to require but little political direction. —To this consideration we ought to ascribe the absence of any regulation, respecting religion, from the Magna-Charta of our coun-

[56] Charles M. Woodman, *Quakers Find a Way* (Indianapolis, 1950), p. 244; Sharpless, *Quaker Government*, p. 223.

[57] Jonathan Elliot, ed., *The Debates in the Several State Conventions on the Adoption of the Federal Constitution . . .*, 2d ed. (Philadelphia and Washington, 1861), I, 385–386.

[58] Papers of Washington, CCCXXXIV, 77–79.

try. . . . To the guidance of the Ministers of the gospel, this important object is, perhaps, more properly committed—It will be your care to instruct the ignorant and to reclaim the devious—and, in the progress of morality and science, to which our government will give every furtherance, we may confidently expect the advancement of true religion, and the completion of our happiness."[59] Although this response was tactfully phrased, there is every reason to believe that the policy of "friendly separation" which he enunciated here represented both his own considered opinions and those of most of his associates in the Constitutional Convention.

Not all Americans agreed with the Eastward Presbytery in regarding religious tests as instruments of persecution. Many of the states continued, as in the colonial period, to restrict office-holding to Protestants in the constitutions they adopted during the Revolutionary period. Moreover, there was some grumbling about the omission of religious tests in the federal Constitution on the ground that the national government might fall under the control of Roman Catholics, Jews, and infidels.[60] One writer even warned that there was "a very serious danger, that the pope of Rome might be elected President." Probably few people took such talk seriously. Most Americans undoubtedly shared James Iredell's impatience with such absurd warnings. "A native American," he declared with some irritation in the North Carolina ratifying convention, "must have very singular good fortune who, after residing fourteen years in his own country, should come to Europe, enter Romish orders, obtain the promotion of cardinal, afterward that of Pope, and at length be so much in the confidence of his country as to be elected President. It would be still more extraordinary, if he should give up his popedom for our presidency."[61]

Nevertheless, a few days after Washington's inauguration, an article appeared on the front page of the *Gazette of the United States* insisting that the foundations of the American Republic had been laid by the Protestant religion and that Protestants therefore

[59] *Ibid.*, p. 80.

[60] Oscar Straus, *Religious Liberty in the United States* (New York, 1896), p. 6.

[61] Elliot, *Debates in the State Conventions*, IV, 195–196.

deserved special consideration under the federal government.[62] In a long letter to the *Gazette* the following month, Father John Carroll vigorously challenged this point of view. "Every friend to the rights of conscience," he declared, "must have felt pain" at this evidence of "religious intolerance." "Perhaps," he continued, the writer "is one of those who think it consistent with justice to exclude certain citizens from the honors and emoluments of society merely on account of their religious opinions, provided they be not restrained by racks and forfeitures from the exercise of that worship which their consciences approve. If such be his views, in vain then have Americans associated into one great national Union, under the firm persuasion that they were to retain, when associated, every natural right not expressly surrendered." Pointing out that the "blood of Catholics flowed as freely" as that of "any of their fellow citizens" during the Revolution and that American Catholics had "concurred with perhaps greater unanimity than any other body of men" in the work of the Constitutional Convention, Father Carroll concluded: "The establishment of the American empire was not the work of this or that religion, but arose from the exertion of all her citizens to redress their wrongs, to assert their rights, and lay its foundations on the soundest principles of justice and equal liberty."[63]

It is not surprising, then, that American Catholics looked upon the friendly sentiments that Washington expressed to them a few months later, in response to their congratulatory address of March 15, 1790, as of major importance in the development of religious toleration in the new nation. To the Catholics of 1790 the "encomium of the first President meant much in the way of patience and encouragement."[64]

Like the Catholics, American citizens of Jewish faith heartily

[62] *Gazette of the United States* (New York), May 6–9, 1789.

[63] *Ibid.,* June 10, 1789.

[64] Guilday, *John Carroll,* I, 367. Washington stated that "those who conduct themselves as worthy members of the community, are equally entitled to the protection of civil government," and hoped Americans would not forget "the patriotic part which you took in . . . their revolution, and the establishment of their government; or the important assistance which they received from a nation in which the Roman Catholic religion is professed." Papers of Washington, CCCXXXIV, 100.

endorsed the work of the Constitutional Convention and rejoiced that religious tests were forbidden under the Constitution. There were probably less than three thousand American Jews (with congregations in New York, Newport, Philadelphia, Savannah, Charleston, and Richmond) when Washington became President. Early in 1790 Shearith Israel in New York, the oldest congregation, began making plans for a joint address to Washington by all six congregations, pledging support to the new federal government and expressing gratitude for "the Enfranchisement which is secured to us *Jews* by the Federal Constitution."[65] But slow communication and lack of experience in united action produced so many delays that the Savannah Jews finally decided to go ahead on their own. On May 6, 1790, Levi Sheftall, president of the congregation, sent a letter to Washington; to this, Washington responded cordially.[66] Similarly, Yeshuat Israel in Newport, learning that the President was planning a trip to Rhode Island in August and impatient of any further delay, composed for the occasion what David de Sola Pool calls a "historic address."[67] The Newport congregation began by formally welcoming Washington to that city and then went on to say: "Deprived as we have been hitherto of the invaluable rights of free citizens, we now . . . behold a Government which to bigotry gives no sanction, to persecution no assistance—but generously affording to All liberty of conscience, and immunities of citizenship—deeming everyone, of whatever nation, tongue, or language equal parts of the great governmental machine. . . . For all the blessings of civil and religious liberty which we enjoy under an equal and benign administration we desire to send up our thanks to the Antient of days. . . ."[68]

In his reply, which he read in person, Washington emphasized the important point that religious freedom is something more than mere toleration—it is a right:

[65] "Items Relating to Correspondence of Jews with George Washington," *American Jewish Historical Society, Publications,* XXVII (Philadelphia, 1920), 217–222.
[66] Papers of Washington, CCCXXXIV, 129–132.
[67] David de Sola Pool, *An Old Faith in a New World* (New York, 1955), p. 323.
[68] Papers of Washington, CCCXXXV, 17–18.

The Citizens of the United States of America [he said] have a right to applaud themselves for having given to Mankind examples of an enlarged and liberal policy: a policy worthy of imitation. All possess alike liberty of conscience and immunities of citizenship. It is now no more that toleration is spoken of, as if it was by the indulgence of one class of people, that another enjoyed the exercise of their inherent natural rights. For happily the Government of the United States, which gives to bigotry no sanction, to persecution no assistance, requires only that they who live under its protection, should demean themselves as good citizens, in giving it on all occasions their effectual support. . . .[69]

In December, 1790, Manuel Josephson, president of the Philadelphia congregation, finally presented an address to Washington on behalf of the remaining four congregations. Like the others, the joint address of the Philadelphia, New York, Charleston, and Richmond congregations praised Washington's "character and Person," lauded the achievements of the "late glorious revolution," and rejoiced that with Washington as chief of state the "reign of freedom" had been made "perfectly secure" for citizens of all faiths.[70] Again the President expressed kindest regards for his Jewish fellow citizens and applauded the fact that the "liberal sentiments towards each other which marks every political and religious denomination of men in this country stands unrivalled in the history of nations."[71]

Washington's replies to the three Jewish addresses have been highly prized by later generations of American Jews. Jewish historians commonly regard them as "of great historic interest as well as of importance."[72] Washington's Newport statement, in particular, with its assertion of the primacy of "inherent natural rights" over toleration and its inclusion of the phrase, "to bigotry no sanction," has, as Lee M. Friedman points out, become "famous

[69] Papers of Washington, CCCXXXV, 19–20.
[70] *Ibid.*, pp. 30–31.
[71] *Ibid.*, pp. 32–33.
[72] Morris U. Schappes, ed., *A Documentary History of the Jews of the United States, 1654–1875* (New York, 1950), p. 77. "These three letters of Washington," according to Lee M. Friedman, "deserve to rank with the Constitutional interpretations of Chief Justice Marshall and of Alexander Hamilton's *Federalist*. . . ." *Jewish Pioneers and Patriots* (Philadelphia, 1942), p. 21.

in American Jewish history."[73] It has been enshrined on the
pedestal of the monument erected to the memory of Haym Salo-
mon in Chicago in December, 1941, and on the tablet placed on
the southern wall of the Newport synagogue when it became a
national historic site in the summer of 1947.[74]

Two years after his exchanges with the American Jewish congregations, Washington had an interesting encounter in Baltimore
with a group of Swedenborgians. In January, 1793, the tiny New
Church Society presented him with a copy of Emmanuel Sweden-
borg's *The True Christian Religion,* together with an "energetic"
address[75] rejoicing that "Priestcraft and Kingcraft, those banes of
human felicity, are hiding their diminished heads" and that "equality in State, as well as in Church, proportionably to merit, are
considered the true criterion of the majesty of the people."[76] In
what Swedenborgian writers regard as a "rational" and "manful"
reply,[77] Washington paid tribute to freedom of religion and then
added significantly: "In this enlightened age and in this Land of
equal Liberty it is our boast that a man's religious tenets will not
forfeit the protection of the Laws, nor deprive him of the right of
attaining and holding the highest offices that are known in the
United States."[78] This was Washington's final public insistence
upon "real *Equality"* rather than "mere *Toleration"* for citizens of
every faith in the young Republic.

In September, 1796, the President issued his Farewell Address
to the nation. The "wisdom of Providence," he declared, in a
passage reminiscent of the notes he had jotted down at the be-

[73] Friedman, *Pilgrims in a New Land* (Philadelphia, 1948), p. 134.
Jewish writers have described the statement as "immortal," "a classic definition of American democracy," "a classic phrase of American humanism,"
and as one of the "most outstanding expressions on religious liberty and
equality in America." De Sola Pool, *An Old Faith,* pp. 284, 494; Harry
Simonhoff, *Jewish Notables in America, 1776–1865* (New York, 1956), p.
73; Morris A. Gutstein, *To Bigotry No Sanction: A Jewish Shrine in
America, 1658–1958* (New York, 1958), p. 88.

[74] Rufus Learsi, *The Jews in America* (Cleveland, 1954), pp. 45–46;
Gutstein, *Bigotry No Sanction,* p. 151.

[75] Robert Hindmarsh, *Rise and Progress of the New Jerusalem Church*
(London, 1861), p. 154.

[76] Papers of Washington, CCCXXXV, 108–110.

[77] Hindmarsh, *New Jerusalem Church,* p. 154.

[78] Papers of Washington, CCCXXXV, 110.

ginning of his eight years in office, "has ordained that men, on the same subjects, shall not always think alike." Nevertheless, "charity and benevolence when they happen to differ," he continued, "may so far shed their benign influence as to banish those invectives which proceed from illiberal prejudices and jealousies."[79] A few months later, responding to an address delivered by twenty-four clergymen in Philadelphia on the occasion of his retirement from office, he expressed his "unspeakable pleasure" at viewing the "harmony and Brotherly Love which characterizes the clergy of different denominations—as well in this, as in other parts of the United States; exhibiting to the world a new and interesting spectacle, at once the pride of our Country and the surest basis of universal Harmony."[80]

The Philadelphia clergymen doubtless realized that Washington himself had played a leading role in producing this "new and interesting spectacle." He had labored to banish "illiberal prejudices and jealousies" in religious matters from the nation and had thrown his weight and the weight of his office against the "power of bigotry and superstition" in the young Republic. At the same time, minority groups everywhere were quick to use his name, freely given, in support of their own sometimes precarious positions. By the example he set in word and deed during the Revolution and while he was President, George Washington unquestionably deserves major credit, along with Jefferson and Madison, for establishing religious liberty and freedom of conscience firmly in the American tradition.

[79] *Writings of Washington* (Fitzpatrick ed.), XXXV, 55–56.
[80] Papers of Washington, CCCXXXVI, 282.

PAUL F. BOLLER, JR.

✪

Washington, the Quakers, and Slavery

George Washington was born a slaveholder and he grew to maturity in a society that took slavery as much for granted as it did the
rising of the sun in the east. Until he assumed command of the
Continental Army at Cambridge in July, 1775, there is no reason
for supposing that he had ever questioned the necessity and
righteousness of the institution of slavery. The American Revolution, however, gradually wrought a change in his views.[1] He came
to accept the enlistment of free Negroes in New England, discussed with interest Lieutenant-Colonel John Laurens' proposal
for recruiting soldiers among Negro slaves in South Carolina and
Georgia,[2] invited the Negro poetess Phillis Wheatley to visit him
at his headquarters,[3] and commented sympathetically on Lafayette's plan to "unite in purchasing a small estate, where we may try

[1] For detailed studies of the development of Washington's attitude toward
the American Negro, see Walter H. Mazyck, *George Washington and the
Negro* (Washington, 1932) and Matthew T. Mellon, *Early American Views
on Negro Slavery* (Boston, 1934), pp. 38–85.

[2] Washington to Lieutenant-Colonel John Laurens, Headquarters, July 10,
1782, John C. Fitzpatrick, ed., *The Writings of George Washington* (Washington, D.C., 1931–1944), XXIV, 421.

[3] Washington to Phillis Wheatley, Cambridge, February 28, 1776, *Writings of Washington*, IV, 360–361. See also Edward D. Seeber, "Phillis
Wheatley," *The Journal of Negro History*, XXIV (July 1939), 259–262.

Reprinted from Paul F. Boller, Jr., "Washington, the Quakers, and
Slavery," *The Journal of Negro History*, XLVI (1961), pp. 83–88, by permission of the Association for the Study of Negro Life and History, Inc.

the experiment to free the Negroes, and use them only as tenants."[4]
After the war, he expressed more than once his conviction that
slavery "by degrees assuredly ought" to be abolished "by legislative authority."[5]

But Washington held more than two hundred slaves until his
death (his will provided for emancipating his slaves after the death
of his wife), and although on several occasions he voiced his
"great repugnance to encreasing my slaves by purchase," he continued to assert firmly the right of slaveholders to their property in
slaves, pending the adoption of some plan of gradual emancipation
by law.[6] He was, moreover, anxious that the union of the states
effected by the Constitution of 1787 not be jeopardized by a too
vigorous agitation of the slavery issue. His conservative views on
the slavery question inevitably brought him into conflict with the
Quakers.[7]

On April 12, 1786, Washington wrote Robert Morris from
Mount Vernon to complain of the activities of a Quaker abolitionist society in Philadelphia. A Mr. Dalby of Alexandria, Virginia, according to Washington, "is called to Philadelphia to attend
what he conceives to be a vexatious lawsuit respecting a slave of
his, which a Society of Quakers in the city (formed for such
purposes) have attempted to liberate. . . ." From what Dalby had
told him, Washington continued,

it should seem that this Society is not only acting repugnant to justice
so far as its conduct concerns strangers, but, in my opinion extremely
impolitickly with respect to the State, the City in particular; and
without being able, (but by acts of tyranny and oppression) to accomplish their own ends. He says the conduct of this society is not
sanctioned by Law: had the case been otherwise, whatever my opinion
of the Law might have been, my respect for the policy of the State
would on this occasion have appeared in my silence; because against

---

[4] Washington to Marquis de Lafayette, Head Qrs., Newburgh, April 5,
1783, *Writings of Washington*, XXVI, 300 and note.

[5] *Writings of Washington*, XXVIII, 408 and 424.

[6] *Ibid.*, XXIX, 56.

[7] For a comprehensive study of Washington's relations with the Society of
Friends, see Paul F. Boller, Jr., "George Washington and the Quakers," *The
Bulletin of Friends Historical Association*, XLIX (Autumn 1960), 67–83.

the penalties of promulgated Laws one may guard; but there is no avoiding the snares of individuals, or of private societies. And if the practice of this Society of which Mr. Dalby speaks, is not discountenanced, none of those whose *misfortune* it is to have slaves as attendants, will visit the city if they can possibly avoid it; because by so doing they hazard their property; or they must be at the expence (and this will not always succeed) of providing servants of another description for the trip.

Washington hastened to assure Morris that it was not his "wish to hold the unhappy people, who are the subject of this letter, in slavery." "I can only say," he added,

that there is not a man living who wishes more sincerely than I do, to see a plan adopted for the abolition of it; but there is only one proper and effectual mode by which it can be accomplished, and that is by Legislative authority; and this, as far as my suffrage will go, shall never be wanting. But when slaves who are happy and contented with their present masters, are tampered with and seduced to leave them; when masters are taken unaware by these practices; when a conduct of this sort begets discontent on one side and resentment on the other, and when it happens to fall on a man, whose purse will not measure with that of the Society, and he looses [*sic*] his property for want of means to defend it; it is oppression in the latter case and not humanity in any; because it introduces more evils than it can cure.

Nothing that Washington ever wrote is more revealing of the confusion which the conflict between his opposition to slavery in principle and his accommodation to the system for its economic advantages in practice had produced in his mind. It was a *"misfortune"* to own slaves; they are an "unhappy people." Yet some slaves—Mr. Dalby's, at any rate—are "happy and contented." Washington is anxious for a plan of abolition to be adopted by "Legislative authority"; yet if Pennsylvania had such a law, he is not sure what his "opinion of the Law might have been." Moreover, one may guard against "the penalties of promulgated Laws." And it did not occur to Washington that if Mr. Dalby's "purse will not measure with that of the Society," neither would the "purse" of the Negro in question "measure with" that of Mr. Dalby. Washington had come a long way since 1775 and it is perhaps unreasonable to have expected more of him. At the end of his letter he seems to have realized that he had overreacted to the situation, for he acknowledged to Morris that he "may have been too precipitate" in the matter.[8]

The abolition society whose activities disturbed Washington was organized by Philadelphia Quakers in 1775, became inactive during the Revolution, and was revived by them in 1784. In 1787, it was reorganized on a broader basis as the Pennsylvania Abolition Society, with Benjamin Franklin as honorary president. In February, 1790, the Society sent a petition to Congress (similar to one already submitted by Philadelphia and New York Quakers) urging that immediate steps be taken to end the slave trade. After a stormy debate, during which opponents of the petition revived stories of Quaker treachery (because of their pacifism) during the Revolution, the House of Representatives voted to refer the petition to a committee.[9] While the committee report was pending, Washington received a letter from his Virginia friend, David Stuart, warning him that the Quaker petition was upsetting sectional harmony. "A spirit of jealousy," declared Stuart,

which may become dangerous to the Union, toward the Eastern States, seems to be growing fast among us. It is represented, that the Northern phalanx is so firmly united, as to bear down all opposition, while Virginia is unsupported, even by those whose interests are similar to hers. It is the language of all, I have seen on their return from New York. Coll: Lee [Richard Henry Lee] tells me, that many who were warm supporters of the government, are changing their sentiments, from a conviction of the impracticability of Union with States, whose interests are so dissimilar to those of Virginia. I fear the Coll: is one of their number. The late applications to Congress respecting the slaves, will certainly tend to promote this spirit. It gives particular umbrage, that the Quakers should be so busy in this business. That they will raise up a storm against themselves, appears to me very certain.[10]

[8] *Writings of Washington,* XXVIII, 407–408.
[9] Thomas E. Drake, *Quakers and Slavery in America* (New Haven, Connecticut, 1950), pp. 90–106.
[10] David Stuart to Washington, March 15, 1790, *Writings of Washington,* XXXI, 28 n.

Before Washington had got round to answering Stuart's letter, Warner Mifflin, prominent Philadelphia Quaker, called on behalf of the Abolition Society to urge the President's support of the measure before Congress. On March 16, Washington noted in his diary:

> I was visited (having given permisn.) by a Mr. Warner Mifflin, one of the People called Quakers; active in pursuit of the Measures laid before Congress for emancipating the Slaves; after much general conversation, and an endeavor to remove the prejudices which he said had been entertained of the motives by which the attending deputation from their society were actuated, he used arguments to show the immorality—injustice—and impolicy of keeping these people in a state of Slavery; with declarations, however, that he did not wish for more than a gradual abolition, or to see any infraction of the Constitution to effect it. To these I replied, that as it was a matter which might come before me for official decision I was not inclined to express any sentimts [sic] on merits of the question before this should happen.[11]

Although Washington did not think it proper for him to comment on the Quaker petition while it was still under consideration in Congress, he seems to have listened to Mifflin's views with sympathy and respect.[12] In his reply to David Stuart's letter some days later, however, he expressed somewhat different sentiments. By this time, Congress had adopted an amended version of the committee's report stating that Congress could not interfere with the slave trade until 1808, as provided in the Constitution, and Washington was obviously relieved that the matter had been laid to rest.[13] "The memorial of the Quakers (and a very mal-apropos one it was) has at length been put to sleep," he told Stuart, "and will scarcely awake before the year 1808."[14] When Stuart wrote

[11] John C. Fitzpatrick, ed., *The Diaries of George Washington, 1748–1799* (Boston, 1925), IV, 103–104.

[12] It was during this interview that Washington, after hearing an exposition of Quaker views on war, declared: "Mr. Mifflin, I honor your sentiments; there is more in that than mankind have generally considered." *The Friend of Peace* (Cambridge, Massachusetts), (January 1820), II, 8.

[13] Drake, *Quakers and Slavery*, p. 106.

[14] Washington to Stuart, New York, March 28, 1790, *Writings of Washington*, XXXI, 30.

again to elaborate on how the Quaker petition had "soured the public mind," especially in Virginia,[15] Washington said simply:

The introduction of the Memorial respecting Slavery, was to be sure, not only an illjudged piece of business, but occasioned a great waste of time. The final decision thereon, however, was as favorable as the proprietors of that species of property could have expected considering the great dereliction of Slavery in a large part of this Union.[16]

The Quaker memorial may have been a waste of time so far as immediate practical results were concerned. Nevertheless, it undoubtedly played some part in impressing Washington with the "great dereliction of Slavery," as he put it, in many parts of the United States. The fact is that Washington was finding his position as slaveholder in the new nation increasingly embarrassing. In 1791, fearing that slaves with Mrs. Washington might avail themselves of a Pennsylvania law to prevent their removal from the state, he sent secret instructions to his private secretary, Tobias Lear, from Richmond directing him to send the slaves back to Mount Vernon, if it seemed likely that any of them would "attempt their freedom," but to do so "under pretext that may deceive both them and the Public."[17] A similar feeling of embarrassment about his role as slave-master is seen in his directions, a few years later, in advertising for a runaway slave, that his name not appear in the advertisement, north of Virginia.[18] In 1794, he told Tobias Lear that he wanted to dispose of some of his western land and that his "chief motive" was to liberate the slaves there.[19] And two years before his death he expressed the hearty wish to his nephew, Lawrence Lewis, that the Virginia legislature would adopt some plan of gradual abolition.[20] It was doubtless with a great sense of relief that Washington drafted a provision for the gradual emanci-

---

[15] Stuart to Washington, June 2, 1790, *Writings of Washington,* XXXI, 49–50 n.

[16] Washington to Stuart, New York, June 15, 1790, *Writings of Washington,* XXXI, 50–52.

[17] Washington to Tobias Lear, Richmond, April 12, 1791, *Writings of Washington,* XXXVII, 573–574.

[18] *Writings of Washington,* XXXIV, 154 and 171.

[19] *Ibid.,* XXXIII, 358.

[20] *Ibid.,* XXXVI, 2.

pation of his slaves when he was drawing up his will in 1798. When they learned the contents of Washington's will after his death the following year Quakers everywhere were overjoyed. According to Robert M. Hazelton, the Quakers "felt they had won a most important point in the campaign for freedom."[21]

[21] Robert M. Hazelton, *Let Freedom Ring! A Biography of Moses Brown* (New York, 1957), pp. 120–121.

ESMOND WRIGHT

✪

President of the United States (1789-1797)

Washington's journey from Mount Vernon to New York was a
triumphal progress. At Philadelphia he was greeted by flower-
decked maidens and an arch of victory. At Trenton, "Virgins fair
and Matrons grave" welcomed him in song and strewed flowers in
his path. As his barge sailed up the Hudson, it was greeted by
sloops on which choirs sang odes composed for the occasion, one
of them tactlessly set to the tune of "God Save the King." Such
was the noise of thirteen-gun salutes from ship and shore batteries
that the church bells of New York could not be heard. Washington
took up residence, in a house previously used by the President of
Congress, in Cherry Street—now lost among the abutments of
Brooklyn Bridge.

Washington was inaugurated on 30th April, 1789, in a ceremony in Federal Hall, at the corner of Wall Street. He wore a suit
of brown broadcloth, specially spun in Connecticut, with the
buttons carrying the device of a wing-spread eagle; his stockings
were of white silk, his shoe-buckles of silver; at his side hung a
dress-sword; his hair was powdered and worn in a queue. The oath
was administered on the balcony of the hall, by Chancellor Livingston of New York, before a vast crowd, and in an atmosphere
not only of carnival but of dedication. The circumstances of the
election, wrote the New York correspondent of the *Federal*

Reprinted from Esmond Wright, *Washington and the American Revolution* (The English Universities Press, 1957), pp. 146–173, by permission of
the publisher.

Gazette of Philadelphia, "the impression of his past services, the
concourse of spectators, the devout fervency with which he repeated the oath, and the reverential manner in which he bowed
down and kissed the sacred volume—all these conspired to render
it one of the most august and interesting spectacles ever exhibited
on this globe. It seemed, from the number of witnesses, to be a
solemn appeal to Heaven and earth at once. Upon the subject of
this great and Good man, I may perhaps be an enthusiast; but I
confess that I was under an awful and religious persuasion that the
gracious Ruler of the Universe was looking down at that moment
with peculiar complacency. . . ."

The Inaugural Address was delivered in a low voice; observers
noted the awkward gestures now and then, and the restless hands.
The President expressed again his strong sense of inadequacy, his
"inferior endowments"; he hoped that no local attachments,
"separate views nor party animosities" would misdirect the purposes of Congress; he asked that the expenses of his office be met,
but he wanted no salary. (In the end Congress decided to pay him
a salary of twenty-five thousand dollars per year and to leave him
to spend it as he pleased.) It was not an orator's effort, and there
were critics of the fumbling delivery, but the awkwardness was
further evidence of the man's sincerity and won sympathy. Fisher
Ames, a judge of public speeches, sat, he said, "entranced"—
Washington's "aspect grave, almost to sadness; his modesty, actually shaking" seeming "an allegory in which virtue was personified." The French Minister went further: the President had "the
soul, look and figure of a hero united in him."

He did not find it difficult to become the part. His natural
dignity of manner was now enhanced by age—"Time has made
havoc upon his face," said Ames. And Washington sensed the
value to an unformed nation of some measure of pomp and
circumstance. It does not seem to be true that he wanted to be
called "His Mightiness, the President of the United States and
Protector of their Liberties"; a letter to David Stuart echoes what
his experience with the Cincinnati had proved—that titles were apt
to arouse resentment. The Senate favored "His Highness," and
"His Elective Majesty" and "His Excellency" were proposed, but

the House decided to use merely the simple title "The President of the United States."

Yet there was considerable formality. There were fourteen white servants and seven slaves in the house on Cherry Street, and then in the Macomb House on Broadway, to which he moved in 1790. At his wife's Friday evening levees Washington's deportment was "invariably grave"; there were no handshakes, but formal bows; remarks were brief, and the President withdrew at nine P.M. He used a canary-colored chariot imported from England, decorated with gilded nymphs and cupids and his own coat-of-arms. It was drawn on formal occasions by six cream horses. This was again less a case of the man adapting himself to the office as of the office reflecting the character and dignity of the man and the tastes of a successful planter. Martha, who joined him in May and was "Lady Washington" to all the world, did not take to it so easily—"I lead a very dull life here . . . I never goe to any public place. . . . I am more like a state prisoner than anything else, there is certain bounds set for me which I must not depart from—and as I cannot doe as I like I am obstinate and stay at home a great deal."

Washington spent eighteen months in New York, organizing a government. He inherited from the Confederation only a handful of unpaid clerks and a large number of debts. North Carolina and Rhode Island were not yet in the Union; Vermont was still intriguing with Canada; Britain held on to the western posts and was dangerously friendly with the Indians—and in 1790, against the possibility of war with Spain, she sought permission in advance from the United States to move troops through the western territory. The American Army had 840 officers and men; there was no navy at all. Hamilton thought the Constitution "frail and worthless"; his opinion seemed nearer reality than Washington's talk of a "hopeful experiment."

Washington was on, he knew, "untrodden ground"; everything he did would set a precedent. What distinguished his work in creating the administrative system was his sense of order, his discretion and his freedom from advocacy. What he wrote to his favorite nephew, Bushrod Washington, in refusing his application for appointment as United States District Attorney for Virginia, held of his attitude generally: "My political conduct in nominations, even if I was uninfluenced by principle, must be exceedingly circumspect and proof against just criticism, for the eyes of Argus are upon me." He regarded the executive branch as distinct from but equal to the Legislature; the choice and form of legislation was a matter for Congress, but the President had the right to remove and, subject to Congressional endorsement, to appoint officials. This was not an easy task; there were some three thousand applications for federal employment even before a single job was created. The effect was that control of administrative and diplomatic officials fell to the Executive, not Congress.

One of the first products of the new Establishment was a judiciary, "the firmest pillar of good government." The Constitution had provided only for a Supreme Court; the Judiciary Act of 1789 set up the system of which the basic features are still in operation—district courts, circuit courts of appeal and a Supreme Court of one Chief Justice and of five (now eight) Associates. To ensure uniform legal interpretations throughout the nation, the Supreme Court was to rule on the constitutionality of state court decisions. John Jay was appointed Chief Justice, and the Court sat for the first time in February, 1790, resplendent in judicial robes but without the white wigs of their English counterparts.

Treaty making was a more difficult matter. Washington took quite literally the constitutional provision that treaties be made with "the advice and consent" of the Senate. He thought that on some occasions it should be possible for the President to appear before the Senate, to explain the purpose of a treaty and to obtain forthwith a "yes" or "no" on the points he raised. In order to settle the long-standing boundary dispute between the Creek Indians and the State of Georgia, Washington proposed negotiations with the Creeks, to attempt to wean them from the temptations of an alliance with the Spanish in Louisiana. In August, 1789, with this in mind, he appeared before the Senate in person with a series of proposals. The most vigorous dissenter from them among the Senators, William Maclay, asked that the treaty be deferred to a committee. According to Maclay, whose portraits were often etched with acid, Washington stalked out with a "discontented air," declaring that deferment "defeats every purpose of my coming here." He got the Senate's approval two days later, but the incident had important consequences: it became the rule for treaties to be presented to the Senate for approval after, and not before, they were negotiated; in the Senate the committee system began to develop; and the Senate made it clear that in its own estimation it was not a Council of State but a legislative body, in no way subordinate to the President.

Congress established three executive departments—State, Treasury and War. It was, however, Washington's wish to obtain advice from his aides before making decisions that gradually made of these officials an American cabinet. They were responsible to the President only, not to Congress, and they became the originators of the policy of the administration; they were all consulted on all matters, not merely on their specialisms. The cabinet, unmentioned in the Constitution, thus became a privy council, which the Founding Fathers had clearly meant the Senate to be.

To the State Department, Washington appointed Thomas Jefferson, a forty-six-year-old fellow-Virginian whose path so far had rarely crossed his own and who had just completed five years as the United States Minister to France. Hamilton, thirty-two years old and his war-time secretary, with his ambition greater than ever as the result of his marriage to the daughter of General Schuyler, became Secretary of the Treasury. Henry Knox, Washington's corpulent old Chief of Artillery, continued as Secretary of War, an office he had held under the Confederation. Edmund Randolph, former Governor of Virginia and for a time critic of the Constitution, became Attorney General.

While Hamilton was becoming familiar with his task—Jefferson did not arrive in New York until March, 1790—Washington undertook in October and November, 1789, a tour of New England, going as far north as Portsmouth, and returning, as John Trumbull remarked, "all fragrant with the odor of incense." His *Diaries* contain some revealing glimpses of his Northern tour. He compelled gouty Governor Hancock of Massachusetts, his old rival for the post of commander-in-chief in 1775, to pay his respects to the President, and not vice versa. Pleased by the kindness shown him in a humble home near Uxbridge, Massachusetts, he sent presents to the daughter of the house—"As I do not give these things with a view to have it talked of, or even to its being known, the less there is said about the matter the better you will please me." He had some dull days in Connecticut:

"It being contrary to law and disagreeable to the People of this State to travel on the Sabbath day—and my horses, after passing through such intolerable roads, wanting rest, I stayed at Perkins' tavern (which, by the bye, is not a good one) all day—and a meeting-house being within a few rods of the door, I attended morning and evening service, and heard very lame discourses from a Mr. Pond."

On his return, he issued a proclamation that 26 November, 1789, should be a Day of Thanksgiving. These activities strengthened the sense of national unity. The only criticism they evoked was an occasional mild protest in New England at the degree of ceremony that appeared to hedge a President.

It was another matter with the nationally inspired financial program of his first lieutenant. That program gave energy and direction to the government, and made its author the driving spirit, in some ways the prime minister, of the administration. But it heralded controversy. The three great state papers of Alexander Hamilton were his reports on *Publick Credit* (January, 1790), on *A National Bank* (December, 1790) and on *Manufactures* (December, 1791). The first of these did not cause but further widened differences already apparent between Federalists and Antifederalists, between what Maclay called the party, on the one hand, of the speculators and the courtiers ("the party of interest"), and, on the other, "the party of principle." But Hamilton, if a courtier, had his own principles in abundance, even if the most avowed of them was the advancement of their author.

Hamilton was convinced that the efficiency of the newly created federal government depended, first, on energy in the executive branch—on what he called "Executive impulse," and second, in no way inferior, on the establishment of sound public credit. He urged that all outstanding foreign and domestic debts incurred by the states or by Congress be assumed and paid by the federal government. This would serve a political as well as an economic purpose; it would impress foreign governments and would bind creditors to the national cause; "a public debt," he argued, "is a public blessing." Of illegitimate birth in the West Indies, he became the great protagonist of birth and connection. Of poor origins, he believed that government was the preserve of "the rich and the well-born," that man's prevailing passions "are ambition and interest." Nor did he hide his contempt for democracy— "your people, Sir, is a great beast." He proposed that a Bank of the United States should be established, and that a system of tariff duties and excises should be used to provide revenue. His proposals have been the core of that Federalist economic program that, later, Whigs and, later still, Republicans have made their own.

Despite the appeal of these measures to commercial and financial interests, they were far from popular. Suspicious Congressmen like Madison and crotchety Senators like Maclay objected to paying off the domestic debt of the Confederation at face value to bond-holders who were often merely speculators. Madison argued that federal assumption of state debts did injustice to those states, mainly Southern, that had already done their duty by their creditors but that would now be called upon to contribute to those states, mainly Northern, that had not. In any event, assumption would strengthen the federal government and would weaken the states. Patrick Henry argued with customary vehemence that the Constitution gave no authority to the federal government to assume the obligations of the states. On the bank and excise questions South and North were in opposing camps, the South against, the North for them.

The debate on these issues was not confined to Congress. If Fenno's *Gazette of the United States* became the Hamiltonian vehicle, critics appeared in the pages of the *New-York Journal* and of the *Pennsylvania Gazette:*

> Each day a fresh report he broaches,
> That Spies and Jews may ride in coaches,
> Soldiers and farmers, don't despair,
> Untaxed as yet are Earth and Air.

In the debate on the assumption of state debts, Congress was evenly divided, and Washington was determined to remain above the battle. At its height, in May, 1790, he was seriously ill with pneumonia and feared likely to die. This was his second illness within a year, and his recovery was slow. The thought of a con-valescence at Mount Vernon when Congress recessed became more attractive than ever.

By the time Congress rose, it had found an answer to its dead-lock on the assumption of the state debts. Jefferson, recently arrived from Paris, brought pressure on his Southern friends to support assumption on condition that the federal government should ultimately be sited on the Potomac. Robert Morris was also a party to the deal, and it was agreed that Philadelphia should become the temporary seat of government—no doubt he had hopes of its becoming permanent.

After a decade in Philadelphia (1790–1800) the "Federal City" was to be built near Georgetown on the Potomac. This compromise, though vaunted by later historians, was a matter of much bitterness at the time. Jefferson later claimed, not entirely convincingly, that he did not appreciate all that was involved in the deal, that he had not wanted to provide "pabulum for stock-jobbers." New Yorkers were indignant, and the *New-York Journal* charged that "Miss Assumption" had given birth to two illegiti-mate children "Philadelphia" and "Potowmacus," as a result of the seductive promises of "Mr. Residence." More sensitive New Englanders were glad to move away from Manhattan's dram-shops. Pennsylvanians were angry at the idea of an artificial capital being built in a muddy and mosquito-ridden swamp in preference to the facilities of Philadelphia (the only city at that time with paved streets and a rudimentary water-supply). Their testy junior Senator saw a conspiracy on the part of the President, "who pushes the Potomac." "The President has become in the hands of Hamilton, the dish-clout of every dirty speculation, as his name goes to wipe away blame and silence all murmuring."

The charges would soon grow more savage than this, but there is no evidence that Washington sought to influence Congress in any way on the choice of site. On the contrary; on visiting Rhode Island in August, in order to welcome it into the Union, he was seeing his task more than ever as a national one. "We must drive far away the daemon of party spirit and local reproach." No doubt he was privately happy at the thought of a Federal City within range, even perhaps within sight, of his own broad acres, though he was not to live to see it. In September, 1790, the capital was transferred to Philadelphia, and for two months the President was able to revisit Mount Vernon.

The first two years of the administration were years of unusual harmony. The country was prosperous. The site of the new Federal City was agreed upon, L'Enfant was drawing his grandiose plans and commissioners had been appointed to superintend the work. The anniversary of the President's birthday, 22nd February, 1791, was treated as a national festival.

The President was as concerned to see the various sections of the country as he was to establish a unifying government and the public credit. Having visited the North in 1789–1790, he spent two months in 1791 on a Southern journey—through the sandy roads of the Carolina pine barrens, thin in population and in soil, to Charleston and Savannah, returning by way of Augusta and Guilford and the scene of the Southern battles—"a Journey of 1,887 miles . . . without meeting with any interruption."

His diary of the Southern tour is unusually full and frank, and reflects not only physical but social endurance. In Charleston, which he had not seen before, he spent a week; during that time he held three receptions, attended two breakfasts, ate seven formal dinners, listened and replied to four addresses, attended two assemblies and a concert, visited the sites of the sieges and drank sixty toasts. He enjoyed particularly the "elegant dancing" of Southern ladies, "respectable" and "superbly dressed," wearing ribbons or bandeaux that carried sentimental tributes to him.

He was gratified by the evidence of his own popularity, but even more by the discovery that the country was in an "improving state." There were problems ahead—"the direful effect of slavery," careless farming and sterility of soil which would in a few years drive people west. But "tranquility reigns among the people with that disposition towards the general government which is likely to preserve it. They begin to feel the good effects of equal laws and equal protection."

Yet 1791 brought problems to try the domestic peace. France was now in the throes of revolution and faced a slave rebellion in Santo Domingo, her richest West Indian possession. Washington promised all possible help to France in the Caribbean, meanwhile expressing to Lafayette, now grown into a leading personality in Paris, the hope that a government might emerge in France that would be "respectfully energetic and founded on the broad basis of liberality and the rights of man." The temper and situation of France might, however, push Britain and Spain into alliance. It might even involve a request by France that the United States fulfill the terms of the military alliance of 1778. A war might break out among the powers of Europe that could imperil American frontiers. From these political disputes Washington hoped to stay aloof; what distance of itself did not do might be helped by "a conduct of circumspection, moderation and forbearance." And there were signs that this conduct was bringing dividends. Relations with Britain seemed more cordial with the arrival in October, 1791, of George Hammond as British Minister—the first British diplomatic agent formally accredited to America.

Whatever she might be in Philadelphia, however, in the Ohio country Britain was still a frontier ally of the Indians, and these were an immediate and not a contingent problem. The attempt to settle the persistent troubles of Georgia with Choctaw, Creek and Cherokee had led Washington, in 1790, to invite the Creek chiefs to New York. Their leader, the colorful half-breed Alexander McGillivray, signed a treaty in which the Creek tribes were guaranteed their hunting-grounds. The chiefs were dined and fêted by the Tammany Society, and Washington believed—optimistically, as it proved—that the treaty had brought peace to the southwestern border. In the Northwest the situation remained uglier, with Britain not Spain, in connivance. The Miami and Wabash tribes had raided in Ohio and Kentucky, and General Harmar's punitive column, based on Fort Washington in Ohio (the present Cincinnati), had failed to curb them. "I expected *little,*" said Washington, "from the moment I heard he was a *drunkard.*" In 1790 General St. Clair had been instructed to establish a strong military post in the Northwest, at Miami Village (the present Fort Wayne). Treaties were to be attempted with the tribes that seemed well-disposed, but St. Clair was to "seek the enemy." Jefferson agreed —the Indians must be given "a thorough drubbing."

The event was a repetition of Braddock's disaster on the Monongahela: fifteen miles from his goal, St. Clair was attacked and overwhelmed, and nearly one thousand of his force were casualties. The legend has grown that the news of the disaster reached Washington during one of Mrs. Washington's Friday levees, that he concealed his feelings until the guests had gone, and that then a storm broke in the Morris house like that that had struck St. Clair. In fact, the newspapers had carried plausible reports of the disaster for a day or two beforehand, and the dispatches from St. Clair were addressed not to the President but to the Secretary of War. The President can hardly have been unprepared for the disaster. Congress was promptly and fully informed, and a new force was raised, with Anthony Wayne at its head. Though a sense of alarm swept through the West and with it a mounting nationalism, there were no political repercussions.

By the end of 1791, however, political partisanship was being generated in domestic matters. In November, 1791, Fisher Ames wrote that "tranquility has smoothed the surface" but that "faction glows within like a coalpit." It was not merely a clash of political philosophy, of Hamilton versus Jefferson, or of the discussions for or against assumption, the excise tax and the Bank proposals. There was still a widespread fear of centralized government—"I do not believe," said Ames, "that the hatred of the Jacobites towards the House of Hanover was ever more deadly than that which is borne by many of the partisans of State power towards the government of the United States." The fiscal policy of the government and the preferred position of the Bank of the United States were believed by many to be responsible for the speculative mania of 1791. The *National Gazette* campaigned against the excise tax and against what it thought the unconstitutionality of the Hamiltonian program. "The free citizens of America will not quietly suffer the well-born few to trample them under foot." "Another revolution must and will be brought about in favour of the people."

These differences, though not limited to, were most acute inside the administration. They had emerged first in August, 1790, when the Cabinet had discussed American policy in the event of a British war with Spain and of a British attempt to conquer Louisiana and the Floridas. To avert this, Jefferson was ready for war with Britain; his colleagues would not go beyond remonstrance. The differences became clearer on the assumption question and on the constitutionality of the Bank. Washington was particularly embarrassed by the conflicting views on this last question, for Jefferson, Madison and Attorney General Randolph denied that Congress had the right to establish such a corporation. Hamilton took the view that anything could be done so long as it was not expressly forbidden by the Constitution. As with the drafting of the document, so with the interpretation, Washington favored strength and authority at the center, and this took him into the Hamiltonian camp; he signed the bill establishing the Bank in February, 1791. Yet he was fully sympathetic to Jefferson's warning—"if the pro and con hang so even as to balance his [the President's] judgment, a just respect for the wisdom of the Legislature would naturally decide the balance in favour of their opinion." He was careful to honor this advice, and indeed to follow Hamilton's own insistence that "it is always best for the chief magistrate to be as little implicated as possible in the specific approbation of a particular measure proceeding from a particular officer."

This was proving increasingly difficult in a team in which, as Oliver Wolcott put it (October, 1791)—"The principles of dissension exist, but the principles are the merest trifles." "Mr. H. and Mr. J." he found, were ready to quarrel over most matters, especially whether "Tom Paine or Edmund Burke are the greatest fools." Jefferson was a frank admirer of Paine's *Rights of Man,* which was dedicated to Washington. To Jefferson, as to Paine, the French Revolution and the American were closely linked, and he was suspicious of what he thought Hamilton's over-frank admiration of the British constitution. He gave a post as translator in the State Department to Philip Freneau, who proceeded to edit the *National Gazette,* and to make of it a journal increasingly critical of the Federalists.

Despite Wolcott's warnings, Washington tried to regard this conflict as one of principle rather than of personality—a view it was increasingly hard to maintain. He did not think in personal terms, and could not conceive of anything being more important than the establishment of the government on firm foundations. Once it was established, it was to be "a government of accommodation as well as a government of laws." The clash was alarming, because it was echoed in some of the states and in Congress, and because it suggested a geographical division on policy between North and South. Washington himself was not involved in the conflict, and only indirectly in the public charges and countercharges. Nevertheless, the prospect of retirement in March, 1793, became ever more attractive.

This mood of hesitation, though familiar, seems by 1792 to have been something more than gentlemanly affectation. Washington was growing deaf, and his memory, he said, was beginning to fail him. There is little evidence for this where Mount Vernon is concerned—in the winter of 1792–3 he wrote twenty-one letters to his manager at Mount Vernon, of which the first ran to some three thousand words, and they all showed a minute knowledge of its affairs. In the spring of 1792, however, he had had a number of discussions with Madison on the shape of a farewell address. He found him a convinced opponent of the idea of retirement: the rise of party spirit was a reason rather for staying on, than for withdrawing; another four years would save the country from the risks of a new regime or the dangers of monarchy, and would give "tone and firmness." Hamilton, Knox and Randolph endorsed this advice. Jefferson's original assumption was that the President's mind was made up—"I knew we were some day to try to walk alone, and if the essay should be made while you should be alive and looking on, we should derive confidence from that circumstance, and resource, if it failed." But in the summer of 1792 Jefferson, too, was urging Washington to consent to serve again, and used an argument that had influence—"North and South will hang together if they have you to hang on."

The summer was full of rumors: of Indian troubles, of the arrival in New Orleans of five regiments of Spanish troops, of the formation of a Jacobin club in Philadelphia, of efforts in Pennsylvania to obstruct the excise laws. These tensions brought the factional clash into the open. In May Jefferson had listed a series of charges against the Secretary of the Treasury. Washington drew these up under twenty-one headings and invited Hamilton's comments, "to obtain light and to pursue truth." The reply ran to fourteen thousand words; Hamilton admitted that speculation in government securities had had some bad effects on those engaged in it, but denied that a single member of Congress could "properly" be called a stock-jobber. For the rest, there was a complete refutation of all the charges.

To both men Washington appealed for compromise and moderation, for "liberal allowances, mutual forbearances and temporizing yieldings," instead of "wounding suspicions and irritable charges." He appealed in vain. Jefferson thought Hamilton's principles were "adverse to liberty" and that he was exerting a dangerous influence over the Legislature. Hamilton charged Jefferson with "whispers and insinuations." But both agreed that Washington was indispensable, "the only man in the United States who possessed the confidence of the whole . . . no other person . . . would be thought anything more than the head of a party."

When the time came for his Annual Message to Congress in November, 1792—the date he had suggested to Madison, months before, as appropriate for a farewell message—Washington said nothing of his intention to resign. Though later letters suggest that he had not yet finally closed the door on the possibility, failure then to announce withdrawal made his re-election certain. By that time the states were preparing to name electors. The party battle was transferred to the Vice-Presidency. When the votes were counted, 13th February, 1793, Washington was again unanimously chosen; Adams was re-elected to the Vice-Presidency with seventy-seven votes against fifty for Hamilton's rival in New York politics, George Clinton. And Virginia's entire electoral vote of twenty-one had gone to the New Yorker. This, seeming a paradox, was to be a portent. The alliance of rural South and urban North was to become the nucleus of the Jeffersonian party. The Senate, not yet established as the senior chamber, remained Federalist, but there was an Antifederalist, Republican or "Democratick" majority—the terms were interchangeable and pejorative—in the Lower House. There were other portents in 1793; despite the unanimous choice for President, Freneau's paper had begun to train its guns not only on the Cabinet but on its Head, to sneer at "the drawing Room," "those apparent trifles, birthday odes" and the Friday evening levees. There was a certain symbolism in the fact that on 18th September, 1793, Washington laid the cornerstone of the federal Capitol; in four years the foundations had been laid, but an uglier term lay ahead.

On 4th March, 1793, Washington was inaugurated President for a second time. Already the European scene was darker: Louis XVI was guillotined in January; on 1st February, France declared war on Britain and a great European coalition was formed to resist the Revolution. This situation made explicit what had hitherto been implicit in Washington's attitude. When the French Revolution broke out in 1789, the fact on which he seized was American remoteness. "We, at this great distance . . . hear of wars and rumors of wars, as if they were the events or reports of another planet." At times, particularly in his letters to Lafayette, he expressed sympathy with the Revolution, and he received from the Marquis a picture of the captured Bastille, with the main key of the fortress—"a tribute, which I owe as a son to my adopted father, as an aid-de-camp to my general, as a missionary of liberty to its patriarch." In acknowledging the gift, Washington referred to the key as a "token of victory gained by liberty over despotism."

Yet to Lafayette he could also be frank in avowing the threats to America presented by a war in Europe. He wanted, he wrote in 1790, to be "unentangled in the crooked policies of Europe," and sought only the free navigation of the Mississippi. He sensed the tumult and the paroxysms of France, the "more haste than good speed in their innovations," and wanted no part in the attendant political disputes of Europe. These views were reinforced by the events of 1790–1793, domestic as well as foreign, and by the alarms in Florida and New Orleans, in the Caribbean and in the Ohio country.

With the declaration of war by France on Britain in 1793, the United States issued a proclamation (April) declaring her intention to pursue "a conduct friendly and impartial towards the belligerent powers." It was drawn up by Randolph, and it did not contain the word "neutrality." This proclamation marks the real beginning of the break between President and Secretary of State. For Washington it was an expression of neutrality, in fact if not in word. Jefferson's view was more devious. Publicly, he argued that by holding back a declaration of neutrality, the United States might induce the European powers to bid for it, and thus secure "the broadest privileges of neutral nations." Privately, however, he thought it pusillanimous, a "milk-and-water" instrument, which disregarded American obligations both to the cause of France under the alliance of 1778 and to the larger cause of liberty. When "Pacificus" Hamilton came out in support of the proclamation, Jefferson encouraged "Helvidius" Madison to attack him—"For God's sake, my dear Sir, take up your pen, select the most striking heresies and cut him to pieces in the face of the public." However much idealism lay behind Jefferson's methods, they appear less noble and infinitely less discreet than Washington's.

Washington was convinced of the wisdom of neutrality. His purpose, he later declared to Henry, was "to keep the United States free from political connections with *every* other country, to see them independent of all and under the influence of none. In a word, I want an *American* character, that the powers of Europe may be convinced we act for *ourselves* and not for *others*."

He admitted a friendship for, even some obligation toward, Lafayette, and requested Gouverneur Morris, the American Minister in Paris, to convey informally to the French the regard of all Americans for him; but when Henry Lee informed Washington that he was considering enlistment in the French Army, and requested advice, the reply was impeccable and magisterial:

"As a public character, I can say *nothing* on the subject. . . . As a private man, I am unwilling to say much. Give advice I shall not. All I can do, then . . . is to declare that if the case which you have suggested was mine, I should ponder well before I resolved, not only for private considerations, but on public grounds."

And then, just to be sure, he advised Lee to burn the letter. If Lee failed to act on one piece of advice, he saw the point, however guarded, of the other.

The problems posed by the war in Europe were not just matters of personal alignment and personal sympathy. Some three-quarters of America's trade was with Britain, and 90 per cent of her imports came from Britain. New England favored Britain, therefore, as surely as Southern agrarians did not. But it was still hard for the friends of Britain in America to raise their voices; Britain on the seas and in the Western posts was still an arrogant power.

The first real challenge to the Federalist quest for neutrality was presented, however, by the arrival of Edmund Charles Genêt as the French Girondin Minister to the United States. France could hardly have selected a more tactless ambassador—a man, Gouverneur Morris warned Washington, with "more of genius than ability," with "at first blush the manner and look of an upstart." As luck would have it, his ship was blown out of its course, and he landed, in April, 1793, at Charleston, in "Democratick" territory. His twenty-eight-day journey, by easy stages, to Philadelphia, was a procession which evoked an enthusiasm reminiscent of the President's own, four years before. It gave him a quite false notion of his popularity and of his role. Genêt was deterred neither by the announcement of neutrality nor by a chilly reception from Washington in Philadelphia. He saw himself, apparently, as the Minister, not of a government to a government, but of a people to a people. With the support of the Jeffersonians, he proceeded to act in most undiplomatic fashion. As he lyrically reported to his changing masters in Paris—"I provision the Antilles, I excite the Canadians to free themselves from the yoke of England, I arm the Kentuckians." He organized expeditions against Florida and Louisiana—George Rogers Clark found himself "Commander-in-chief of the French Revolutionary Legion on the Mississippi River." He sent out privateers and he sponsored Jacobin clubs.

By June, even Jefferson was alarmed at this—"indefensible"; "never was so calamitous an appointment made; hot-headed, all imagination, no judgment, passionate." By August he was, thought Jefferson, "absolutely incorrigible," and the Cabinet unanimously demanded his recall. The responsibility, however, was not Genêt's alone, but Jefferson's, who had at first abetted his schemes.

By 1793 Madison and Jefferson were becoming afraid that behind the mask of neutrality lay "a secret Anglomanny." Jefferson's five years in Paris had left him with no love of the English— "those rich, proud, hectoring, swearing, squibbling, carnivorous animals who live on the other side of the Channel"—or of those in America who admired their institutions or imitated their ways. And though his own naïveté made him an easy victim, Genêt became the instrument of Jefferson's policy. Four years later, he accused Jefferson of encouraging him and of persuading him that Washington, "that excellent man," was "controlled by the English." He also charged Jefferson with denouncing him to "Roberts-pierre," and said that had he attempted to return to Paris he would certainly have been executed. He expressed his thanks to Washington for saving him from this fate. Another fate awaited him. In the phrase of Professor Bailey, "hand in hand with the daughter of Governor Clinton, he faced the altar instead of the guillotine," and died, appropriately enough, on Bastille Day, 14th July, 1834.

Washington was kind to Genêt, but resolute in his neutrality. He believed that "the defensive alliance" with France had ended with the treaty of peace with Britain in 1783. His first obligation was to the United States, and to the facts of a revolution in Europe from which, if possible, the United States must be protected. He told Congress:

> There is a rank due to the United States among nations, which will be withheld, if not absolutely lost, by the reputation of weakness. If we desire to avoid insult, we must be able to repel it; if we desire to secure peace, one of the most powerful instruments of our rising prosperity, it must be known that we are at all times ready for War.

The *affaire Genêt* added zest to the domestic party battle.

Years later, in correspondence with Jefferson and with memory blurred, Adams wrote of the "thousands" in the Philadelphia mobs who threatened to drag Washington from his house and to overturn the government. He was convinced that revolution was averted only by the coming to Philadelphia in the late summer of a still more deadly scourge—yellow fever. Out of a population of some 45,000, 4,000 died. Hamilton was stricken, but, aided by his remarkable vitality, survived. Washington, like other members of the administration, spent part of the period away from the city. He returned from Mount Vernon as the weather grew cold. The political temperature stayed high. The Marseillaise and "Ça Ira" were now the marching songs of Antifederalism. To the Jeffersonians the Federalists were "British boot-lickers," and some of their editors, like Callender and Duane, had choicer epithets. The Democratic Societies or Jacobin Clubs, the *National Gazette* and the *Philadelphia Aurora* were now the instruments of a party, of which Jefferson was clearly becoming the leader. To Fenno and Cobbett and the Federalist *Gazette of the United States,* the

Republicans were "Democraticks," "filthy Jacobins," "frog-eating, man-eating, blood-drinking cannibals."

Believing in the soundness of the new American institutions that were now repeatedly being attacked, convinced of the importance of neutrality toward and aloofness from revolutionary Europe, distrustful not only of revolutionary doctrines but of any theory that was joined to fanaticism and sophistry, Washington's idea of good government was by 1794 almost identical with Hamilton's. The identity was never complete; Hamilton was bolder and brasher than Washington, with a gift of words and a grasp of finance—and of intrigue—far surpassing the President's. Washington, though less intellectual, was infinitely superior to Hamilton in judgment. Jefferson's range was wider than either of theirs, his cast of mind more contemplative and contradictory. But Washington could have little sympathy with Jeffersonian ideas; and the man of affairs found himself much more attuned to the administrative emphasis and to the concrete program of the Hamiltonians. From 1789 to 1794 he was above party, an enemy of what he called "faction," a Federalist. By 1794 he went further and became a Hamiltonian. The partisanship spread. Madison went the other way, and Jefferson resigned the Secretaryship of State on 31st December, 1793, to be replaced by Edmund Randolph.

It was therefore with alarm that Washington viewed the so-called Whisky Rebellion of 1794. The excise tax was a heavy burden on the Western farmers, who, unable to transport their corn and rye across the Alleghenies or down the Mississippi, converted it into whisky. Every farmer in the back-country manufactured it. In 1794 open rebellion against the excise tax broke out among the farmers of western Pennsylvania, and federal Treasury officials, like state officials before them, were driven back. Under Hamilton's persuasions, Washington saw in the rebellion "the first *formidable* fruit" of the Democratic Societies, and of "their diabolical leader, Genêt." Unless it were broken, "we may bid adieu to all government in this country, except mob and club government."

There were no federal police to enforce the law, but the Constitution empowered the federal government to call out the state militia when necessary. But would the states acknowledge this authority? Washington put the matter to the test, called out the militia, and talked of leading it in person over the mountains. Hamilton accompanied the troops as a kind of political commissar. By the time the militia appeared—and 15,000 turned out at the call—the rebellion had come to an end. Having displayed the power of the federal government—and satisfied conservative opinion as much as he alarmed Jeffersonians—the President, in July, 1795, pardoned the insurgents. For him firmness again was allied to clemency. Hamilton's prestige was more seriously affected; when he played the double role of man on horseback and Grand Inquisitor, he became more than ever the butt of the Jeffersonians.

The same Hamiltonian policy led Washington to attempt a settlement of the disputes with Britain. Anthony Wayne's victory over the Indians at Fallen Timbers in 1794 opened up the Ohio country and weakened British influence over her forest allies. But Britain still held the fur-posts, still excluded American ships from her West Indian ports and still dickered over the boundary with Maine. She was countering the revived and lucrative American trade with the French West Indies by invoking the Rule of 1756 (that trade closed in time of peace could not be opened in time of war) and, under its cloak, seizing American ships. She claimed the right also to search American ships for British deserters at a time of lax naturalization laws and inadequate proof of citizenship. This interference was particularly resented in New England, the Federalist stronghold, and in the debates in the House of Representatives in 1794 New England and the Middle States seemed in process of aligning on this issue with the South. Despite the unpopularity of any suggestion of rapprochement with Britain, Washington felt that an effort should be made to settle these outstanding problems, and that it should be done by a special mission and a treaty requiring only Cabinet and Senate approval. Accordingly, in April, 1794, he dispatched John Jay as special envoy to London. Not the least important of Jay's discoveries, so he wrote to Washington, was that "No other man enjoys so completely the esteem and confidence of this nation as you do; nor, except the King, is any one so popular."

When the news of the treaty signed by Jay (November, 1794)

reached the United States in the following March, Washington's popularity at home was given its severest test. Jay knew that his work would meet with opposition, but thought that the terms were the best that could be obtained: Britain agreed to evacuate the fur posts by 1796, and to open her East Indian ports to American ships; she agreed to open her West Indian ports also, but only to vessels under seventy tons; the United States agreed not to export sugar, molasses, coffee, cotton or cocoa; joint commissions were to settle the Maine boundary dispute and claims for damages arising from seizures, but nothing was said about impressment, the trade of neutrals with France or about Indians. Washington did not pretend to like these terms, and kept the treaty for three months before submitting it to the Senate. The Senate ratified the treaty after long discussions, in June, 1795, by the minimum number of votes necessary, but rejected the West Indian clauses and the ban on exports.

When the terms of the treaty leaked to the press, they met a wave of popular protest. "The cry against the Treaty," Washington wrote to Hamilton, "is like that against a mad-dog; and every one, in a manner, seemed engaged on running it down." There was worse than this waiting for Hamilton, whose support for the treaty led to his being stoned in the streets. A placard appeared: "D—— John Jay! D—— every one who won't d—— John Jay! D—— every one who won't put lights in his windows and sit up all night d——ing John Jay!" For a time the House refused to appropriate the money called for by the treaty and requested a copy of Jay's instructions. Washington refused—"The nature of foreign negotiations requires caution, and their success must often depend upon secrecy." This was, he claimed, the reason for vesting the treaty-making power in the President, acting with the advice and consent of the Senate. Washington saw the dispute not as one on the merits of the treaty alone, but on the treaty-making power and the Constitution itself. It was only "the Colossus of the President's merits with the people," wrote Jefferson, that had allowed the "Anglomen" to get their handiwork enacted, after months of wrangling. The President signed the treaty in August, 1795.

Though the Treaty of 1795 failed to make clear what were the rights of neutrals and he had his reservations about it, Washington was right in thinking that it was the best treaty that could be won at the time. It represented, on however small a scale, the beginnings of arbitration in Anglo-American disputes. Spain became so alarmed at the prospect of a closer Anglo-American accord that she proceeded to negotiate a settlement of her own disputes with the United States in the Godoy-Pinckney Treaty, or the Treaty of San Lorenzo, signed in the shadow of that Escorial Palace that symbolized the power of a now fading empire.

This treaty got little attention and less applause, but it was a complete diplomatic success for Pinckney: Spain granted to the United States the rights of navigation on the Mississippi and the right of deposit at New Orleans free of duty for ocean-going American goods; she recognised the thirty-first parallel as the northern boundary of Florida and agreed to try to restrain the Indians from border raids. The treaty helped the United States to retain the fluctuating loyalty of the Kentucky and Tennessee area, now becoming states, it pointed the way South and West, and for a generation it made the nation Mississippi-minded. The President who had forty years before marched into the then West and seen its potentialities, and who twenty years before had considered retreating over the Alleghenies with his weary and dwindling forces, had good reason for satisfaction with the settlement of 1795.

By 1795 the domestic scene, however, had become completely partisan. Randolph, who had succeeded Jefferson as Secretary of State in 1793, was dismissed in 1795 on the doubtful grounds of receiving bribes from France. Washington was angered by what he thought the intrigues of one whom he had always befriended, for his own, for his uncle's, and even for his father's sake. In fact, Randolph appears to have been imprudent and unstable rather than dishonest, and may well have been the victim of High Federalist intrigues. Hamilton returned to the practice of law in order to maintain a steadily increasing family. Henry Knox, too, resigned; a good general, he had become "a furious Federalist" but an administrator of only modest capacity. By 1796 the government was completely recast; conscientous and combative Timothy Pickering at the State Department, the efficient and self-effacing Oliver Wolcott at the Treasury, the inefficient Irishman James

McHenry as Secretary of War. New men—and by now an avowed principle. "I shall not," Washington wrote to Pickering, "whilst I have the honor to administer the government, bring a man into any office of consequence knowingly, whose political tenets are adverse to the measures which the general government are pursuing; for this, in my opinion, would be a sort of political suicide." Washington had come to a position he disliked and for which the Constitution gave no warrant; the pattern of party rivalry in the United States, like the pattern of government itself, stems from the years of his administration.

The partisanship of the press made Washington's last year in Philadelphia one of acute misery. He was particularly hurt by a reference of Jefferson's to the "men who were Samsons in the field and Solomons in the council, but who have had their heads shorn by the harlot England." He had, thundered the *Aurora,* "the ostentation of an eastern bashaw." He was alarmed at what, in his Farewell Address, he called "the banefull effects of the Spirit of Party"; the American people, he wrote in 1796, seemed "more disposed to promote the views of another nation than to establish a national character of their own"; he was being compared, he said, to a Nero, or even to a common pickpocket, after forty-five years of public service; he was tired of being "buffeted in the public prints by a set of infamous scribblers." His thoughts turned again to Addison's *Cato*—and to the idea of retirement.

The decision was not one of principle—though the refusal to consider a third term has subsequently become a hallowed convention, which all but one of his successors has honored and which is now a Constitutional provision. But Washington was tired physically and mentally of the strains of office—and of the personal attacks. No one so sensitive about his "reputation" could long continue in a post now vulnerable to partisan attack, to innuendo and to public censure.

There has been much debate over the authorship of the Farewell Address (September, 1796). Washington had always sought secretaries who, as he put it, would "possess the soul of the General"; though he left the writing of the Address to others, and especially to Hamilton, it incorporated—as he insisted it should—much of Madison's draft of 1792, and he went over it carefully himself. It is a Federalist document, the nearest approach in his writings to a declaration of the Washington *credo*. The unity of government he held to be primary; sectionalism and partisanship open the door "to foreign influence and corruption." More than anything else, Washington counselled against "the insidious wiles of foreign influence." It was not so much a policy of isolation from Europe that he advocated as the exclusion of Europe from America, and the maintenance thereby of an independent American national character. The "primary interests" of Europe and America were quite distinct. There should be no "permanent inveterate antipathies against particular nations, and passionate attachments for others," but constant vigilance, preparedness, and, if necessary, temporary alliances on extraordinary occasions.

Washington, though bequeathing a legacy and no doubt fully conscious of it, was also speaking in a particular situation, deploring the meddling of Genêt and Adet in American affairs, and the intrigues of Jefferson and Freneau, and advocating that the United States should have the strength to resist insults, whether from the Barbary pirates or the French revolutionaries or the captains of British frigates. He was speaking as a realist out of long experience, and concluded that nations, like men, must depend in the end on themselves alone—the lesson of all revolutions, the goal of all national movements. "There can be no greater error than to expect, or calculate upon real favours, from Nation to Nation." Not Isolation for all time, then, but Independence; not sectionalism or partisanship, though it appeared to be "inseparable from our nature," but loyalty to the national cause; not party controversy, but "strength and consistency" to give the country "the command of its own fortunes"; this was the legacy of 1776 as well as of 1796. Like all else he did, it set a precedent, and one of the wisest. The passing of the years has made Washington's Farewell Address almost as important a bequest of the first President as the drafting of the Constitution itself. It is read in both the Senate and the House of Representatives at noon on each 22nd February, as a tribute and as a reminder.

Washington's last speech to Congress was given on 7th December, 1796. In it he pressed the case for a naval force, for a military academy and for a national university. It was dangerous, when revolution and war ravaged Europe, to send young Americans abroad at their most impressionable age. In a republic they should be taught "the science of government," and taught it at home. On 3rd March, 1797, he presided at a dinner in honor of the President-elect, John Adams, and watched his inauguration on the following day. His diary is, as usual, laconic—"Much such a day as yesterday in all respects. Mercury at 41." The new President, who had not failed to criticize his predecessor, described the occasion to Abigail in more fulsome terms:

> A solemn scene it was indeed, and it was made more affecting to me by the presence of the General, whose countenance was as serene and unclouded as the day. He seemed to me to enjoy a triumph over me. Methought I heard him say "Ay I am fairly out and you fairly in."

The role of Washington as President remains difficult to assess. It is clear that he began with a belief (shared by John Adams) in an independent executive, but that he moved steadily toward the Hamiltonians in his sympathies, especially after 1793; on financial matters he was completely dependent on Hamilton's guidance. Yet to the end Washington deplored the growth of parties; one reason he cited for refusing to consider a third term was that by 1796 party bitterness prevented universal acceptance of the President. The country would be no more united by him than by anyone else.

He does not appear as a very forceful leader in his own administration: he provided few ideas; the problems that aroused him were those in which he had direct personal experience—relations with the Indians, military affairs, defense of the frontier, the maintenance of national unity. His Farewell Address says nothing about "the rights of man" and nothing about slavery, the basic threat to those rights in the next two generations; its theme is Washington's own even if the language is Hamilton's—the need for union and the danger of foreign entanglements.

Beginning as a Head of State and hoping to remain above faction, concerned to exalt the office of President and the authority of the new government, Washington found that his Federalism itself rapidly generated partisanship. He was both hurt and baffled at the development, at the attacks of "the rascally Freneau," and at the savagery of Tom Paine's "Open Letter" from Paris in 1796. To use the language of an anonymous Philadelphia editor on the situation in 1788—"Thirteen staves and ne'er a hoop will not make a barrel." Washington sought to provide the hoop for the barrel. During his Presidency, five new states were added to the eleven that had accepted the Constitution: North Carolina (1789), Rhode Island (1790), Vermont (1791), Kentucky (1792) and Tennessee (1796). He moved away from a Virginian to a national, at times a nationalist, position; the break was not only with Jefferson, but with Madison, with Monroe and with Henry, despite the talk of nominating the last for Secretary of State in 1795. His system, he said, was to overlook all personal, local and partial considerations and "to contemplate the United States as one great whole."

Looking back, it appears surprising that Washington did not foresee the likelihood of the rise of party feeling. But Adams did not see it either, or if he did refused to face the consequences. He, too, tried to act as though the Executive were above party, representing the national interest, and paid the price in 1800. In Washington's case, the attitude is explicable enough. He was no theorist; his concern was with sound administration—of his estates, or of the Army, or of the nation. He could hardly be expected to know how bitter and irresponsible the press charges would be, nor how savagely they would treat his concern with "respectability." "I was no party man myself," he wrote to Jefferson in 1796, "and the first wish of my heart was, if parties did exist, to reconcile them." What he did understand was the threat of sectionalism, and of states' rights, to the unity won in 1783, and the threat of international revolution to the institutions of 1787. In this he was remarkably farsighted. He was the first leader of a successful national revolt against imperialism in modern history, but for him, unlike Jefferson and Monroe and Paine, America's national revolt was not part of an international revolution. It was not part of a crusade to be launched across the world, but the product of a particular situation in America in 1776. By 1797 the new and free country had to be protected against revolution, as the Constitution protected it against democracy. The America that became the guide to Latin America in the 1820's, to Greece and Hungary, Italy and Ireland, was Jefferson's not Washington's America.

The legacy of Washington's two terms was less political than administrative. Washington was a gifted and experienced administrator, and the federal government, after all, had fewer employees in 1790 than Mount Vernon. As discipline was the soul of an army, so, he said, "system to all things was the soul of business." System involved industry, integrity, impartiality and firmness. "No man," said John Adams, "has influence with the President. He seeks information from all quarters, and judges more independently than any man I ever knew." His standards for appointments were very high—higher than those in contemporary Britain or France, higher than those of most of his successors. He sought, and found, men who "would give dignity and luster to our National Character."

He was helped by rising prosperity. Though not an era of good feelings, his Presidency was an era of good times. One reason for the popularity of the Constitution was that it coincided with this upswing. All sections of the nation and all ranks of society shared in it, and the federal government, regardless of the party group in control, was the beneficiary. In foreign affairs, too, Europe's ordeal was America's advantage; it produced settlement with Britain and Spain, it eased the tension on the western border, and it made closer the ties between the Tidewater and the trans-Allegheny country. There were associated problems; the French Revolution gave further impetus to American democracy, and foreign refugees and foreign ideas brought the risk of dangerous involvement in Europe. But in its prosperity at home and its policy of peace abroad, the Washington administration laid a sound foundation for the new Republic. Never before had a republican government attempted to organize so vast an area on a federal pattern. Rarely before had an executive been so directly responsive to the popular assemblies. Rarely has an office, that was to grow into the most important elective office in the world, been so clearly given the stamp of one man's character.

Washington sensed that Europe's distress could be for America destiny as well as advantage. "Sure I am," he wrote, "if this country is preserved in tranquillity twenty years longer, it may bid defiance in a just cause to any power whatever; such in that time will be its population, wealth and resources."

LEONARD D. WHITE

✪

George Washington as an Administrator

When Washington took the oath of office as President of the United States, the character and quality of the Presidency were defined merely by the appropriate sentences of the Constitution. When he issued his Farewell Address in September, 1796, the impact of events and the personality of Washington on the office had given it living form and substance. The character of Washington was one of the most significant single influences which gave identity to the Presidency as an administrative, as well as a ceremonial, political, and military office, and it is accordingly appropriate to round out an account of its formation with an analysis of the qualities of mind and of the understanding of administration which he brought to his task.

The character of Washington, combined with his long public service, was one that inspired confidence in the new general government. Confidence was the greatest single asset that any man could have brought to the new enterprise. Again and again in the early debates on the Presidency, acknowledgment was made of the universal respect in which Washington was held. "The President," said James Madison in 1793, "was the last man in the

Reprinted from *The Federalists: A Study in Administrative History* (Macmillan, 1956), pp. 97–115, by Leonard D. White. Copyright 1948 by Leonard D. White.

world to whom any measure whatever of a deceptive tendency could be credibly attributed."[1]

The simplicity and the dignity of Washington's personality have often been touched upon. The words of a contemporary English visitor to the President, Thomas Twining, speak eloquently of the impact which Washington must have had upon his time.

13th May.—At one o'clock to-day I called at General Washington's with the picture and letter I had for him. He lived in a small red brick house on the left side of High Street, not much higher up than Fourth Street. There was nothing in the exterior of the house that denoted the rank of its possessor. Next door was a hair-dresser. Having stated my object to a servant who came to the door, I was conducted up a neat but rather narrow staircase, carpeted in the middle, and was shown into a middling-sized well-furnished drawing-room on the left of the passage. Nearly opposite the door was the fireplace, with a wood-fire in it. The floor was carpeted. On the left of the fireplace was a sofa, which sloped across the room. There were no pictures on the walls, no ornaments on the chimney-piece. Two windows on the right of the entrance looked into the street. There was nobody in the room, but in a minute Mrs. Washington came in, when I repeated the object of my calling, and put into her hands the letter for General Washington, and his miniature. She said she would deliver them to the President, and, inviting me to sit down, retired for that purpose. She soon returned, and said the President would come presently. Mrs. Washington was a middle-sized lady, rather stout; her manner extremely kind and un-affected. She sat down on the sofa, and invited me to sit by her. I spoke of the pleasant days I had passed at Washington, and of the attentions I had received from her granddaughter, Mrs. Law.

While engaged in this conversation, but with my thoughts turned to the expected arrival of the General, the door opened, and Mrs. Washington and myself rising, she said, "The President," and introduced me to him. Never did I feel more interest than at this moment, when I saw the tall, upright, venerable figure of this great man advancing towards

[1] *Debates and Proceedings in the Congress of the United States, 1789–1825* (Washington, 1834–1856), III [March 1, 1793], 943 (hereafter cited as *Annals*). Adams' fulsome praise in the Senate, April 21, 1789, may be discounted (Charles Francis Adams, ed., *Works of John Adams* [Boston, 1853], VIII, 486–487). See Madison's comparison of Washington and Adams in Gaillard Hunt, ed., *The Writings of James Madison, 9 vols.* (New York: G. P. Putnam's Sons, 1900–1910), VI, 310, Madison to Jefferson, February 1798.

me to take me by the hand. There was a seriousness in his manner which seemed to contribute to the impressive dignity of his person, without diminishing the confidence and ease which the benevolence of his countenance and the kindness of his address inspired. There are persons in whose appearance one looks in vain for the qualities they are known to possess, but the appearance of General Washington harmonized in a singular manner with the dignity and modesty of his public life. So completely did he *look* the great and good man he really was, that I felt rather respect than awe in his presence, and experienced neither the surprise nor disappointment with which a personal introduction to distinguished individuals is often accompanied. . . .

The General's age was rather more than sixty-four. In person he was tall, well-proportioned, and upright. His hair was powdered and tied behind. Although his deportment was that of a general, the expression of his features had rather the calm dignity of a legislator than the severity of a soldier. . . .[2]

While during the later years of his administration Washington was the subject of much criticism and abuse, mostly factional in origin, the deep veneration in which he was held expressed itself publicly on the last day of his second term as he turned over the reins of government to his successor. "He came unattended and on foot, with the modest appearance of a private citizen. No sooner was his person seen, than a burst of applause such as I had never before known, and which it would be as impossible for me to describe, as my own sensations produced by it, saluted the venerable Hero and Patriot. . . ."[3]

WASHINGTON'S GENERAL IDEAS ON ADMINISTRATION

The vast importance of good administration of the new system was never out of Washington's mind; frequently he revealed his con-

[2] May 13, 1795, Thomas Twining, *Travels in America 100 Years Ago* (New York: Harper and Brothers, 1902), pp. 128–130, 132–133. Twining had visited Washington, the future seat of government, mentioned in the above quotation. For Jefferson's analysis of Washington's character, see Paul L. Ford, ed., *The Writings of Thomas Jefferson*, XI, 375–377.

[3] Charles R. King, ed., *The Life and Correspondence of Rufus King*, 6 vols. (New York, 1894–1900), II, 159; see also for another eyewitness account Robert G. Harper's Letter to his Constituents, March 13, 1797, American Historical Association, *Annual Report, 1913*, II, 29–30.

cern for the effective conduct of national affairs. Writing on January 21, 1790, to Thomas Jefferson to persuade him to become Secretary of State, he said, "I consider the successful Administration of the general Government as an object of almost infinite consequence to the present and future happiness of the Citizens of the United States."[4]

In all his early actions as President, Washington was acutely aware that he was setting precedents and creating a system. "Many things which appear of little importance in themselves and at the beginning," he stated, "may have great and durable consequences from their having been established at the commencement of a new general government. It will be much easier to commence the administration, upon a well adjusted system, built on tenable grounds, than to correct errors or alter inconveniences after they shall have been confirmed by habit."[5]

Washington never wrote out a systematic view of the functions and appropriate qualities of a chief executive.[6] "With me," he said, "it has always been a maxim, rather to let my designs appear from my works than by my expressions."[7] But that he had a firm grasp of the means of conducting affairs which he put to daily use cannot be doubted by anyone who reads his letters and his public papers. Washington was an able administrator. With a sure and

[4] John C. Fitzpatrick, ed., *The Writings of George Washington*, XXX, 510.

[5] May 10, 1789, *ibid.*, XXX, 321.

[6] In 1792 he described the character of a "judicious and skilful superintendant [of the Federal City]. . . . One in whom is united knowledge of Men and things, industry, integrity, impartiality, and firmness." *Ibid.*, XXXII, 223.

[7] December 21, 1797, *ibid.*, XXXVI, 113. Norman J. Small comments as follows: "Whether Washington, like his successors, was in possession of any definite opinions as to the powers of the Presidency at the date of his entry into that office, or whether he formulated any theory as to the Chief Magistracy during his subsequent years in the service cannot be conclusively determined. . . .

". . . Being essentially a man of deed and not of contemplation, a man for whom facts and not abstraction had any attraction, he was preoccupied with the problem of putting into successful operation the product of the Philadelphia Convention." (*Some Presidential Interpretations of the Presidency*, p. 13.) Vernon Louis Parrington thought so little of Washington's contribution to the thought of his time that he did not include him in his *Main Currents in American Thought* (3 vols., New York: Harcourt, Brace, 1927–1930).

almost intuitive understanding he established in eight years an office with settled relationships to Congress, to the departments of state, and to a public which had to be taught that the head of a state could be powerful without escaping control. In his daily administrative tasks he was systematic, orderly, energetic, solicitous of the opinions of others but independent in his own judgment, insistent upon facts and deliberation but decisive, intent upon general goals and the consistency of particular actions with them. Less inventive than Hamilton, he was not brilliant but steady; he balanced different courses of conduct against each other in the recesses of his mind rather than in argumentation with his associates; always sensitive to public opinion, no criticism could swerve him from the decisions which his intelligence and conscience dictated.

In response to hostile petitions against the Jay Treaty, he uniformly replied,

In every act of my administration, I have sought the happiness of my fellow-citizens. My system for the attainment of this object has uniformly been to overlook all personal, local and partial considerations: to contemplate the United States, as one great whole. . . .

While I feel the most lively gratitude for the many instances of approbation from my country; I can no otherwise deserve it, than by obeying the dictates of my conscience. . . .[8]

His principal success was to plant in the minds of the American people the model of a government which commanded respect by reason of its integrity, energy, and competence.

In his First Inaugural Address, Washington observed that he was "unpracticed in the duties of civil administration."[9] His competent

[8] Letter to the Boston Selectmen, July 28, 1795, *Writings*, XXXIV, 252–253.

[9] At the end of his first term, when contemplating retirement, Washington told Madison that "he had from the beginning found himself deficient in many of the essential qualifications, owing to his inexperience in the forms of public business, his unfitness to judge of legal questions, and questions arising out of the Constitution; that others more conversant in such matters would be better able to execute the trust; that he found himself also in the decline of life, his health becoming sensibly more infirm, & perhaps his faculties also; that the fatigues & disagreeableness of his situation were in fact scarcely tolerable to him. . . ." (Madison, *Writings*, Hunt ed., VI, 108, n.) Washington suffered from a bad memory, to which he referred as early as 1789 (Washington, *Writings*, XXX, 456); it became progressively worse.

performance in administration grew out of two separate aspects of his experience—his life as a plantation manager and his life as a military commander. The former is not to be despised; the number of persons whom Washington supervised directly at Mount Vernon was greater than the number required to carry on the functions of any of the departments of state in New York or Philadelphia (omitting their embryonic field services); and the lessons which he learned in plantation management he applied to public affairs. In his instructions to his manager at Mount Vernon he once wrote,

there is much more in what is called head work, that is in the manner of conducting business, than is generally imagined. For take two Managers and give to each the same number of labourers, and let these labourers be equal in all respects. Let both these Managers rise equally early, go equally late to rest, be equally active, sober and industrious, and yet, in the course of the year, one of them, without pushing the hands that are under him more than the other, shall have performed infinitely more work. To what is this owing? Why, simply to contrivance resulting from that forethought and arrangement which will guard against the mis-application of labour, and doing it unseasonably. . . .[10]

As a military commander Washington encountered a wide range of administrative problems, not the least of which were his relations to the Congress. Not until he assumed command of the Continental Army in Cambridge in 1775 had he directly encountered important public management responsibilities. During the hard years which followed he learned much by experience, but what he learned was consonant with the underlying common-sense dictates which plantation management since 1759 had already confirmed.

While Washington never committed to paper an organized philosophy of government or of administration, his working rules stand out with remarkable clarity. He attached great importance to system and plan; he insisted upon energetic handling of public affairs, promptly and decisively; he based his actions solidly upon facts; he understood the necessity of freedom from detail although he was not too successful in avoiding it; and he set much store upon the dignity of the Presidential office, not to gratify a personal

---

[10] January 1, 1789, *ibid.*, XXX, 175–176, n. 4; cf. *ibid.*, XXXIII, 389; and especially *ibid.*, XXXVII, 460.

sense of station but to lend prestige to the infant general government. These rules, implicit in what Washington did rather than in what he said, are examined in the following pages.

SYSTEM AND PLAN

"System," wrote Washington, "to all things is the soul of business. To deliberate maturely, and execute promptly is the way to conduct it to advantage."[11] Addressing Benjamin Stoddert in 1792 on the duties of the commissioners in conducting the affairs of the Federal City, he advised,

there is in my judgmt. but one line of conduct proper for these Gentlemen to pursue, and that is to take a comprehensive view of the trust reposed in them, the general expectation of the community at large, and the means to effect it, form their plans agreeably thereto upon sound and just principles and to see that they are carried into effect by whomsoever they shall employ in the Execution thereof, without regard to any local concern or interest whatsoever. . . .[12]

Toward the end of his life he put into a sentence the essence of his greatness as an administrator: ". . . for the more combined, and distant things are seen, the more likely they are to be turned to advantage."[13] Perspective on distant goals and the combination of many things to their achievement, patience meanwhile, were close to the heart of Washington's character.

These maxims were illustrated in Washington's working habits.[14] After taking office and before the new government was organized, he read extensively among the papers of the Confederation period and digested them for future reference. On June 8, 1789, he requested the acting heads of the former departments for "a clear account" in writing of their respective agencies.[15] From

[11] *Ibid.*, XXXVI, 113.
[12] *Ibid.*, XXXII, 224.
[13] Washington to James Anderson, December 21, 1797, *ibid.*, XXXVI, 113.
[14] Paul Leland Haworth declares in his *George Washington: Country Gentleman* (Indianapolis: Bobbs-Merrill, 1925), p. 76, that Washington was the most methodical man that ever lived.
[15] Washington, *Writings*, XXX, 344.

time to time he requested a statement of those duties which required the "agency" of the Presidency, to be sure that he omitted
no task imposed upon him. Before leaving New York or Philadelphia he regularly asked each secretary to review any pending
business which might require his attention.[16] Well before each
session of Congress, he requested his secretary, Tobias Lear, and
the department heads, as well as Madison and others, to organize
material and present ideas for his messages. When Jefferson finally
arrived to become Secretary of State, Washington spent the greater
part of a week in almost unbroken conference with him. Washington was, in short, an exceptionally orderly chief magistrate, and in
his daily routine kept within the framework of general plans. But
planning in the sense of forming a national economy either in the
Hamiltonian or Jeffersonian pattern was not among his preoccupations.

ENERGY

Energy and firmness were cardinal virtues in Washington's sense of
administration. While awaiting inauguration as President he observed with indignation the incompetence of the Confederation
authorities. On April 10, 1789, he wrote to the Acting Secretary of
War,

the stupor, or listlessness with which our public measures seem to be
pervaded, is, to me, matter of deep regret. Indeed it has so strange an
appearance that I cannot but wonder how men who sollicit public confidence or who are even prevailed upon to accept of it can reconcile such
conduct with their own feelings of propriety.

The delay is inauspicious to say the best of it, and the World must
condemn it.[17]

He expected the heads of departments to give close attention to
business and reminded them of this duty. ". . . let me, in a
friendly way, impress the following maxims," he said, "upon the
Executive Officers. In all important matters, to deliberate maturely, but to execute promptly and vigorously. And not to put

[16] For example, *ibid.,* XXXI, 91–92.
[17] *Ibid.,* XXX, 280.

things off until the Morrow which can be done, and require to be done to day. Without an adherence to these rules, business never will be *well* done, or done in an easy manner; but will always be in arrear, with one thing treading upon the heels of another."[18] In dealing with his department heads, Washington was prompt and decisive. He cleared quickly the business they brought to him, and pushed them for expedition in the discharge of their duties.

Washington was greatly annoyed by the failure of some officials to attend to their duties and not infrequently wrote sharp letters to them. On July 2, 1792, for example, he caused Lear to write Woodbury Langdon, one of the commissioners for settling accounts between the United States and the individual states,

I am commanded by the President of the United States to inform you, that it is indispensably necessary you should without delay repair to the seat of Government to prosecute jointly with your colleagues the business of your office as Commissioner. . . . I am further instructed by the President to say, that if any circumstances in your situation should be incompatible with your immediate and steady attendance, it is proper you should resign the Office. . . .[19]

The decisiveness with which Washington met the challenge of the disorderly distillers of whisky in western Pennsylvania is one of the most dramatic examples of his energy and firmness. . . . The tone and temper of the Chief Executive in this crisis of law enforcement are revealed in his correspondence. "When . . . lenient and temporizing means have been used, and serve only to increase the disorder; longer forbearance would become unjustifiable remissness, and a neglect of that duty which is enjoined on the

18 *Ibid.*, XXXV, 138. In a letter to the Secretary of War written at Mount Vernon, September 24, 1792, Washington referred to "some remissness on the part of the Contractors at Pittsburgh. This ought not to be suffered in the smallest degree; for one neglect or omission, is too apt to beget another, to the discontentment of the Troops and injury of the Service; whereas a rigid exaction in every case checks a departure on their part from the Contract in any; and no indulgence is ever allowed by them to the public." *Ibid.*, XXXII, 162.

19 *Ibid.*, XXXII, 82–83. Cf. his remark to the commissioners of the District of Columbia, "Coaxing a man to stay in Office, or to do his duty while he is in it is not the way to accomplish the object." *Ibid.*, XXXV, 111.

President."[20] And again, "neither the Military nor Civil government shall be trampled upon with impunity whilst I have the honor to be at the head of them."[21] Washington himself left Philadelphia and journeyed to Bedford as commander in chief to be certain that the militia was well organized and the expedition was properly directed. Nor did he fail to provide a compelling argument to the rebellious distillers; no less than 15,000 militia were assembled from Pennsylvania and neighboring states.

FACTS

In reaching decisions Washington required all available facts. Throughout his official correspondence there is repeated insistence upon facts rather than opinions. On September 14, 1791, he wrote Governor Clinton of New York with reference to British occupancy of the Western posts; while recognizing the gravity of the situation he declined to take action other than to dispatch a "gentleman to the spot," so that his eventual decision could be based "upon the ground of well authenticated facts."[22] Commenting on General Wayne's plan for an Indian campaign, he noted that "The latter will be *right,* or *wrong,* according to the actual State of things at *those places* at the time it is proposed to make them, (to be ascertained from indubitable information). . . ."[23] Replying to a letter recommending a young Alexandrian as an ensign because a number of young country-born men would enlist under him, he answered, let him "ascertain *that* fact, and then apply with the list of them."[24]

Toward the end of his administration he wrote to Pickering, referring to a forthcoming statement on relations with France:

I have no doubt that you have taken care, and will continue to be assured, of your facts; for as this business will certainly come before the public, not only the facts, but the candour also, the expression, and force of every word, will be examined with the most scrutinizing eye,

[20] September 17, 1792, *ibid.,* XXXII, 154.
[21] September 24, 1792, *ibid.,* XXXII, 161.
[22] *Ibid.,* XXXI, 370.
[23] *Ibid.,* XXXII, 145.
[24] *Ibid.,* XXXII, 161.

and compared with everything that will admit of a different construction, and if there is the least ground for it, we shall be charged with unfairness, and an intention to impose on, and to mislead the public judgment.

Hence, and from a desire that the statement may be full, fair, calm and argumentative; without asperity, or anything more irritating in the comments, than the narration of facts, which expose unfounded charges and assertions, do themselves produce, I have wished that this letter to Mr. Pinckney may be revised over, and over again. . . .[25]

AVOIDANCE OF DETAIL

Washington was more clear in principle about the necessity of avoiding detail than he was successful in practice. The interchange of correspondence between Hamilton, Jefferson, Knox, and the President reveals a mass of business which the heads of departments thought it essential to clear with the Chief Executive, and which Washington continued to accept throughout his two terms. Appointments, great and small, were of direct concern to Washington, and no collector of customs, captain of a cutter, keeper of a lighthouse, or surveyor of revenue was appointed except after specific consideration by the President. In signing contracts for the construction of a lighthouse the President took time to enjoin economy in the selection of materials. Leaves of absence of important officials were requested from and approved by the President himself.

General Uriah Forrest remarked to McHenry, "You know Genl. Washington is in all respects singularly attentive to any thing, and perhaps the Federal City (being rather a Hobby Horse of his) more than anything else had his attention. . . ."[26] This was partly on account of the feuds and quarrels which developed there, partly by reason of his intense interest in the new capital. Thus on August 29, 1791, we find Washington writing to Jefferson, "Ought there to be any wood houses in the town? . . . Ought not Stoups, and projections of every sort and kind into the Streets, to be prohibited *absolutely?*"[27] On July 23, 1794, he wrote the com-

[25] January 4, 1797, *ibid.,* XXXV, 351–352.
[26] *Publications of the Southern History Association,* X (1906), 33.
[27] Washington, *Writings,* XXXI, 352.

missioners of the District of Columbia, "I wish, however, you had declared that so much of the stone walls, on which the railing in the Street is to be placed, as shall appear above the pavement (or surface of the ground before it is paved) should be of freestone hewed."[28] His repeated efforts to relieve himself of the details of laying out the Federal City by pointing out the proper duties of the commissioners and of the superintendent were unavailing.

In military administration Washington grasped completely the importance of thrusting detail into other hands. Few better statements of the concept of a military staff as an aid to a commander have been made than that contained in a letter of Washington's to the Secretary of War on July 29, 1798, the main purpose of which was to protect himself against demands for appointment as his aide.

Of the propriety of remaining *perfectly* free from all engagements respecting my Aids, I am more and more convinced as the applications encrease and the little knowledge displayed of the qualifications which the Aids of the Commander in Chief out to possess, is discovered by the Applicants. The variegated, and important duties of the Aids of a Commander in Chief, or, the Commander of a seperate Army, require experienced Officers, men of judgment, and men of business, *ready pens* to execute them properly and with dispatch. A great deal more is required of them than attending him at a Parade, or delivering verbal orders here and there; or copying a written one. They ought if I may be allowed to use the expression, to possess the Soul of the General; and from a *single* Idea given to them, to convey his meaning in the clearest and fullest manner. This, young men unacquainted with the Service and diffident, would not do; be their abilities what they may. . . .[29]

DIGNITY

In his own personality Washington was reserved and aloof; an easy congeniality did not come naturally to him. His personality coincided with his considered view concerning the public importance of surrounding the office of the Chief Executive with an impressive

[28] *Ibid.,* XXXIII, 440–441.
[29] *Ibid.,* XXXVI, 374–375.

dignity.[30] The salary of the office, fixed by the first Congress at $25,000 a year, a figure far in excess of any other official salary and probably equaled by few of his American contemporaries, was an early proof of the general desire to form an office of great prestige. Washington's own choice of title was "His High Mightiness, the President of the United States and Protector of their Liberties"; fortunately a less "high toned" formalism was devised.[31] In his public appearances on official occasions, Washington rode in a coach drawn by four horses, sometimes six, followed by his official family in other coaches. At the outset, "to preserve the dignity and respect that was due to the first Magistrate," he decided to give invitations to dinner only "to official characters and strangers of distinction," and to receive no invitations.[32] His encounter with the gouty John Hancock, then Governor of Massachusetts, at the time of his eastern trip is well known; he declined to call on Hancock until the Governor had first paid his respects to the President of the United States.

One aspect of Presidential formality which Washington did not enjoy, and for which he was criticized in Republican circles, was his weekly levee.[33] The levees were held every Tuesday between

[30] John Adams shared this attitude toward the external show of public office. "Neither dignity nor authority," he once wrote, "can be supported in human minds, collected into nations or any great numbers, without a splendor and majesty in some degree proportioned to them," *Works*, VIII, 493.

[31] Max Farrand, *The Framing of the Constitution of the United States* (New Haven: Yale University Press, 1913), p. 163. For the House debate on the Presidential title, *Annals*, I, 318–324 (May 11, 1789).

[32] One of Washington's duties was to entertain Indian chiefs on formal occasions. John Adams noted on December 4, 1796, that "The President dined four sets of Indians on four several days the last week." *Letters of John Adams, addressed to his wife*, II, 231. An early precedent (which curiously connected the first President with Franklin D. Roosevelt) occurred when Washington declined to attend the funeral ceremonies of Mrs. Isaac Roosevelt. Different accounts have been preserved of the atmosphere of Washington's dinners. Senator Maclay found them very formal, stiff, and almost oppressive (*Journal*, pp. 137–138, 206); but Jacob Hiltzheimer in his diary repeatedly commented upon Washington's ease; "an unassuming, easy and sociable man" (p. 171); "exceedingly affable to all" (p. 213). Jacob Cox Parsons, ed., *Extracts from the Diary of Jacob Hiltzheimer of Philadelphia, 1765–1798* (Philadelphia: Wm. F. Fell, 1893).

[33] Maclay, *Journal*, p. 351, December 14, 1790: "This was levee day, and I accordingly dressed and did the needful. . . . The practice, however, considered as a feature of royalty, is certainly anti-republican."

three and four o'clock in the afternoon. Visitors were introduced by Tobias Lear or by some gentleman acquainted with the President. Washington dressed for the part

in black velvet; his hair in full dress, powdered and gathered behind in a large silk bag; yellow gloves on his hands; holding a cocked hat with cockade in it, and the edges adorned with a black feather about an inch deep. He wore knee and shoe buckles; and a long sword, with a finely wrought and polished steel hilt, which appeared at the left hip; the coat worn over the sword, so that the hilt, and the part below the folds of the coat behind, were in view. The scabbard was white polished leather.

He stood always in front of the fire-place, with his face towards the door of entrance. . . . He received his visitor with a dignified bow, while his hands were so disposed of as to indicate, that the salutation was not to be accompanied with shaking hands. This ceremony never occurred in these visits, even with his most near friends, that no distinction might be made.

As visitors came in, they formed a circle around the room. At a quarter past three, the door was closed, and the circle was formed for that day. He then began on the right, and spoke to each visitor, calling him by name, and exchanging a few words with him. When he had completed his circuit, he resumed his first position, and the visitors approached him in succession, bowed and retired. By four o'clock this ceremony was over.[34]

While Washington was reserved in personality he had no fondness for display, and on repeated occasions urged the avoidance of public notice or excessive ceremony. In this respect he differed from John Adams, whose pretension aroused much adverse criticism; Patrick Henry commented that it squinted toward monarchy. At the other extreme stood Jefferson who according to dubious tradition hitched his saddle horse before the capital as he walked in for his first inauguration. Hamilton, as might have been expected, insisted upon regard for the dignity of the Presidential office, an attribute which, despite Republican abuse, had been well established at the conclusion of Washington's service as chief executive.

[34] William Sullivan, *The Public Men of the Revolution* (Philadelphia: Carey and Hart, 1847), p. 120.

THE PRESIDENT AND PUBLIC OPINION

Washington was alert to the importance of a favorable public opinion in support of the new government and of the particular administrative decisions which were taken from time to time. From his correspondence it is clear that he took pains to ascertain what people were thinking and saying; that his decisions were affected, although not governed, by probable public reaction; and that on rare occasions he was prepared to influence public opinion.

At his invitation, a number of friends from different parts of the country, often not in public life, became informal reporters of public opinion to the President. On July 26, 1789, he wrote David Stuart of Virginia, "I should like to be informed, through so good a medium of the public opinion of both men and measures, and of none more than myself; not so much of what may be thought commendable parts, if any, of my conduct, as of those which are conceived to be of a different complexion."[35] On many occasions he directed his secretary, Tobias Lear, to sound out public opinion, especially on appointments.[36] On February 9, 1792, he wrote Jefferson with respect to a resident of Georgetown newly arrived in Philadelphia to "contrive to get him to his house," and "learn the sentiments of the people of that place, Carrolsburg &ca., with respect to the dispute between the Comrs. and Majr. L', and generally of the State of the business."[37]

To assess the state of opinion about the yeasty Pennsylvania whisky distillers became a matter of prime importance; and it is not surprising to find Washington writing on August 10, 1794, to Burges Ball, "What (under the rose I ask it) is said, or thought, as far as it has appeared to you, of the conduct of the People in the Western Counties of this State (Pennsylvania) towards the excise Officers? and does there seem to be a disposition among those with

---

[35] Washington, *Writings*, XXX, 360; see also *ibid.*, XXXI, 28–30 for an example of this correspondence.
[36] *Ibid.*, XXXI, 296.
[37] *Ibid.*, XXXI, 477–478.

whom you converse, to bring them to a Sense of their duty, and obedience to law, by coercion . . .?"[38]

Washington's *major* decisions of policy and administration were affected to a very slight extent by what he learned of public opinion. The hostility to the Jay Treaty did not swerve him. On lesser matters, however, he weighed the opinion of the community carefully and in some instances it was a decisive factor. Writing to Comte de Rochambeau in the summer of 1790 he said, "In a government which depends so much in its first stages on public opinion, much circumspection is still necessary for those who are engaged in its administration."[39]

Washington entertained a progressively unfavorable opinion of the value of newspapers, and was privately deeply wounded by their intemperate attacks upon his policy. As early as the spring of 1790 he wrote David Stuart, "It is to be lamented that the Editors of the different Gazettes in the Union, do not more generally, and more correctly (instead of stuffing their papers with scurrility, and nonsensical declamation, which few would read if they were apprised of the contents) publish the debates in Congress on all great national questions. . . ."[40]

In the autumn of 1791 Philip Freneau began publication of the *National Gazette,* which rapidly became the major instrument of opposition to the Federalist policy and program. In August, 1792, Washington privately referred to its attacks upon almost every measure of the government and expressed his concern.[41] In October he wrote Gouverneur Morris: "From the complexion of some of our Newspapers Foreigners would be led to believe that inveterate political dissensions existed among us, and that we are on the very verge of disunion; but the fact is otherwise. . . ."[42]

Although Freneau's *National Gazette* expired in the fall of 1793 Republican editors continued their abuse, to Washington's constant discomfort. In a letter to Jefferson he revealed his anger at the hostile press.

[38] *Ibid.,* XXXIII, 463.
[39] *Ibid.,* XXXI, 83–84.
[40] *Ibid.,* XXXI, 30.
[41] *Ibid.,* XXXII, 136.
[42] *Ibid.,* XXXII, 189.

Perceiving, and probably, hearing, that no abuse in the Gazettes would induce me to take notice of anonymous publications, against me; those who were disposed to do me *such friendly Offices,* have embraced without restraint every opportunity to weaken the confidence of the People; and, by having the *whole* game in their hands, they have scrupled not to publish things that do not, as well as those which do exist; and to mutilate the latter, so as to make them subserve the purposes which they have in view.

Later in the same letter he referred to the abuse by his critics as couched "in such exaggerated and indecent terms as could scarcely be applied to a Nero; a notorious defaulter; or even to a common pickpocket."[43] In public, however, Washington maintained a resolute and unbroken silence.

There is little evidence that Washington attempted to "manage" opinion, although Federalist and Republican leaders alike were alert to the importance both of the press and the post office in this respect. The distribution of large contracts for shipbuilding in different parts of the country was undoubtedly determined in part by the desire to secure a favorable public reaction. Two early examples were the construction of revenue cutters in 1790, and of frigates in 1794. In the first instance, Hamilton wrote the President, "To avoid dissatisfaction, it may appear best to build them in different ports of the Union," and specified where ten could be built from New Hampshire to Savannah; Washington endorsed this plan.[44] In the second instance the President directed frigates to be built at Baltimore and at Norfolk: "The wealth, and populousness of the two states will not only warrant, but require this change, if there is an equality in other respects."[45]

At times Washington took steps to influence public opinion. On January 16, 1792, he directed the Secretary of War to publish a statement on the Indian War, adding, "When the Community are called upon for considerable exertions to relieve a part which is suffering under the hand of an enemy, it is desirable to manifest

[43] July 6, 1796, *ibid.,* XXXV, 119, 120.
[44] September 10, 1790, John C. Hamilton, ed., *The Works of Alexander Hamilton* (New York, 1850–1851), IV, 46–47; Washington, *Writings,* XXXI, 118 (September 20, 1790).
[45] Washington to the Secretary of War, April 16, 1794, *ibid.,* XXXIII, 333.

that due pains have been taken by those entrusted with the administration of their affairs to avoid the evil."[46] In the early effort to enforce the tax on distilled spirits, he instructed the Attorney General to attend in person the Circuit Court at York, "for the further purpose, also, of giving to this measure of Government a more solemn and serious aspect."[47] Writing Jefferson concerning suggestions for rephrasing of his Fourth Annual Message in 1792, he remarked, "For while so many unpleasant things are announced as the Speech contains, it cannot be amiss to accompany them with communications of a more agreeable nature."[48] In discussing the recall of Monroe from Paris, Washington wrote Pickering, the Secretary of State, "As the measure, when known, will excite much speculation, and set all the envenomed pens to work; it is worthy of consideration what part, and how much of the causes which have produced this event, should be spoken of *unofficially* by the officers of Government."[49]

So far as interference in the course of elections is concerned, Washington pursued a policy of complete nonintervention. In the elections of 1792 Colonel John F. Mercer of Maryland[50] asserted that Washington had told his nephew, Bushrod, that Mercer was the best representative "that now goes or ever did go to that Body from this State." Washington immediately commissioned an intermediary to deny this assertion, and shortly thereafter wrote directly to Colonel Mercer:

I was not a little displeased to find . . . that my name had been freely used by you or your friends, for electioneering purposes, when I had never associated your name and the Election together; and when there had been the most scrupulous and pointed caution observed on my part, not to express a sentiment respecting the fitness, or unfitness of any Candidate for representation. . . . Conceiving that the exercise of an

[46] *Ibid.*, XXXI, 459.
[47] October 1, 1792, *ibid.*, XXXII, 171–172.
[48] *Ibid.*, XXXII, 200.
[49] *Ibid.*, XXXV, 174.
[50] John F. Mercer, of a distinguished Virginia family, was a Virginia delegate to the Confederation Congress from 1782–1785. After his marriage in 1785, he moved to Maryland, and was a representative to Congress from that state, 1792–1794. He served as Governor of Maryland from 1801–1803.

influence (if I really possessed any) however remote, would be highly improper. . . .[51]

On broader grounds Washington conceived his principal duty to be to weld together a numerous body of states, scattered over an area immense under the conditions of the eighteenth century, diverse in many of their interests and conflicting in some, jealous and suspicious of each other and tending to fall into three principal sections, or even two. The great trends of opinion which he saw crystallizing around the Southern and Northern interests consequently disturbed him deeply. Less than a year after his inauguration his correspondent, David Stuart, had written Washington about "A spirit of jealousy which may become dangerous to the Union, towards the Eastern States."[52] Washington replied,

Was it not always believed that there are some points which peculiarly interest the eastern States? and did any One, who reads human nature, and more especially the character of the eastern people conceive that they would not pursue them steadily by a combination of their force? Are there not other points which equally concern the southern States? If these States are less tenacious of their interest, or, if whilst the eastern move in a solid phalanx to effect their views, the southern are always divided, which of the two is most to be blamed? That there is a diversity of interests in the Union none has denied. That this is the case also in every State is equally certain. And that it even extends to the Counties of individual States can be as readily proved. . . .

. . . to accommodate differences, temper and mutual forbearance are requisite. Common danger brought the States into confederacy, and on their union our safety and importance depend. . . .[53]

On matters great and small, therefore, Washington recognized that he must measure his public acts against the tone and temper of public opinion. His personal fortunes counted for nothing in the outcome, but his task of consolidating the new general government counted for everything. While Hamilton sought to conciliate the mercantile and professional "persons of property," Washington with a broader perspective was seeking to cultivate a favorable opinion in the far-flung sections of the Union and among all

[51] Washington, *Writings,* XXXII, 165.
[52] *Ibid.,* XXXI, 28, n. 54.
[53] *Ibid.,* XXXI, 28–29.

groups and interests so far as possible. Here, again, Washington preferred to let his deeds speak rather than his promises.[54]

The contribution of Washington's personality and sense of administration to the office of Presidency as an administrative agency was thus of great significance. He possessed a deep-seated understanding of the importance of good administration both as a means of consolidating popular support for the general government, and as an essential source of strength of the government itself. He understood good administration to be characterized by integrity, system, energy, reliance on facts, relative freedom from detail, and due responsibility to Congress. These understandings came partly from his experience as a plantation manager and as a military commander, but they also reflected the habitual cast of Washington's mind. He was as an administrator what he was as a man.

---

[54] Brooks Adams' estimate of Washington as an administrator is contained in the following passage: "The original union and the original administrative system of the government was, as far as so complex an organism might be, the product of Washington's single mind and of his commanding personality." Henry Adams, *The Degradation of the Democratic Dogma* (New York: Macmillan, 1919), p. 108.

ALEXANDER DE CONDE

✪

Washington's Farewell, the French Alliance, and the Election of 1796

When in 1789 George Washington became the nation's first President the French alliance was the cornerstone of American foreign policy. It largely had made possible American independence and had established American foreign policy orientation. At the end of Washington's second term, in fact as he prepared his farewell to public life, the life-giving alliance was practically dead and the United States was virtually at war with France. Why, in eight formative years, did such a drastic reversal in foreign policy take place?[1] A full answer to this question would be long and complex; yet by looking closely at the election of 1796 and by reviewing the Farewell Address in its political context we may find a partial answer as to how the alliance received its mortal wound. We may also find additional reason for revising the traditional interpretation of the Farewell Address as a wise, timeless, and unbiased warning to the nation.

[1] A few months after Washington had left office, the French, in taking stock of the defunct alliance of 1778 and the serious state of American relations, asked the same question. Louis-Guillaume Otto, "Considerations sur la Conduite du gouvernment des États-Unis envers la France, depuis 1789 jusqu'en 1797," Paris, June 17, 1797, Archives des Affaires Étrangères, Correspondance Politique, États-Unis (Reproductions in the Library of Congress), XLVII, 401–418.

Reprinted from Alexander DeConde, "Washington's Farewell, the French Alliance, and the Election of 1796," *The Mississippi Valley Historical Review*, XLIII (1956), pp. 641–658.

The blow from which the alliance never recovered was the Jay Treaty of 1794.[2] While this Federalist-negotiated treaty averted a war with England, a war which Federalists feared, the major objectives which John Jay had been expected to win were not realized. Because it failed to obtain specific concessions on impressments, ship seizures, and Indian raids on the frontier, the treaty infuriated Republicans and others who still nurtured a Revolution-bred hatred of England.[3] At the same time it blighted Franco-American relations. Successive French revolutionary governments were convinced that the Jay Treaty violated the Franco-American treaties of 1778 and that the American government had accepted it against the will of an overwhelming public sentiment. Believing that the bulk of the American people were pro-French even though Washington's Federalist government was pro-English, the French sought to arouse their allies, the American people, to their true interest. This true interest was alliance with France and disassociation with England, America's natural enemy and France's major antagonist in war since February, 1793.[4]

[2] For background on the Jay Treaty see Samuel F. Bemis, *Jay's Treaty: A Study in Commerce and Diplomacy* (New York, 1923); Frank Monaghan, *John Jay: Defender of Liberty* (New York, 1935), 361–404; Joseph Charles, "The Jay Treaty: The Origins of the American Party System," *William and Mary Quarterly,* Ser. III, Vol. XII (October 1955), 581–630; Bradford Perkins, *The First Rapprochement: England and the United States* (Philadelphia, 1955), 1–6.

[3] That the treaty violated the "rights of friendship, gratitude and alliance which the republic of France may justly claim from the United States" was a foremost criticism of Jay's work, a criticism which had great popular appeal. See the memorial emanating from a mass meeting of citizens in Philadelphia, July 25, 1795, cited in Margaret Woodbury, "Public Opinion in Philadelphia, 1789–1801," *Smith College Studies in History* (Northampton, Mass.), V, nos. 1–2 (1919–1920), 88. "Junius Americanus," in New York *Herald,* reprinted in *Virginia Herald and Fredericksburg Advertiser,* June 26, 1795, attacked the administration for neglecting France and surrendering to Great Britain's tyranny. For a French commentary on American public opinion in regard to the Jay Treaty see François de La Rochefoucauld-Liancourt, *Travels through the United Etates of North America in the Years 1795, 1796, and 1797,* 2 vols. (London, 1799), I, 381–382.

[4] See, for example, Joseph Fauchet to Committee of Public Safety, April 19, 25, 1795, Frederick J. Turner, ed., *Correspondence of the French Ministers to the United States, 1791–1797* (American Historical Association, *Annual Report,* 1903, II, Washington, 1904), 649–650, 662–663. For an astute French analysis of the status of the alliance at the time of the Jay negotiations see Philipe A. J. Létombe to Commission of Foreign Relations,

To arouse the American people in defense of the 1778 alliance the French Directory in June, 1795, sent to the United States a new minister, a young man in his early thirties, Pierre Auguste Adet. To the French the Jay Treaty created an intimate alliance between the United States and France's worst enemy. In Adet's instructions, therefore, the idea that the treaty violated the French alliance stood out as the foremost grievance against the Washington administration.[5]

Despite French anger, and despite Adet's attempts to prevent ratification, the Senate approved the Jay Treaty eleven days after Adet had landed in Philadelphia. Two months later, while Adet continued his efforts to kill it, Washington ratified the treaty.[6] England accepted the ratified treaty and in April, 1796, after a long, last-ditch battle in which Adet used all the influence he could

---

[1794], Archives des Affaires Étrangeres, Correspondance Politique, États-Unis, XL, 241–247.

[5] Adet's instructions, dated October 23, 1794, are in *Correspondence of French Ministers*, 721–730. For biographical details on Adet see *Nouvelle Biographie Générale*, I (1852), 278; Jean Kaulek, ed., *Papiers de Barthelemy: Ambassadeur de France en Suisse, 1792–1797*, 6 vols. Paris, 1886–1910), VI, 151 n. Adet was second choice for the American mission. Alphonse Bertrand, "Les États-Unis et la Révolution Française," *Revue des Deux Mondes*, XXXIII (May 15, 1906), 422 n.

[6] Adet wrote that "the President has just countersigned the dishonor of his old age and the shame of the United States." Adet to Committee of Public Safety, September 2, 1795, *Correspondence of French Ministers*, 776–777. The despatch is printed in translation in Gilbert Chinard, ed., *George Washington as the French Knew Him* (Princeton, 1940), 106–109. In France, of course, Washington's support of the Jay Treaty was considered a tragic mistake and inimical to the 1778 alliance. See George Duruy, ed., *Memoirs of Barras: Member of the Directorate*, trans. by Charles E. Roche, 4 vols. (London, 1895–1896), II, 103 (entry of March 22, 1795); Michele de Mangourit to ———, December 23, 1795, Archives des Affaires Étrangeres, Correspondance Politique, États-Unis, XLIV, 103. In the United States, Washington's signing of the treaty infuriated Republicans; Republican newspaper editors embarked on a concerted effort to make public life so unpalatable that Washington would virtually be driven from office. See the diary of Dr. Nathaniel Ames, August 14, 1795, in Charles Warren, *Jacobin and Junto* (Cambridge, 1931), 12, 63; Donald H. Stewart, "The Press and Political Corruption during the Federalist Administrations," *Political Science Quarterly*, LXVII (September 1952), 436. William Vans Murray, a moderate Federalist, believed that Washington ran the "risk of the most alarming discontent if he ratifies & war if he does not." William Vans Murray Papers, Commonplace Book, August 15, 1795 (Princeton University Library, microfilm copies).

ALEXANDER DECONDE

muster against the treaty, the House of Representatives voted funds to implement it. To Adet as to other Frenchmen this meant the end of the 1778 alliance and another triumph for England and English gold.

Not knowing that Washington already had decided to retire from the Presidency, Adet now saw the overthrow of Washington and his Federalist administration as the only salvation for the 1778 alliance. Adet and the French Directory viewed the Washington administration as the captive of English policy; to save the alliance it had to be replaced by a pro-French Republican administration.[7] Charles Delacroix, French foreign minister, advocated inciting an uprising against Washington to break the Jay Treaty and to invigorate the alliance. Thomas Jefferson, he believed, would replace Washington and thus France would command the influence in the United States which she deserved. Prospects for the defeat of Washington were good, he believed, since the President, once the idol of the American people, had become to some an object of scorn and even hatred as the result of the Jay Treaty; already the journals attacked him, his principles, and his conduct.[8]

Taking into account what it conceived to be the temper of American popular opinion, and with the objective of destroying English influence in the United States and salvaging the 1778 alliance, the French government intervened actively in the Presidential election of 1796. Through Adet and other French officials in the United States the Directory openly supported the Republican party and wherever possible attacked the Federalist party.[9] French intervention in the election became, therefore, one of the

[7] Adet to Minister of Foreign Relations, May 3, 1796, *Correspondence of French Ministers*, 900–906.

[8] "Rapport au Directoire Exécutif par le Ministere des Relations Exterieures," January 16, 1796, Archives des Affaires Étrangeres, Correspondance Politique, États-Unis, XLV, 41–51. Part of the document is printed in Samuel F. Bemis, "Washington's Farewell Address: A Foreign Policy of Independence," *American Historical Review*, XXXIX (January 1934), 257–258.

[9] "Mémoire sur les effets du dernier traité des États-Unis et de l'Angleterre, et les remèdes à employer," (May 1796), Archives des Affaires Étrangeres, Correspondance Politique, États-Unis, XLV, 323–351; Adet to Minister of Foreign Relations, May 3, 1796, *Correspondence of French Ministers*, 900–906.

main issues in the campaign of 1796. The fate of the alliance hung on the outcome of the election.

The decision of the Directory to intervene in the 1796 election, while a decisive factor, contributed but one element to the complex politics of the election. Domestic issues and the Jay Treaty itself contributed others. Final acceptance of the treaty plunged Franco-American relations to their lowest depths since independence and marked a great political triumph for Federalists. Yet to Republicans all hope of ultimately defeating the treaty did not appear lost. Seeing the extent of the Jay Treaty's unpopularity, Republican leaders believed that it would make an excellent campaign issue in the 1796 election as an unrivaled party rallying point for national sentiment. Thomas Jefferson, James Madison, and other party leaders believed that popular opinion remained still largely pro-French and anti-British. Being politicians they reacted logically. Their party had ready-made national issues; they had only to exploit them properly and victory would be theirs. Republicans, consequently, carried over into the election of 1796 their campaign against the Jay Treaty and the pro-British "system" of Alexander Hamilton.[10]

Granted the logic and appeal of the Republican campaign plan, a towering obstacle—the person and prestige of George Washington—stood in the way of success, as was clear to the French. So deep was the impression Washington had made on fellow Americans that to attack him would be to risk injuring the attacker. Twice he had been chosen President without a dissenting vote. Had he so desired he could undoubtedly have held office for a third term, for, as a foreign observer remarked, "there is a Magic in his name more powerful in this Country than the Abilities of any other man."[11] No man, moreover, was better aware of this

[10] Phineas Bond, British consul in Philadelphia, for example, maintained that it was pretty well understood that Republican opposition to the Jay Treaty was planned by Jefferson "for the double purpose of promoting the interests of France and of advancing" his candidacy for President. Bond to Lord Grenville, May 4, 1796, British Foreign Correspondence: America (Henry Adams Transcripts, Library of Congress). See also Harry Ammon, "The Formation of the Republican Party in Virginia, 1789–1796," *Journal of Southern History*, XIX (August 1953), 309–310.

[11] Robert Liston, British minister in Philadelphia, to Grenville, October 13, 1796, Henry Adams Transcripts. The quotation is from Henrietta Liston

than Jefferson. "Republicanism," he advised, "must lie on it's [*sic*] oars, resign the vessel to it's pilot [Washington], and themselves to the course he thinks best for them."[12]

Despite Washington's great political strength the situation in 1796 was far different from 1789 and 1792; Washington probably could have had a third term, but not by unanimous choice. In political battles over neutrality, the Jay Treaty, and other issues, he had divested himself of nonpartisanship. To Republicans and Francophiles the guise of being above party and of working for the welfare of the nation as a whole, in view of his intimate connections with his Federalist subordinates and his consistent practice of acting in accord with their principles, appeared the sheerest hypocrisy.[13] In town and country some men now spat at the mention of his name, denounced him as a monocrat and an Anglomaniac, and prayed for his removal from office. Washington in 1796 had become a central figure in emerging party politics; he was a principal target for the violent personal politics of the time; and to the French he was the main barrier to reactivation of the 1778 alliance.[14]

---

to James Jackson, October 16, 1796, Bradford Perkins, ed., "A Diplomat's Wife in Philadelphia: Letters of Henrietta Liston, 1796–1800," *William and Mary Quarterly*, Ser. III, Vol. XI (October 1954), 604.

[12] Jefferson to James Monroe, June 12, 1796, Paul L. Ford, ed., *The Writings of Thomas Jefferson*, 10 vols. (New York, 1892–1899), VII, 80; James Madison, too, complained of Washington's prestige. Madison to Jefferson, May 22, 1796, Madison Papers, Library of Congress, XIX, 68, cited in Nathan Schachner, *Thomas Jefferson: A Biography*, 2 vols. (New York, 1951), II, 581.

[13] John Quincy Adams believed that Republican efforts to associate Washington with "an English party" was "a party manoeuvre," a trick "to make their adversaries unpopular by fixing upon them odious imputations." Adams to Joseph Pitcairn, March 9, 1797, Worthington C. Ford, ed., *Writings of John Quincy Adams*, 7 vols. (New York, 1913–1917), II, 140.

[14] See, for example, Lexington *Kentucky Gazette*, September 26, 1795; John B. McMaster, *A History of the People of the United States*, 8 vols. (New York, 1883–1913), II, 289. While opposing him, many of Washington's critics still recognized his virtues. One, for instance, remarked that "the best man that ever lived possessing the influence of the P[resident], is a dangerous man; the more so if guided in any of his measures by others who may not be so virtuous. God grant we may never have cause to say 'curse on his virtues; they have undone his country'." Joseph Jones to James Madison, February 17, 1796, Worthington C. Ford, ed., "Letters from Joseph Jones to Madison, 1788–1802," Massachusetts Historical Society, *Proceedings*, Ser. II, Vol. XV (1902), 155.

So bitter was feeling between English and French partisans that domestic issues drifted into relative insignificance. In their conviction that the Federalist administration did not truly represent the American people, the French were encouraged by pro-French partisans among Republicans who indicated that the Federalist government would topple if only France were to take a strong stand.[15] As the election year of 1796 opened, Republicans intensified their attacks against the Federalist administration. The Jay Treaty and the loud cry of aristocracy, monarchy, and plutocracy aroused deep popular emotions. Mutual hatred characterized the two large political segments of the American public.

With his government under fire on both domestic and foreign policy and with himself the target of unrestrained scurrility, Washington found the demands of his office increasingly difficult to endure. Publicly he maintained a dignified silence, but privately he revealed the strain.[16] Even he had come to see that the myth of nonpartisanship was shattered, and that his concept of an administration above party and the tumult of politics had been illusory. Foreign relations had exploded the myth while serving as a catalyst in the formation of national political parties. This was an issue capable of transforming the opposing local alliances of Federalist and Antifederalist into integrated national parties—an emotional foreign policy issue capable of capturing public imagination in a way which abstruse problems of finance could not.[17]

Despite his increasing distaste for the office and the increasing speculation about his not wishing to be a candidate for a third term, the President remained silent as to future plans. Leaders of both political parties, however, had little doubt that he would not run. "He gave me intimations enough," asserted John Adams, "that his reign would be very short." Early in 1796, and even

15 At this time La Rochefoucauld-Liancourt, for example, reported that the common people in the United States were overwhelmingly pro-French and anti-British. *Travels*, II, 64–65, 139.

16 See, for example, Washington to Jefferson, July 6, 1796, and to Charles C. Pinckney, July 8, 1796, John C. Fitzpatrick, ed., *The Writings of George Washington, 1745–1799* (Washington, D.C., 1931–1944), XXXV, 120, 130.

17 Ammon, "Formation of the Republican Party in Virginia," *Journal of Southern History*, XIX (August 1953), 300.

before, both parties had laid tentative plans which did not include Washington as a candidate.[18]

The attacks on Washington grew increasingly bitter during the year. Opponents charged that he had betrayed a solemn pledge to France by destroying the French alliance. Personal attacks accused him of taking more salary than was allotted him. His mail was tampered with for political advantage, and forged letters of 1777 were refurbished and printed as genuine. Particularly cutting was Tom Paine's bitter attack from Paris, which city was the source, Federalists were convinced, of the anti-Washington campaign.[19] Jefferson, too, had lost patience with the exalted role of Washington. The President, he wrote, like Samson had had his head "shorn by the harlot England."[20]

Despite pressures to stay and ride out the storm, Washington disclosed in May, 1796, that he intended definitely to retire.[21] If he had nurtured at all the desire to seek a third term it was killed by the acid criticism to which he had been subjected. The President decided not to seek a third term not only because he sought retirement in his old age but also because he was disgusted with the abuse from political opponents. "The true cause of the general's retiring," declared one of his staunchest supporters, "was

[18] The quotation is from John Adams to Abigail Adams, March 25, 1796, Charles F. Adams, ed., *Letters of John Adams Addressed to His Wife*, 2 vols. (Boston, 1841), II, 214. Republicans shared the same rumors. Madison to Monroe, February 26, 1796, *Letters and Other Writings of James Madison*, 4 vols. (Philadelphia, 1865), II, 83; Madison to Monroe, May 14, 1796, Gaillard Hunt, ed., *The Writings of James Madison*, 9 vols. (New York, 1900–1910), VI, 301 n. For about a year George Hammond, the British minister, had heard rumors that Washington would retire in 1797. Hammond to Grenville, January 5, 1796, Henry Adams Transcripts.

[19] John Quincy Adams to John Adams, August 13, 1796, *Writings of John Quincy Adams*, II, 21; Paine to Washington, July 30, 1796, Philip S. Foner, ed., *The Complete Writings of Thomas Paine* (New York, 1945), II, 691–723. For other details see Nathaniel W. Stephenson and Waldo H. Dunn, *George Washington*, 2 vols. (New York, 1940), II, 409; McMaster, *History of the People of the United States*, II, 249–250.

[20] Jefferson to Philip Mazzei, April 24, 1796. See Howard R. Marraro, "The Four Versions of Jefferson's Letter to Mazzei," *William and Mary Quarterly*, Ser. II, Vol. XXII (January 1942), 24–25; Schachner, *Jefferson*, II, 578–679.

[21] Washington to John Jay, May 8, 1796, *Writings of Washington*, XXXV, 36–37.

. . . the *loss of popularity* which he had experienced, and the further loss which he apprehended from the rupture with France, which he looked upon as inevitable."[22]

Once the decision to retire was made, Washington turned to Hamilton, as usual, for advice. When, he asked, would be the best time for publication of his farewell to the nation? Hamilton, with his eye on the coming election, advised that the public announcement be held off as long as possible. "The proper period now for your declaration," wrote Hamilton, "seems to be *Two months* before the time for the Meeting of the Electors. This will be sufficient. The parties will in the meantime electioneer conditionally, that is to say, *if you decline;* for a serious opposition to you will I think hardly be risked."[23]

Three months before the gathering of electors Washington announced to the nation his intention to retire. Although in 1792 he had planned a valedictory to the nation and James Madison had drafted one, the September, 1796, version, in which Hamilton's hand was prominent, became a piece of partisan politics directed specifically against Republicans and Francophiles who had made Washington's last years miserable. At the time, it was recognized for what it was: a political manifesto, a campaign document. The 1792 version, drawn up before popular passions had been stirred by war in Europe, did not, for example, stress politics nor did it touch on foreign affairs. In the 1796 version partisan politics and foreign affairs were central.[24]

[22] William Cobbett, *Porcupine's Works,* 12 vols. (London, 1801), IV, 444 n. The italics are in the original.

[23] Washington to Hamilton, June 26, 1796, *Writings of Washington,* XXXV, 103–104. See also Washington's letter to Hamilton, May 15, 1796, *ibid.,* 50; Hamilton to Washington, July 5, 1796, *ibid.,* 104 n., and in Henry Cabot Lodge, ed., *The Works of Alexander Hamilton,* 9 vols. (New York, 1885–1886), VIII, 408–409. Republicans recognized that Washington's delayed announcement of retirement was a political scheme emanating from Hamilton. Noble E. Cunningham, "The Jeffersonian Party to 1801: A Study of the Formation of a Party Organization" (Ph.D. dissertation, Duke University, 1952), p. 142.

[24] A copy of Madison's suggestions for the 1792 version of the Farewell Address is incorporated in Washington to Hamilton, May 15, 1796, *Writings of Washington,* XXXV, 51–61; the September 19, 1796, version is on pp. 214–238. For a detailed analysis of the address and its various contributors see Victor H. Paltsits, ed., *Washington's Farewell Address* (New York,

Washington's specific target in foreign affairs, heartily seconded by Hamilton, was the alliance with France. He struck at Adet's partisan activities, at French meddling in American politics (while passing over British meddling), and at the allegedly dangerous implications of the French alliance. Washington told Hamilton that had it not been for the status of "party disputes" and of foreign affairs he would not have considered it necessary to revise his valedictory. He was convinced that a warning to the nation was necessary to combat foreign (French) intrigue "in the internal concerns of our country." It is indeed easy "to foresee," he warned, "that it may involve us in disputes and finally in War, to fulfill political alliances." This was the crux of the matter; Washington believed that the French alliance was no longer an asset to the country.[25]

Washington's valedictory trumpeted the Federalist answer to Republican accusations that the administration had sold the country to the British; it countered the anti-administration furor over the Jay Treaty; it was a justification and defense of his policies. As such it was designed and as such it became the opening blast in the Presidential campaign, contrived to prevent the election of Thomas

---

1935). Usually Washington's advice on foreign policy is taken as the substance of the Farewell. See Albert K. Weinberg, "Washington's 'Great Rule' in Its Historical Evolution," in Eric F. Goldman, ed., *Historiography and Urbanization* (Baltimore, 1941), p. 113. Marshall Smelser, in "George Washington and the Alien and Sedition Acts," *American Historical Review,* LIX (January 1954), 326, and in "The Jacobin Phrenzy: Federalism and Liberty, Equality, and Fraternity," *Review of Politics,* XIII (October 1951), 476, and Joseph Charles, in "Hamilton and Washington: The Origins of the American Party System," *William and Mary Quarterly,* Ser. III, Vol. XII (April 1955), 262, have placed the Farewell in its context as a political document.

[25] Bemis, "Washington's Farewell Address," *American Historical Review,* XXXIX (January 1934), 262–263. Washington understood that basic in any nation's foreign policy was self-interest, and that at this stage of American development it was to the nation's advantage, particularly from his Federalist viewpoint, not to be bound by the French alliance. Sound though this view may be in the perspective of mid-twentieth century, in 1796 it appeared to political opponents to be a partisan political view. To Republicans, loyalty to the alliance and hostility to England appeared the best means of promoting national self-interest. Roland G. Usher, "Washington and Entangling Alliances," *North American Review,* CCIV (July 1916), 29–38; James G. Randall, "George Washington and 'Entangling Alliances'," *South Atlantic Quarterly,* XXX (July 1931), 221–229.

Jefferson. The Farewell laid the basis for Federalist strategy of using Washington's great prestige to appeal to patriotism, as against the evil of foreign machinations, to make "Federalist" and "patriot" synonyms in the minds of the electorate. Under the banner of patriotism the Farewell spearheaded the attack on the opposition party and on French diplomacy.[26]

In the address Washington opened with the announcement that he would not be a candidate for a third term and then stressed the advantages of union and the evils of political parties. Having in mind, undoubtedly, the French Republic, he advised against "a passionate attachment of one Nation for another." Such "sympathy for the favourite nation," he warned, leads to wars and quarrels "without adequate inducement or justification." Then followed the oft-quoted "Great rule of conduct" that with foreign nations we should have "as little *political* connection as possible." While stressing fidelity to "already formed engagements," he announced that "'tis our true policy to steer clear of permanent Alliances with any portion of the foreign world." Washington deplored the growth of political opposition, chastised the public for its attachment to France, and concluded with a defense of his foreign policy, particularly his much criticized policy of neutrality which was based on the Proclamation of April 22, 1793. He called this the "index" to his plan or policy.[27]

Although cloaked in phrases of universal or timeless application, the objectives of the address were practical, immediate, and partisan. Men often attempt to rationalize their partisan political views in pronouncements studded with timeless patriotic appeals; so it was with Washington and Hamilton. The valedictory bore directly on the coming election, on the French alliance, and on the status of Franco-American relations in general.

While expressed cogently and linked forever with Washington's

26 Wilfred E. Binkley, *American Political Parties: Their Natural Histories* (New York, 1943), p. 51. For a stimulating discussion of the Farewell Address which vigorously attacks the persistent myth that Washington's words constituted an inspired charter for a permanent foreign policy based on isolationism, see Louis B. Wright, "The Founding Fathers and 'Splendid Isolation'," *Huntington Library Quarterly*, VI (February 1943), 173–178.

27 The quotations follow the text printed in *Writings of Washington*, XXXV, 214–238.

name, the main ideas and foreign policy principles of the Farewell were not unique with either Hamilton or Washington. They were prevalent Federalist ideas on current foreign policy and politics, and can be found expressed in various ways in the polemical literature of the time. The concept of no entanglement with Europe, for instance, was a common one among Federalists and others. More often than not it was a universalized reaction against a specific annoyance—the French alliance. Stated as noninvolvement with Europe an attack against the alliance had great psychological appeal. In time this specific meaning was lost and only the generalization remained.[28]

As partisans had expected, Washington's words stoked an already hot political situation. "It will serve as a signal," exclaimed New England Federalist Fisher Ames, "like dropping a hat, for the party racers to start."[29] The Farewell was indeed soon under partisan attack. Washington's advice for the future, taunted William Duane, "is but a defence for the past." Referring to the warning against "permanent alliances," he exclaimed, "this extraordinary advice is fully exemplified in your departure from the spirit and principle of the treaty with France, which was declared to be permanent, and exhibits this very infidelity you reprobate in a most striking and lamentable light." The President had not, Duane continued, "adhered to that rigid and neutral justice which you profess—every concession to Britain in prejudice of France was a deviation from neutrality." Much of the evil which Washing-

[28] For a discussion of this point see Weinberg, "Washington's 'Great Rule' in Its Historical Evolution," in Goldman, ed., *Historiography and Urbanization,* 109–138. The foreign policy ideas reflected in the Farewell were not even unique American principles; they can be found in the writings of certain eighteenth-century *philosophes.* See Felix Gilbert, "The 'New Diplomacy' of the Eighteenth Century," *World Politics,* IV (October 1951), 13–14, 28. For earlier expressions of the idea of nonentanglement with Europe, see the discussions relative to the Congressional resolution of June 12, 1783, in Samuel F. Bemis, *The Diplomacy of the American Revolution* (New York, 1935), pp. 166–167, and Alexander DeConde, "William Vans Murray's *Political Sketches:* A Defense of the American Experiment," *Mississippi Valley Historical Review,* XLI (March 1955), 637–638.

[29] Fisher Ames to Oliver Wolcott, September 26, 1796, George Gibbs, ed., *Memoirs of the Administrations of Washington and John Adams, edited from the Papers of Oliver Wolcott, Secretary of the Treasury,* 2 vols. (New York, 1846), I, 384–385.

ton attributed to faction, he claimed, came from the Federalist party. "Your examples of party influence are uniformly drawn from occasions wherein your personal opinions, your pride and passions, have been involved."³⁰ As to Washington's advice to steer clear of permanent alliances, why, critics asked, was it unwise to extend the nation's political engagements? Was not the Jay Treaty a political connection, practically an alliance with England?³¹

To James Madison—who earlier had feared that under Hamilton's influence the address would become a campaign document—the valedictory confirmed his assumptions; it was all politics. Under the complete influence of the British faction, Madison wrote, Washington obviously sought to destroy the French alliance. "It has been known," he continued, "that every channel has been latterly opened that could convey to his mind a rancor against that country [France] and suspicion of all who are thought to sympathize with its revolution and who support the policy of extending our commerce and in general of standing well with it. But it was not easy to suppose his mind wrought up to the tone that could dictate or rather adopt some parts of the performance."³²

30 [William Duane], *A Letter to George Washington, President of the United States: Containing Strictures on His Address of the Seventeenth of September, 1796, Notifying His Relinquishment of the Presidential Office,* by Jasper Dwight of Vermont [pseud.] (Philadelphia, 1796), 31, 40–45. In later years politicians and others referred to Washington's advice as an enduring guide to policy. See, for example, Henry Cabot Lodge's address of February 16, 1916, at Morristown, New Jersey, entitled, "Washington's Policies of Neutrality and National Defence," in his *War Addresses* (Boston, 1917), 117–136.

31 John C. Hamilton, *History of the Republic of the United States of America, as Traced in the Writings of Alexander Hamilton and of His Contemporaries,* 7 vols. (New York, 1857–1864), VI, 536–537. Although Americans viewed the Farewell in many instances as purely a political document, this is not to deny that some men wanted a genuine neutrality which would save the United States "from the exactions and insolence of both" England and France. See, for example, James Kent to Moss Kent, September 19, 1796, William Kent, ed., *Memoirs and Letters of James Kent* (Boston, 1898), p. 174.

32 Madison to Monroe, September 29, 1796, quoted in Irving Brant, *James Madison: Father of the Constitution, 1787–1800* (Indianapolis, 1950), p. 442. As Washington had anticipated, opponents claimed that the motive

Minister Adet believed wrongly that the address would arouse the indignation of pro-French "patriots" and would not have the effect on the people that the British faction hoped it would. He consequently plunged into the campaign to see to it that the address would not have its intended effect.[33] Looking upon John Adams as an enemy of France and a friend of England, he electioneered brazenly for Jefferson. The future conduct of France toward America, he made clear to Americans, would be governed by the election's outcome.[34]

Beginning at the end of October and timing himself carefully, Adet began publication of a series of public manifestoes designed to influence the electorate. He conjured up the prospect of war with France, stressing that Jefferson's election would eliminate such a possibility. With the Quakers of Pennsylvania, Federalists lamented, Adet's strategy of fear worked. Fearing a Federalist-sponsored war against France, Quakers cast their votes for Repub-

---

behind the Farewell was his knowledge that if he ran he would not be re-elected. McMaster, *History of the People of the United States*, II, 290–291. Federalists were convinced that Republicans created French animosity against Washington for political reasons. See Timothy Pickering to John Quincy Adams, December 9, 1796, Pickering Papers (Massachusetts Historical Society, Boston); John Quincy Adams to John Adams, April 4, 1796, *Writings of John Quincy Adams*, I, 484. Young Adams praised the address. He wrote Washington that he hoped "it may serve as the foundation" for future American policy. Letter of February 11, 1797, *ibid.*, II, 119–120. Samuel F. Bemis, "John Quincy Adams and George Washington," Massachusetts Historical Society, *Proceedings*, LXVII (1945), 365–384, maintains that young Adams' ideas influenced Washington and the Farewell.

[33] Adet to Minister of Foreign Relations, October 12, 1796, *Correspondence of French Ministers*, 954; Bemis, "Washington's Farewell Address," *American Historical Review*, XXXIX (January 1934), 263.

[34] Adet to Minister of Foreign Relations, September 24, 1796, *Correspondence of French Ministers*, 947–949. The Directory, of course, approved of Adet's meddling and counted on Jefferson's election. Delacroix wrote to Adet on November 2, 1796, that his despatches confirmed what the Directory had expected would result from its measures directed against Washington's government. Archives des Affaires Étrangères, Correspondance Politique, États-Unis, XLVI, 355–357. The British, too, had a vital stake in the election. Bond to Grenville, May 4, 1796, Henry Adams Transcripts. For a discussion of the 1796 election with emphasis on John Adams and domestic politics see Manning J. Dauer, *The Adams Federalists* (Baltimore, 1953), pp. 92–111.

licans.[35] "French influence never appeared so open and unmasked as at this city [Philadelphia] election," cried William Loughton Smith, Hamilton's Congressional mouthpiece. "French flags, french cockades were displayed by the Jefferson party and there is no doubt that french money was not spared. . . . In short there never was so barefaced and disgraceful an interference of a foreign power in any free country."[36]

Adet's procedure was to write an official note to the Secretary of State and then to send a copy for publication to Benjamin Bache's Philadelphia *Aurora*. In his note of October 27, for example, he protested against American foreign policy and appealed to the people to renew their friendship with France by disavowing the Jay Treaty and honoring the French alliance.[37] A few days later (November 5) the pages of the *Aurora* carried Adet's second manifesto, dubbed by Federalists the "cockade proclamation." In the name of the Directory it called on all Frenchmen in the United States—in the land of an ally—to mount the tricolored cockade, symbol of liberty. Those who did not so give public evidence of their support of the French Republic were to be denied the services of French consuls and the protection of the French flag. Immediately the tricolored cockade blossomed in the streets. Americans as well as Frenchmen wore it as a badge of devotion to the French cause. It became, in short, a symbol of republicanism.[38]

[35] Fisher Ames to Christopher Gore, December 3, 1796, Seth Ames, ed., *Works of Fisher Ames*, 2 vols. (Boston, 1854), II, 206; John Adams to Abigail Adams, December 4, 1796, *Letters of John Adams to Wife*, II, 231; Oliver Wolcott to Oliver Wolcott, Sr., November 27, 1796, *Wolcott Papers*, I, 400–401.

[36] William Loughton Smith to Ralph Izard, November 8, 1796, in Ulrich B. Phillips, ed., "South Carolina Federalist Correspondence, 1789–1797," *American Historical Review*, XIV (July 1909), 785.

[37] Adet to Pickering, October 27, 1796, *American State Papers, Foreign Relations*, 6 vols. (Washington, 1832–1859), I, 576–577. For Pickering's response of November 1, 1796, see *ibid.*, 578; see also Pickering to Rufus King, November 14, 1796, Charles R. King, ed., *The Life and Correspondence of Rufus King*, 6 vols. (New York, 1894–1900), II, 108–109.

[38] The proclamation is in Archives des Affaires Étrangères, Correspondance Politique, États-Unis, XLVI, 352, and is reprinted in Cobbett, *Porcupine's Works*, IV, 154–155. Adet's promulgation of the "cockade proclamation" was under orders from his home government. Adet to Minister of Foreign Relations, November 12, 1796, *Correspondence of French Ministers*, 967.

Ten days later Adet followed the "cockade proclamation" with his last and most florid note, which he again sent simultaneously to the Secretary of State and to Bache's *Aurora*. In it he announced that as a result of the Jay Treaty his function as minister had been suspended and that he was returning to France.[39] Adet had timed his announcement so that it might have a maximum political influence, particularly on the electors who were soon to meet to choose Washington's successor.[40]

Adet's notes and Secretary of State Timothy Pickering's replies were used as campaign ammunition by both sides. Federalists, of course, were furious. They denounced Adet's pronouncements for what they were—brazen electioneering maneuvers by a foreign agent. John Adams, against whom the last note was directed, found "it an instrument well calculated to reconcile me to private life. It will purify me from all envy of Mr. Jefferson, or Mr. Pinckney, or Mr. Burr, or Mr. any body who may be chosen President or Vice President."[41] William Cobbett, violent Francophobe and anti-Jeffersonian, published Adet's note under the title of *The Gros Mousqueton Diplomatique; or Diplomatic Blunderbuss*. He ran with it, of course, an adverse commentary.[42]

Friends of France, according to Adet, were delighted. Republican leaders were willing and even eager to use the issue of the French alliance to gain votes. But, contrary to Adet's opinion, they were not happy with the French minister's personal interference. Madison, for instance, maintained that Adet's note announcing his return to France worked "all the evil with which it is pregnant." Its indiscretions, he added, gave comfort to Federalists who had the "impudence" to point out that it was "an electioneering maneuver," and that "the French government had been led into it by the opponents of the British treaty."[43]

[39] Adet to Pickering, November 15, 1796, *American State Papers, Foreign Relations*, I, 579–583.

[40] Adet to Minister of Foreign Relations, [November 1796], *Correspondence of French Ministers*, 969–970.

[41] Adams to Abigail Adams, November 27, 1796, *Letters of John Adams to Wife*, II, 229.

[42] Reprinted in Cobbett, *Porcupine's Works*, IV, 137–206.

[43] Madison to Jefferson, December 5, 1796, Madison Papers, quoted in Brant, *Madison: Father of the Constitution*, 445. See also Fisher Ames to Christopher Gore, December 13, 1796, cited in Harry M. Tinkcom, *The*

Adet did not realize that his activities worked mainly to injure the cause he sought to aid. French popularity, according to competent observers, decreased as a result.[44] Disgusted by Adet's conduct, Washington drew even closer to the British. One piqued New England writer went so far as to declare that since Adet's electioneering on behalf of Jefferson "there is not an elector on this side of the Delaware that would not be sooner shot than vote for him." And Philip Key maintained that Adet's meddling "irretrievably diminished that good will felt for his Government & the people of France by most people here."[45]

Unaware of any adverse reaction, Adet and his intimates believed that his actions and the Directory's measures would influence the Presidential electors decisively in favor of Jefferson.[46]

Republicans and Federalists in Pennsylvania, 1790–1801: A Study of National Stimulus and Local Response (Harrisburg, 1950), p. 173.

[44] Liston to Grenville, November 15 and December 9, 1796, Henry Adams Transcripts. Liston complained that Republicans charged that British gold was being used in the election and confessed "that a persevering repetition of such accusations has at last the effect of procuring them a degree of credit." A prominent Republican Unitarian clergyman was surprised at how people cursed the French at this time. *The Diary of William Bentley,* 4 vols. (Salem, Mass., 1905–1914), II, 207 (entry of November 8, 1796).

[45] For the observation on Washington, Henrietta Liston to James Jackson, 1796, Perkins, ed., "Diplomat's Wife in Philadelphia," *William and Mary Quarterly,* Ser. III, Vol. XI (October 1954), 605. The quotations are from "The People," Hartford, Connecticut, *Courant,* reprinted in *New Hampshire and Vermont Journal: or, The Farmer's Weekly Museum* (Walpole, N.H.), November 22, 1796, and Philip Key to James McHenry, November 28, 1796, in Bernard C. Steiner, *The Life and Correspondence of James McHenry* (Cleveland, 1907), p. 202. Congressman Robert Goodloe Harper wrote to his constituents that if there had been no other objection to Jefferson than French exertions on his behalf it would have been sufficient to oppose him. Letter of January 5, 1797, Elizabeth Donnan, ed., *Papers of James A. Bayard, 1796–1815,* American Historical Association, *Annual Report,* 1913, II (Washington, D.C., 1915), 25. Later, certain French officials came to believe that the activity of Adet coupled with that of his predecessors plus the seeming duplicity of the French government brought victory to the Federalists in 1796. Even Jefferson, it was pointed out, came to believe that the French sought to destroy the American Constitution. See James A. James, "French Opinion as a Factor in Preventing War between France and the United States, 1795–1800," *American Historical Review,* XXX (October 1924), 46.

[46] Adet to Minister of Foreign Relations, [November 22, 1792], *Correspondence of French Ministers,* 972.

What Adet and the Directory had not taken into account was that invariably when a foreign diplomat takes sides openly in the domestic politics of the nation to which he is accredited he makes the party leader he seeks to aid appear to be the pawn of a foreign government. Such a charge, whether or not true, gives the opposition the opportunity of patriotically denouncing foreign interference and of posing as the defender of national honor against foreign subversives. So it was with the Adet case. His activities seemed to confirm the very warnings of foreign interference that were stressed in Washington's Farewell Address.

Sensing the opportunity, Federalists attacked the French alliance, denounced French domestic interference, and pitted the patriotism of Washington and Adams against the Jacobin-tainted Republican campaign. Voters were importuned to beware of foreign influence; to "decide between the address of the President and the [French]"; to follow Washington's counsel. Adet and the Directory, they were told, wished to draw the nation into war and to sever the Western from the Atlantic states. No doubt clouded the Federalist mind; the Union was in danger.[47]

Federalist warnings, persistent though they were, did not stop French interference in American politics; nor did the interference end with the choosing of electors in November. Few of the electors were pledged to a specific candidate, so the campaign continued with increasing tumult until December 7, when the electors cast their ballots. Adet, having suspended his diplomatic functions, remained in Philadelphia to continue his anti-administration campaign. He and the Republicans hammered at similar themes, stressing that if Adams were elected the errors of the Washington administration would be continued, since Adams was committed to Washington's tragic policies; and that such policies would lead to war with France.

Candidate Adams, on the other hand, believed that only time would tell whether "the French Directory have only been drawn in to favor the election of a favorite, or whether in their trances and

----

[47] "Americanus," in *Gazette of the United States* (Philadelphia), reprinted in New York *Herald,* December 3, 1796. William Vans Murray, commenting on a letter from James McHenry, November 19, 1796, Murray Papers, Library of Congress.

delirium of victory they think to terrify America, or whether in their sallies they may not venture on hostilities." He advised that under the circumstances "Americans must be cool and steady if they can."[48]

But Americans were not cool and steady. In newspapers and elsewhere they debated the French alliance, the mounting crisis with France, and the possibility of war.[49] Hamilton, as was his practice in time of crisis, wrote articles for the press to reply to Adet's manifestoes, to defend administration foreign policy, and to attack the French alliance.[50] Another prominent Federalist, Noah Webster, editor of the *American Minerva,* wrote a series of articles in which he also attacked the alliance. His articles were reprinted and widely circulated. In the Federalist press, in fact, attacks on the alliance now became common. Webster in his articles stressed that France had equated the term ally with that of vassal; "an *open* enemy," he declared, "is less dangerous than an *insidious friend.*" Although the British, too, had injured the United States, Webster maintained that the American connection with Great Britain was stronger than the French alliance because "our connection with her is solely *an alliance of interest.* This is the true basis of all

[48] John Adams to Abigail Adams, December 4, 1796, *Letters of John Adams to Wife,* II, 231. A basic charge directed against Adams was that he was too closely connected to the British party. "Cassius," in Philadelphia *New World,* October 28, 1796, cited in Woodbury, "Public Opinion in Philadelphia," *Smith College Studies in History,* V, 126.

[49] William Willcocks, "To the People of the United States," *The Minerva,* reprinted in New York *Herald,* December 28, 1796, January 18, 1797, maintained that France from the beginning had sought to involve the United States in war. Some Federalists saw in the difficulties with France the virtue that the nation might be cured "of extraneous attachments," that the embarrassing French alliance would be destroyed. Chauncey Goodrich to Oliver Wolcott, *Wolcott Papers,* I, 417. Republican Congressman from Virginia, John Clopton, warned his constituents against Federalist "efforts to foment a prejudice in the public mind against the French nation." Clopton to Isaac Youngblood, January 24, 1797, John Clopton Papers (Duke University Library).

[50] Under the signature "Americanus," Hamilton on December 6, 1796, published "The Answer," his reply to Adet, *Works of Hamilton,* V, 348–362. Under the signature "Americus," he published a series of articles, beginning January 27, 1797, entitled "The Warning," in which he warned against French influence and the alliance. *Ibid.,* 363–392.

national connections. We are therefore in no danger from Great Britain."[51]

In the first week of February, 1797, the American people finally learned the results of the election. Although the Federalist victory was narrow, it was enough to sink French hopes for a revived alliance. By "three votes" John Adams, who wisely had perceived that he was "not enough of an Englishman, nor little enough of a Frenchman, for some people," was elected second President of the United States.[52]

Jefferson, however, captured the second highest electoral total and became Vice-President.[53] America's first contested Presidential election therefore, although a clear-cut Federalist victory, gave some comfort to Republicans and struck fear into Federalist ranks. But Republican strength had not been sufficient to overturn the government and hence to reverse the course of Franco-American relations. To staunch Hamiltonian Federalists this aspect of the election was indeed sweet. In various election post-mortems, in New England in particular, such Federalists rejoiced that the "French party is fallen," and that the French alliance was at last valueless. Even Adet, one of them pointed out, "avows, and it is rather a tough point to avow, that our treaty is disadvantageous." Now he might inform the Directory that it has "been deceived by the revolutionary Americans in Paris; that we (at least the

[51] Webster's articles were entitled: "To the People of the United States," and ran from December, 1786, through February, 1797. Harry R. Warfel, *Noah Webster: Schoolmaster to America* (New York, 1936), p. 229. The quotations are from *The Minerva*, reprinted in New York *Herald*, December 17 and 28, 1796.

[52] John Adams to Abigail Adams, December 12, 1796, Charles F. Adams, *The Life of John Adams*, 2 vols., rev. ed. (Philadelphia, 1891), II, 208. The electors' ballots had been announced on the first Wednesday in January but were not counted formally until the first Wednesday in February.

[53] Adet realized before the meeting of electors that Jefferson, "in spite of the intrigues against him," would become Vice-President. Although he rejoiced in Jefferson's election he understood that the Virginian was drawn to France primarily because he feared England. Even Jefferson, declared the French minister, "is an American, and as such, he cannot sincerely be our friend. An American is the born enemy of all the peoples of Europe." Adet to Minister of Foreign Relations, December 31, 1796, *Correspondence of French Ministers*, 982–983.

Yankees) have not been traitors, and have ceased to be dupes."[54]

With the Federalist victory, narrow though it was, the Farewell Address had done its work. The French alliance which had been drawn to last "forever" and which had been the core of American foreign policy when Washington launched the federal government was practically dead as he prepared to leave office. Despite French and Republican efforts to the contrary, and in large part because of the impact of Washington's Farewell, the basic foreign policy orientation of the United States remained pro-British.[55] The Farewell Address now belonged to posterity and posterity has given it meanings to fit its own problems.

[54] *New Hampshire and Vermont Journal,* March 7, 1797.

[55] The son of the new President caught a glimpse of the Farewell in the future of American foreign policy. The failure of the French in their attacks against Washington in the election of 1796, he believed, should reveal to them the "temper" of the American people. "Can France possibly believe," he asked rhetorically, "that Mr. Jefferson, or any other man, would dare to start away from that system of administration which Washington has thus sanctioned, not only by his example, but by his retirement?" John Quincy Adams to Joseph Pitcairn, January 31, 1797, *Writings of John Quincy Adams,* II, 95–96.

DANIEL J. BOORSTIN

✪

The Mythologizing of George Washington

Never did a more incongruous pair than Davy Crockett and
George Washington live together in a national Valhalla. Idolized
by the new nation, the legendary Washington was a kind of anti-
Crockett. The bluster, the crudity, the vulgarity, the monstrous
boosterism of Crockett and his fellow supermen of the subliterature were all qualities which Washington most conspicuously
lacked. At the same time, the dignity, the reverence for God, the
sober judgment, the sense of destiny, and the vision of the distant
future, for all of which Washington was proverbial, were unknown
to the Ring-tailed Roarers of the West. Yet both Crockett and
Washington were popular heroes, and both emerged into legendary
fame during the first half of the nineteenth century.

The legendary Washington, no less than the legendary Crockett,
was a product of the anachronism and abridgment of American
history. Crockett and his kind, however, had first been spawned by
spontaneous generation. They began as by-products of American
life rather than as artifices of an American literature. The legends
of the comic supermen, which had originated in oral anecdote,
never entirely lost the sound and accent of the raconteur's voice,
even when frozen into their crude literary form.

There were elements of spontaneity, of course, in the Washington legend, too, but it was, for the most part, a self-conscious

Reprinted from *The Americans: The National Experience,* by Daniel
J. Boorstin. © Copyright 1965 by Daniel J. Boorstin. Reprinted by permission of Random House, Inc.

product. The Crockett and Fink legends caught the spoken echoes of campfire and saloon, captured and diffused them in crudely printed almanacs, in sporting magazines, and anonymous wheezes. The Demigod Washington was to be a cumbersome figure of literary contrivance. The contrast between the Crockett subliterature (flimsy, ephemeral scraps which seldom could be dignified as "books") and the Washington literature (heavy, elegantly printed works, copiously illustrated by maps and engravings, the proud personal product of eminent statesmen and famous writers) was as striking as that between the legendary characters of the two men themselves.

Although both were peculiar products of America, only Washington became part of the national protocol. How this happened showed how different was the Washington legend from its superficially similar counterparts in the Old World. There, names like Romulus and Remus, Aeneas, Charlemagne, Boadicea, King Alfred, St. Louis, St. Joan, and the Cid, glorified the founding of their nations. Some were more mythical than others, but when the modern nations of Italy, France, England, and Spain became self-conscious, the challenge to national historians was to give these hazy figures some historical reality, to make them more plausible by clothing them in historical fact. These nations, which had attained their nationality gradually over the centuries, already possessed legendary founding heroes when they became nations. The challenging task was to historicize them.

Not so in the United States. Here a new nation sprang into being almost before it had time to acquire a history. At the outbreak of the Civil War, there were men alive who could remember the death of Washington; he was still an emphatically real historical person. The national problem was not how to make Washington historical; quite the contrary: how could he be made into a myth? The very brevity of American history made special demands, but Americans of the age proved equal to them.

A measure of their success is how much has been popularly forgotten of the true story of George Washington, especially of his later years. Few Americans remember that Washington had more than his share of enemies, that for all his life he was a controversial figure, and that during his Presidency he was personally libelled with a venom aimed at few of his successors. We cannot understand how powerful were the marmorealizing forces of the early nineteenth century unless we recall the acrimony, the bitter partisanship, the malicious rumor, and the unscrupulous lies which stormed about Washington during the last decade or so of his life. He had already become the archvillain for all those who opposed the Federalists, including Jefferson and his followers, but the climax of Washington's unpopularity came with Jay's treaty. This had been negotiated with Britain by John Jay, Washington's emissary, to resolve differences left unsettled at the end of the Revolution, or which had newly arisen since then. When the terms of the treaty were published in March, 1795, furor shook the country. Southerners objected to its provisions for payment of pre-Revolutionary debts (in large part owed by Virginians); New Englanders objected to its restrictions on United States shipping to the West Indies. Attacks on Washington, who was held responsible for the treaty, were collected by Benjamin Bache, Franklin's grandson, who printed many of them in his *Aurora* in Philadelphia, to be widely copied by such Republican papers as the New York *Argus,* the Boston *Chronicle,* the Kentucky *Herald,* and the Carolina *Gazette.*

"The American People, Sir," the *Aurora* warned, "will look to death the man who assumes the character of a usurper." "If ever a nation was debauched by a man," it added in December, 1796, "the American nation has been by Washington." "If ever there was a period for rejoicing, it is this moment," Bache announced on March 6, 1797, when Washington left office to be replaced by John Adams. "Every heart, in unison with the freedom and happiness of the people, ought to beat high in exultation, that the name of Washington ceases from this day to give a currency to political iniquity and to legalize corruption." Washington was accused of every kind of crime, including stealing from the public treasury. When the circulation of some of these papers fell off, Jefferson himself urged Republicans to support them by soliciting subscriptions; he called them the last bulwark of free speech and representative institutions. Federalists aimed their notorious Alien and Sedition Acts of 1798 (many of the leading Antifederalist writers were European refugees) at these publications. Then

Washington himself, smarting under the venomous attacks, approved the prosecutions which, on dubious evidence, he called necessary to prevent "a disunion of the States."

When Washington died on December 14, 1799, he was anything but a noncontroversial figure. Not only his judgment but his integrity had been publicly impugned. He had been taunted into condoning means of dubious constitutionality to punish his enemies and to silence their presses. But he was destined to a stature in death which he had never attained in life.

What is most remarkable is not that Washington eventually became a demigod, Father of his Country, but that the transfiguration happened so quickly. There is no better evidence of the desperate need Americans felt for a dignified and worshipful national hero than their passionate haste in elevating Washington to sainthood. Never was there a better example of the special potency of the Will to Believe in this New World. A deification which in European history might have required centuries, was accomplished here in decades.

Between Washington's death in the last month of the last year of the eighteenth century and the outbreak of the Civil War, his worship had acquired a full cultic apparatus. To this end many people had collaborated, but the cult could not have grown so quickly or so vigorously without the peculiar American needs and vacuums.

The Sacred Life. It was appropriate to the cultic character of the Washington legend that its first high priest and one of its leading inventors was a charlatan—an amiable and energetic charlatan, but nevertheless a charlatan. And it was appropriate to the American character of the cult that this high priest should have been a salesman, in fact a supersalesman who had thoroughly mixed religion with salesmanship. The notorious Mason Locke Weems, better known as "Parson Weems," even before Washington's death had been collecting biographical materials. Born in Maryland in 1759, the youngest of nineteen children, he was in Britain studying medicine at the time of the Revolution. In 1784 he became one of the first Americans after the war fully ordained by the Archbishop of Canterbury for the Anglican ministry in the United States. After a brief and desultory clerical career, he turned to bookselling, for which he had both passion and genius. Although he had no permanent pulpit after about 1793, he continued to exercise his ministry with gusto through the printing, writing, and especially the selling of edifying books. Weems, during the last thirty years of his life (1795–1825), traveled the country between New York and Georgia as an itinerant salesman of salvation and printed matter. Besides selling his own books, he was agent for Matthew Carey and C. P. Wayne of Philadelphia. Traveling about in a wagon which carried his wares, he was ready, depending on the circumstances, to deliver a sermon or a political oration, or play his fiddle. After he had gathered his crowd and warmed them to good humor, he would sell the books from his wagon—patent medicine for all the ills of the spirit. "Part Whitefield, part Villon," Albert J. Beveridge accurately characterized him, "a delightful mingling of evangelist and vagabond, lecturer and politician, writer and musician."

Wandering over the countryside, he became a one-man market-research enterprise. Never was a cult devised for an audience better pretested, nor a national hero more calculatedly concocted to satisfy the demand. As early as 1797, Weems pointed out to Carey a rich untapped market. "Experience has taught me that small, i.e. quarter of dollar books, on subjects calculated to *strike* the Popular Curiosity, printed in very large numbers and properly *distributed,* w^d prove an immense revenue to the prudent and industrious Undertakers. If you coud get the life of Gen^1. Wayne, Putnam, Green &c., Men whose courage and Abilities, whose patriotism and Exploits have won the love and admiration of the American people, printed in small volumes and with very interesting frontespieces, you w^d, without doubt, sell an immense number of them. People here think nothing of giving ⅙ (their quarter of a dollar) for anything that pleases their fancy. Let us give them something worth their money." Weems turned to the work himself, and on June 24, 1799, he wrote Carey from his home at Dumfries, Virginia, where he was to raise a family of ten children.

I have nearly ready for the press a piece christen^d, or to be christen^d, "The Beauties of Washington." tis artfully drawn up, enliven^d with anecdotes, and in my humble opinion, marvellously fitted, "ad captandum—gustum populi Americani! ! ! !["] What say you to printing it for me and ordering a copper plate Frontispiece of that HERO, something in this way. George Washington Esqr. The Guardian Angel of his Country "Go thy way old George. Die when thou wilt we shall never look upon thy like again" M. Carey inver.&^{c}.

NB. The whole will make but four sheets and will sell like flax seed at quarter of a dollar. I cou'd make you a world of pence and popularity by it.

In October he again wrote Carey that he now had "on the Anvil and pretty well hammer'd out a piece that will sell to admiration.

THE TRUE PATRIOT

or

BEAUTIES OF WASHINGTON

Abundantly Biographical & Anecdotical

Curious & Marvellous"

Weems, therefore, was ready and waiting with his commodity when the great demand was created by the death of Washington. Less than a month after Washington's death, Weems effervesced to Carey:

I've something to whisper in your lug. Washington, you know is gone! Millions are gaping to read something about him. I am very nearly prim^d and cock^d for 'em. 6 months ago I set myself to collect anecdotes of him. You know I live conveniently for that work. My plan! I give his history, sufficiently minute—I accompany him from his start, thro the French & Indian & British or Revolutionary wars, to the Presidents chair, to the throne in the hearts of 5,000,000 of People. I then go on to show that his unparrelled rise & elevation were owing to his Great Virtues. 1 His Veneration for the Diety, or Religious Principles. 2 His Patriotism. 3^d his Magninmity. 4 his Industry. 5 his Temperance & Sobriety. 6 his Justice, &^{c}. &^{c}. Thus I hold up his great Virtues (as Govr McKean prays) to the imitation of Our Youth. All this I have lin^d and enliven^d with *Anecdotes apropos interesting* and *Entertaining*. I have read it to several Gentlemen whom I thought judges, such as Presbyterian Clergymen, Classical Scholars &^{c}. &^{c}. and they all commend it much. it will not exceed 3 royal sheets on long primer. We may sell it with great rapidity for 25 or 37 Cents and it w^d not cost 10. I read a part of it to one of my Parishioners, a first rate lady, and she wish^d I w^d print it, promising to take one for each of her children (a bakers dozen). I am thinking you coud vend it admirably: as it will be the first. I can send it on, half of it, *immediately*.

Carey was too slow for Weems, who within three weeks had found other means. Four printings of this eighty-page booklet arranged by Weems himself appeared in 1800, but Weems still kept after Carey "to make this thing profitable and beneficial—Everybody will read about Washington. . . . I know you desire to do Good . . . We may preach through the Example and Virtues of Washington—Adams & Jefferson both will approve of our little piece.— I am in expectation of good things shortly for you. You know what I mean—Money." This happy marriage of philanthropy and avarice produced Weems's life of Washington, destined to be perhaps the most widely read, most influential book ever written about American history.

Soon after Washington's death, his nephew Bushrod Washington persuaded Chief Justice John Marshall to undertake the official life. This enterprise too was to have a shaping influence on American thinking about American history, not through its success but through its resounding failure. Weems had been employed by the publisher C. P. Wayne of Philadelphia to sell subscriptions to Marshall's monumental five volumes at $3 a volume. When the first instalment of Marshall's work finally reached subscribers in 1804, it quickly established the book as the publishing catastrophe of the age. The whole volume one, called "Introduction," was consumed by a pedantic account of colonial history beginning with Columbus; toward the end were two casual mentions of Washington. Dull, laborious, rambling, and secondhand, the work lumbered into its third, fourth, and fifth volumes. According to John Adams, Marshall's life was not really a book at all, but rather "a Mausoleum, 100 feet square at the base and 200 feet high."

Weems, seeing a public hungry for a readable story about the National Hero, was frantic with disgust and disappointment. He repeatedly begged Carey to dispose of the Marshall venture and provide something more salable. Even before the Marshall fiasco was fully disposed of, Weems returned in earnest to do the job himself. Profiting from Marshall's mistakes, in 1806 he revised his little pamphlet to give it everything Marshall's work had lacked. Though still only eighty pages, it now had more form, more facts (invented when necessary), and contained a number of appealing new anecdotes. After Marshall's final volume appeared in 1807 and Weems was disburdened of the whole profitless business, he turned his spare energies to enlarging his pamphlet to a book of some two hundred pages ("6th edition," 1808). On the title page Weems styled himself "Formerly Rector of Mount-Vernon Parish," which added authenticity for all readers who did not know that such a parish never existed. After 1808 only minor changes and additions were made.

In substantially this form, Weems's *Life of George Washington: With Curious Anecdotes, Equally Honourable to Himself and Exemplary to His Young Countrymen* went through twenty more "editions" before Weems's death in 1825. Within a decade of its first publication, this work probably sold well over 50,000 copies (Marshall's had sold closer to 5,000!), making it a best seller for its time. Still Weems, who had made the mistake of selling the copyright of his book to Carey in 1808 for a mere $1,000, failed to persuade Carey to let him enlarge the work further or to issue an "elegant edition" at three or four dollars. "You have a great deal of money lying in the bones of old George," Weems wrote Carey in January, 1809, on a theme he repeated again and again, "if you will but exert yourself to extract it."

While Weems aimed to produce a book primarily for "the admiring eyes of our *children*," his book should be classified neither as juvenile nor as nonfiction but as booster literature. Others applied their booster enthusiasm and booster optimism to the future; he applied his to the past. While others were boosters for this or that part of the country, he was one of the first national boosters. Weems, like other boosters, asserted facts for which there was little or no foundation, but we must not forget that, in the contagious vagueness of American life, distinctions which elsewhere seemed sharp—between fact and wish, between history and prophecy—were hard to draw. Thus Weems began his chapter on the birth and education of his Hero:

> To this day numbers of good Christians can hardly find faith to believe that Washington was, bona fide, a *Virginian! "What! a buckskin!"* say they with a smile, *"George Washington a buckskin! pshaw! impossible! he was certainly an European: So great a man could never have been born in America."*
>
> *So great a man could never have been born in America!*—Why

that's the very *prince of reasons* why he should have been born here! Nature, we know, is fond of *harmonies; and paria paribus,* that is, *great things to great,* is the rule she delights to work by. Where, for example, do we look for the *whale* "the biggest born of nature?" not, I trow, in a *millpond,* but in the main ocean; *"there go the great ships,"* and there are the spoutings of whales amidst their boiling foam.

By the same rule, where shall we look for Washington, the greatest among men, but in *America?* That greatest Continent, which, rising from beneath the frozen pole, stretches far and wide to the south, running almost *"whole the length of this vast terrene,"* and sustaining on her ample sides the roaring shock of half the watery globe. And equal to its size, is the furniture of this vast continent, where the Almighty has reared his cloud-capt mountains, and spread his sea-like lakes, and poured his mighty rivers, and hurled down his thundering cataracts in a style of the *sublime,* so far superior to any thing of the kind in the other continents, that we may fairly conclude that great men and great deeds are designed for America.

This seems to be the verdict of honest analogy; and accordingly we find America the honoured cradle of Washington, who was born on Pope's creek, in Westmoreland county, Virginia, the 22nd of February, 1732.

As the work begins, so it ends. The three final chapters, on the character of Washington, describe his religion, his benevolence, his industry, and his patriotism—all as the natural response of the greatest of all men to the greatest of all challenges, America.

George's father, we are told by Weems, took every chance to implant virtues in his son. When the boy was only five, his father and a cousin took him walking one fall in the apple-orchard. "Now, George, said his father, look here, my son! don't you remember when this good cousin of yours brought you that fine large apple last spring, how hardly I could prevail on you to divide with your brothers and sisters; though I promised you that if you would but do it, God Almighty would give you plenty of apples this fall. Poor George could not say a word; but hanging down his head, looked quite confused, while with his little naked toes he scratched in the soft ground. . . . George looked in silence on the wide wilderness of fruit; he marked the busy humming bees, and heard the gay notes of birds, then lifting his eyes filled with shining moisture, to his father, he softly said, 'Well, Pa, oi this time; see if I ever be so stingy any more.' "

And, of course, there is the famous story of the ch

"I can't tell a lie, Pa; you know I can't tell a lie. my hatchet."—Run to my arms, you dearest boy, in transports, run to my arms; glad am I, George, that you killeu ..., tree; for you have paid me for it a thousand fold. Such an act of heroism in my son, is more worth than a thousand trees, though blossomed with silver, and their fruits of purest gold.

And then the story of how George's schoolmates wept when George left them. How George hated to fight, yet performed feats of strength. How, after Braddock's defeat, a "famous Indian warrior" swore that "Washington was not born to be killed by a bullet! For, I had seventeen fair fires at him with my rifle, and after all could not bring him to the ground." How, during her pregnancy with George, his mother dreamed a dream which foretold his greatness and the history of the Revolution.

The great gap in our documentary knowledge of Washington, especially in his early life, Weems filled with materials borrowed, stolen, or invented, describing events which, from their very nature, were virtually impossible to disprove. Who could confidently assert that the cherry tree episode had *not* occurred in the privacy of the elder Washington's household? Or that Mary Washington had *not* experienced such and such a dream? Perhaps, as Marcus Cunliffe ventures, these apocryphal anecdotes survived precisely because they did express, however crudely and inexactly, some sort of general truth about the Hero. Certainly what Weems said was what many people wanted to believe. And by these tales Weems sold his book, and through his book he sold another commodity, the Hero. Was this or wasn't this a hoax? Who could say?

Weems was only one of scores of acolytes of the Washington cult. Before Washington's death, although there were brief biographical sketches in magazines or in general works like Jedidiah Morse's *American Geography* (1789), there seems to have appeared no book-length treatment of his life. Soon after Weems's revised version of 1806, several other more or less readable lives ppeared, but most of these were serious works, not directed to the juvenile audience or the unliterary public. For some years Weems had a virtual monopoly of the popular market. Then in 1829 appeared Anna C. Reed's life, written for the Sunday schools (a newly flourishing American institution), and in the centennial year, 1832, Samuel G. Goodrich, whose literary factory produced over a hundred children's books under the pseudonym of "Peter Parley," offered a successful juvenile biography. The life of the Hero was being celebrated in many other forms—in long poems, plays, and even in *A Life of George Washington in Latin Prose* (1835) by an Ohio schoolteacher.

Meanwhile, the story of Washington's life was being retold in heavy tomes by scholars and men of letters. Perhaps there is no better evidence of the piety which the name of Washington excited than that, in the centennial year of Washington's birth (1832), there appeared a revised edition of Marshall's *Life,* only slightly condensed. It was followed by a one-volume school edition (1838). Others too turned out works that were less readable than monumental. Of these ambitious tomes, the least heavy was the two-volume life (1835) by the novelist James Kirke Paulding. Then came Jared Sparks's pious and ponderous life, which appeared as volume one (1837) of his edition of the *Writings.* The best of these works was Washington Irving's five volumes, but he too was afflicted by the contagion of dullness. Judging from the sets of Irving which survive into the twentieth century with virgin pages, these volumes also were more widely bought than read. But Washington's posthumous life had only begun.

The Sacred Writings. The Washington cult, it is important to note, flourished long before there existed any printed collection of the writings of the Hero. Nowhere could the scholar, much less the citizen, read the authentic words of Washington himself. The more widely Washington was adored, the more superfluous—and in many ways the less interesting—his own writings became.

In this cultic spirit, a third of a century after his death, the first edition of Washington's writings appeared. At an early age Jared Sparks (1789–1866) had begun to think about a collection of the Hero's writings. Sparks was a New Englander of humble birth who, after working his way through Harvard College, had by his social grace established himself among the Boston elite. He studied divinity and then filled a Unitarian pulpit in Baltimore for a few years. Returning to Boston, he took over the *North American Review* which he built into a leading critical journal of national circulation. He was a man of many talents, with a sense for the tastes and book-buying interests of the intellectual community. It was the edition of Washington's writings that established Sparks's national reputation and led to his appointment in 1838 as McLean Professor of Ancient and Modern History at Harvard—the first professor of history (other than ecclesiastical) in a university in the United States—and then to his presidency of Harvard (1849–1853).

Securing permission of the Washington family to publish the writings of their ancestor was no easy matter. George Washington's literary executor and the inheritor of Mount Vernon was his nephew, the rigid and unimaginative Bushrod Washington (Associate Justice of the Supreme Court, 1798–1829), who, in refusing Sparks (March 13, 1826) explained that he and Marshall were planning three volumes of selected letters from the Revolutionary period, to be followed later by a pre-Revolutionary selection. Six months later, Sparks, undiscouraged, tried again to persuade Bushrod Washington to give him access to the papers, adding that he would go ahead anyway, gathering copies of the papers wherever he could find them, and that, since the papers would eventually reach the public eye, Bushrod might better choose to supervise the work. Sparks would allow him to withhold whatever he thought unsuitable for publication. "If the entire works of Washington were presented to the public in a form suited to the dignity of the subject, a national interest and a national feeling would be excited, and a wide and honorable patronage might be expected." Sparks then added an argument more substantial: an offer to give Bushrod Washington half the profits of publication. In January, 1827, (after urging by John Marshall, who had been prodded by Sparks) Bushrod Washington accepted the proposal. Under the final terms, half the profits were to go to Sparks, the other half to be equally divided between Bushrod Washington and John Marshall.

Over the next several years Sparks collected manuscripts, copied official documents, and showed an energy in gathering materials which was unprecedented in American historical scholarship. He soon decided that the number of volumes should be determined by "the probable demand in the market, as well as the nature of the work." Sparks's twelve-volume edition (1834–1837) included eleven volumes of selected writings and Sparks's biography of Washington (1837). Despite the large editorial expenses ($15,357.37) which had to be deducted, the net returns were sizable. In 1837, when Sparks sent the first share of profits to the heirs of Bushrod Washington and John Marshall, the total sum to be divided was $15,384.63. For twenty years Sparks was sending additional shares of the profits to the Washington and the Marshall families.

Spark's *Life and Writings of George Washington* was greeted by loud and indiscriminate applause. Surviving members of the Washington family found it perfect and sent Sparks a cedar cane cut from the tree which shaded Washington's tomb. Sixty-three pages by Edward Everett in the *North American Review* exhausted superlatives: "Not a single trait of indiscretion is disclosed in his work." George Bancroft, still near the beginning of his career, found the work "beyond my praise for its calmness, accuracy, and intense interest of authenticity."

"You are a lucky fellow," Bancroft had written Sparks as early as 1827, "selected by a favoring Providence to conduct a good ship into the haven of immortality, and to have your own name recorded as the careful pilot." And Sparks was less the historian than the acolyte, less the discoverer of the true than the adorer of the good. Appropriately, the founder of historical scholarship in the United States was a high priest of the Washington cult. Sparks again and again went through the motions of strenuous historical research. Before his publication of the diplomatic correspondence of the Revolution (12 vols., 1829–1830), of the writings of Washington, and of Franklin (10 vols., 1836–1840), no substantial printed sources were available on the crucial era of American history. But for the study of modern history in American universities this was, as Samuel Eliot Morison observes, a "false dawn." Sparks, the first professor of his subject, left no disciples, and it would be nearly a half-century before American history would begin to flourish as a profession. One reason must be found in how

Sparks and his contemporaries conceived the subject. The vice of Sparks's historical work was not that it was conceived in sin, but rather that it was conceived in virtue.

Sparks followed the style of his day. His biography, which prefaced the writings, was pious, pallid, and reverential. The Hero was of commanding figure, symmetrical features, indomitable courage, pure character, and perfect judgment; "his moral qualities were in perfect harmony with those of his intellect." Sparks's appendix, "Religious Opinions and Habits," was an ingenious whitewash in which Washington's failure to attend communion became an argument for his religiosity. "He may have believed it improper publicly to partake of an ordinance, which, according to the ideas he entertained of it, imposed severe restrictions on outward conduct, and a sacred pledge to perform duties impracticable in his situation. Such an impression would be natural to a serious mind . . . a man of a delicate conscience and habitual reverence for religion." There was no passage in Washington's writings, Sparks noted, which expressed doubt of the Christian revelation. In a man of such Christian demeanor, what more conclusive proof that he was a true and tolerant Christian?

The writings were edited in a similar spirit. In selecting a mere eleven from what might have filled four times that many volumes, Sparks had ample freedom to ennoble his subject. While Sparks did not actually add passages of his own, he omitted passages at will without warning the reader and he improved the language when it seemed unworthy of the Hero. He explained all this in his introduction: "It would be an act of unpardonable injustice to any author, after his death, to bring forth compositions, and particularly letters, written with no design to their publication, and commit them to the press without previously subjecting them to a careful revision." Challenged later on his editorial methods, Sparks argued with charming naïveté that he was really being true to his subject because Washington himself in his old age had revised his early letters. Wherever Sparks had the choice he preferred Washington's own later revisions (again without warning the reader) in place of what had actually been written in the heat of events. And Sparks made changes on his own. Where, for example, Washington had written of the "rascally crews" of New England privateersmen, Sparks emended the text to read simply "the crews." Washington's reference to the "dirty mercenary spirit" of the Connecticut troops became "the mercenary spirit," and their "scandalous conduct" was softened to their "conduct." "Old Put." became the more dignified "General Putnam." When Washington referred contemptuously to a small sum of money as "but a fleabite at present," Sparks improved it to read "totally inadequate to our demands at this time." Sparks again and again and again changed the words to make them worthy of his Hero.

Nearly fifteen years passed before any respectable public voice objected to Sparks's unobtrusive embellishments of Washington. In 1833, when Sparks sent Justice Joseph Story a specimen volume, Story privately expressed his enthusiastic approval: Sparks had "done exactly what Washington would have desired you to do, if he were living." But Story indicated concern lest a "cynical critic" should sometime in the future cavil over these improvements. Not until 1851 was there so much as a peep from any such "cynical critic," when two letters by an unidentified writer to the *New York Post* compared Sparks's version with another recently published version of certain letters from Washington to Joseph Reed, his military secretary during the Revolution.

The opening gun in a major (though finally unsuccessful) attack on Sparks's editorial integrity was fired by an Englishman, who was a noble lord and an accomplished scholar. The cultic sacredness of Washington's writings was revealed in the indignation against this attack and in the solid support of the American scholarly world for Sparks's way of elevating the American Hero. In December, 1851, Lord Mahon (later Lord Stanhope), a well-known English man of letters, who had been active in the Historical Manuscripts Commission, published the sixth volume of his seven-volume *History of England from the Peace of Utrecht to the Peace of Versailles.* "Mr. Sparks," he observed in the appendix, "has printed no part of the correspondence precisely as Washington wrote it; but has greatly altered, and, as he thinks, corrected and embellished it." He accused Sparks of "tampering with the truth of history." This remark, so inconspicuously placed, might have been little noticed had it not touched so sacred a figure. The immediate reply was an eighty-page counterattack by John Gorham Palfrey, the well-known Unitarian clergyman and historian who had followed Sparks as editor of the *North American Review,* in the form of a review of Mahon's work. In a pamphlet-war that lasted nearly three years, Sparks (then President of Harvard College) defended himself and his Hero; hostilities ended in a personal truce between Lord Mahon and Sparks.

The great significance of this controversy was to reveal an orthodoxy among American scholars who competed with one another in expressions of cultic reverence. Among Sparks's supporters were Francis Parkman, William H. Prescott, Senator Charles Sumner (who hailed Sparks "triumphant"), James S. Mackee (Librarian of the State Department and official custodian of the Washington Papers, which were now owned by the government) and, most appropriately, the eminent Professor Andrews Norton, who had attained fame as a pioneer in the use of new "critical" techniques to establish the genuineness of the New Testament. The best evidence of the general satisfaction with Sparks's way of editing was that, during the half-century after the appearance of Sparks's edition, there was no other edition of the Writings.

The Sacred Remains. The struggle over the possession and proper location of the bodily remains of the Hero, if not equaling that over the Holy Grail, expressed a not dissimilar cultic spirit.

At the death of Washington, Congress unanimously adopted a joint resolution directing "That a marble monument be erected by the United States at the Capitol of the city of Washington, and that the family of General Washington be requested to permit his body to be deposited under it, and that the monument be so designed as to commemorate the great events of his military and political life." Mrs. Washington approved the plan and a year later, in December, 1800, the House passed a bill appropriating $200,000 to construct a marble mausoleum, pyramidal in shape, with a base one hundred feet square, to receive Washington's body. At that time the Capitol building still consisted of only one wing; the present rotunda and crypt below it were not yet built. There seems to have been a notion of somehow including the tomb of Washington in the Capitol complex itself. Some Southerners opposed the project, arguing that the sacred remains properly belonged where they already were, at Mount Vernon. Partly because of the division of opinion, nothing was done. A new House committee in 1830 recommended that "the remains of George Washington and Martha Washington be entombed in the same national sepulchre, that immediately over the centre of his tomb and in the grand floor of the Capitol shall be placed a marble cenotaph in the form of a well-proportioned sarcophagus. . . . Immediately above this, in the centre of the Rotunda, a full length marble equestrian statue of Washington, wrought by the best artist of the present time. . . . These memorials, little costly and ostentatious as they may appear, will better accord with the feelings of this Nation and more appropriately commemorate the pure and elevated character of our Washington than could any the most expensive or splendid monument or mausoleum." Meanwhile, as 1832, the centenary of Washington's birth, approached, sectional passions (sharpened by the South Carolina nullification movement) ran high.

After the British, who occupied the city in 1814, had burned the interior of the Capitol building, Charles Bulfinch had rebuilt the central portion (1818–1829) with a crypt designed to receive Washington's body. The plan of the joint Congressional committee for the Washington centennial celebration centered around the transfer of Washington's body from Mount Vernon to the Capitol crypt. In a bitter Congressional debate during January and February of 1832, Southerners, reluctant to part with the National Relic, concocted all sorts of reasons against allowing the removal. A Representative from Maine charged that the whole debate was a contest between the State of Virginia and the great United States. Henry Clay of Kentucky urged the removal because "he would himself discriminate between Washington and any man who had lived, from Adam down."

Southern Representatives, foreseeing civil war and their separation from the Union, imagined the resulting indignities. "Remove the remains of our venerated Washington," warned Wiley Thompson of Georgia, "from their association with the remains of his consort and his ancestors, from Mount Vernon and from his native State, and deposit them in this capitol, and then let a severance of the Union occur, and behold! the remains of Washington on a shore foreign to his native soil." Others objected that, with the westward movement of the population, the Capitol would doubtless also be moved: "Shall the remains of our Washington be left amidst the ruins of this capitol, surrounded by the desolation of this city?" If our population is to reach to the Western Ocean," replied Joel B. Sutherland of Pennsylvania, "and the seat of Government is to be removed, when we carry away the ensigns of power from this place, we will carry with us the sacred bones of Washington." Others argued that the very presence of Washington's remains would somehow mollify and sanctify the deliberations of Congress. "No act can be done by the Government," pleaded Jonathan Hunt of Vermont, "that would have so deep and permanent a moral influence in uniting the people and cementing the Union of this confederacy, as the burial of Washington in the capitol."

The debate came to an abrupt end on February 16, when, less than a week before the proposed ceremony, John Augustine Washington, then the occupant of Mount Vernon, flatly refused to allow removal of the Hero's body. After a mysterious attempt to steal Washington's body from his tomb at Mount Vernon in the 1830's, a new tomb was completed there; it was locked, and the key was thrown into the Potomac.

The Annual Rites and a Declamatory Liturgy. In the mid-twentieth century, the only birthday anniversary (other than December 25) celebrated as a legal holiday by every state of the Union is February 22, the birthday of Washington. In the early nineteenth century, when the new nation still had almost no history, the birthday of Washington shared with the Fourth of July—the birthday of the Republic itself—the annual patriotic rites. On both these occasions, the center of interest, the usual ritual, was an oration. Repetitious, florid, pompous, bombastic, and interminable, the oration followed a pattern that was as set as if it had been prescribed by a liturgical authority. One example will do almost as well as another. Daniel Webster declared at the centennial of Washington's birth on February 22, 1832:

Washington stands at the commencement of a new era, as well as at the head of the New World. A century from the birth of Washington has changed the world. The country of Washington has been the theatre on which a great part of the change has been wrought; and Washington himself a principal agent by which it has been accomplished. His age and his country are equally full of wonders; and of both he is the chief.

Orators said the brevity of American history was more than offset by the grandeur of a Washington. John Tyler (later President) declared at Yorktown in 1837 that the Hero was greater than Leonidas or Moses, for, conspicuously unlike Washington, the one died with his men and the other never entered the Promised Land. John Quincy Adams found combined in Washington, more than in Aeneas or King David, "the spirit of command and the spirit of meekness." "To add brightness to the sun or glory to the name of Washington," Abraham Lincoln said at Springfield on February 22, 1842, "is alike impossible. Let none attempt it. In solemn awe pronounce the name, and in its naked deathless splendor leave it shining on."

Most popular and most repeated was Edward Everett's oration, which he delivered on circuit for the Mount Vernon Association to raise funds to purchase Washington's residence as a public shrine. From 1856 to 1860, Everett traveled over the country, and by delivering the same two-hour oration some 129 times, he raised about $90,000. His oration, "The Character of Washington," immediately became a classic in the national liturgy. Starting with the young Washington—"twenty-four years of age, a model of manly strength and beauty, perfect in all the qualities and accomplishments of the gentleman and the soldier, but wise and thoughtful beyond his years, inspiring at the outset of his career that love and confidence which are usually earned only by a life of service"—Everett sketched the heroic career. In an age "first in the annals of our race for great names, great events, great reforms, and the general progress of intelligence," Washington was greatest of all. Shining above the tawdry tyrannies of Peter the Great of Russia, Frederick the Great of Prussia, and Napoleon the Great of France, was the star of Washington.

A great and venerated character like that of Washington, which commands the respect of an entire population, however divided on other questions, is not an isolated fact in History to be regarded with barren admiration,—it is a dispensation of Providence for good. It was well said by Mr. Jefferson in 1792, writing to Washington to dissuade him from declining a renomination: "North and South will hang together while they have you to hang to." Washington in the flesh is taken from us; we shall never behold him as our fathers did; but his memory remains, and I say, let us hang to his memory. Let us make a national festival and holiday of his birthday; and ever, as the 22d of February returns, let us remember, that while with these solemn and joyous rites of observance we celebrate the great anniversary, our fellow-citizens on the Hudson, on the Potomac, from the Southern plains to the Western lakes, are engaged in the same offices of gratitude and love. Nor we, nor they alone,—beyond the Ohio, beyond the Mississippi, along that stupendous trail of immigration from East to West, which, bursting into States as it moves westward, is already threading the Western prairies, swarming through the portals of the Rocky Mountains and winding down their slopes, the name and the memory of Washington on that gracious night will travel with the silver queen of heaven through sixty degrees of longitude, nor part company with her till she walks in her brightness through the golden gate of California, and passes serenely on to hold midnight court with her Australian stars. There and there only, in barbarous archipelagos, as yet untrodden by civilized man, the name of Washington is unknown; and there, too, when they swarm with enlightened millions, new honors shall be paid with ours to his memory.

As sectional antagonisms sharpened, Washington's light was made to illuminate more brightly one side or the other. For Calhoun, he became the patron saint of Independence; for Webster and Lincoln, the patron saint of Union.

Washington had become the Savior as well as the Father of his Country. "From the first ages of the world," Representative Benjamin C. Howard of Maryland observed in Congress (February 13, 1832), "the records of all time furnished only two instances of birthdays being commemorated after the death of the individual: those two were the 22d of February and the 25th of December." "To 'Mary the Mother of Washington,' whose incomplete monument at Fredericksburg lies shamefully neglected," said the Rev. J. N. Danforth in Virginia on July 4, 1847, "we owe all the mighty debt due from mankind to her immortal son."

The Icon. Nothing better reveals the cultic, sacred character of Washington than the conventional appearance of his familiar portrait. Seldom has a historic figure been cast so universally in a single mold: the stereotype of Washington was cast by Gilbert Stuart. Many contemporary portraits of Washington were painted or sculpted between 1772 and 1799 by the best artists of the age: the Peales (Charles Willson, James, and Rembrandt), John Trumbull, William Dunlap, Edward Savage, Du Simitière, Houdon, Ceracchi, and others. Every known medium was employed, not only oils and marble, but wood, ivory, wax-reliefs, life-masks, shadow-pictures, and profile-drawings with the aid of a mechanical pantograph called the "physionotrace." Washington became inured to long and repeated sittings. What became the classic portrait was highly idealized. Lasting popular devotion significantly fixed on Gilbert Stuart's unfinished portrait (the "Atheneum") that was suffused with an unworldly haze.

Gilbert Stuart, who had been born in Rhode Island, decided at the age of twenty that the American colonies were no place for a painter. In 1775 he went to England, where he spent five years in the studio of another expatriate American, Benjamin West. Quickly acquiring a rich and fashionable portrait clientele, he competed successfully with Ramsay, Reynolds, Romney, and Gainsborough. When he returned to the United States in about 1793, possibly to escape imprisonment for debt, his avowed object was to recoup his fortunes by painting Washington; Stuart hoped eventually to make "a plurality of his portraits" with which to repay English and Irish creditors. His first painting of Washington, done from life in 1795, brought him orders from thirty-one subscribers for thirty-nine "copies." This was only a beginning, for no one knows precisely how many copies of his portraits were made by Stuart or his disciples or imitators.

The peculiar appeal of the Stuart portraits may be their very stiffness, which seems a kind of idealization. In human vividness they are much inferior to the portraits by Rembrandt Peale, which never had the vogue or appeal of Stuart's. The explanation, as Rembrandt Peale himself recounts it, is quite irreverently commonplace.

Judge Washington informed me . . . that the day his Uncle first sat to Stuart, he had placed in his mouth a new sett of teeth, made by the elder Gardette: they were clumsily formed of Sea-horse Ivory, to imitate both teeth & Gums, and filled his mouth very uncomfortably, so as to prevent his speaking, but with difficulty; giving to his mouth the appearance of *being rinced with Water*—(these were Judge Washington's Words). At a subsequent period, Mr. Stuart himself told me that he never had painted a Man so difficult to engage in conversation, as was his custom, in order to elicit the natural expression, which can only be selected and caught in varied discourse. The teeth were at fault; and, unfortunately for Mr. Stuart, they were always again put in at each sitting, with the expectation that eventually they would become easy—but they were finally rejected. It was fortunate for me that my Study was begun *before* the new teeth were finished, and that my Sitter each time came to me with the old Sett furnished him in New York many years before.

These dental circumstances, combined with Stuart's genius for idealizing his subject, produced a portrait perfectly suited to the American's ideal of his Hero.

Not oil, but marble, seemed the most appropriate material for the character and the image of Washington. A catalogue of the sculptured icons itself fills a volume. There was the famous life-size bust by the French sculptor, Houdon, of which countless replicas were made and which has become standard. There was the bust made from life by the Italian adventurer Ceracchi, which he then repeated in colossal size. There was the statue by the celebrated Canova.

Most impressive (and controversial) of all was the work of Horatio Greenough, the New England sculptor who had been given a government commission in 1832 to make a statue of Washington for the Capitol rotunda, at a fee of $5,000. After eight years' labor in his studio in Florence, Italy, Greenough produced the statue; it was ten and a half feet high and weighed twenty tons. The freight bill across the Atlantic was $7,700 and the cost of removal from the Navy Yard to the Capitol rotunda was another $5,000. The Capitol entrance had to be widened to admit the colossus, but, when in place, its weight was too much for the floor; it was removed outdoors to the east front. The bill to this point was $21,000. By now it had become a public scandal, not only because of its cost, but because, ironically, Greenough's very effort to deify the Hero had outraged public decency and seemed itself a kind of blasphemy.

Greenough's statue, modelled after Phidias' colossal ivory and gold Zeus for the temple at Olympia, showed Washington seated on a carved throne, naked to the waist, with drapery over his legs and sandals on his feet. Patriotic Americans were shocked that Washington, of all people, should be displayed without clothing. "Washington was too prudent, and careful of his health," wrote the New York socialite, Philip Hone, "to expose himself thus in a climate so uncertain as ours, to say nothing of the indecency of such an exposure, a subject on which he was known to be exceedingly fastidious." The same public whose committee of clergymen had approved Hiram Powers' totally naked female *Greek Slave* and had approved the nakedness of Greenough's earlier *Chanting Cherubs* "awoke," as Greenough said, "with a roar at the colossal nakedness of Washington's manly breast." The statue remained controversial until, a half-century later, it was removed to the decent obscurity of an alcove in the Smithsonian Institution where it remains. "Did anybody ever see Washington nude?" Nathaniel Hawthorne asked in 1858. "It is inconceivable. He had no nakedness, but I imagine he was born with his clothes on, and his hair powdered, and made a stately bow on his first appearance in the world."

The public shock at this fleshly version of the Hero made it easier for the Washington Monument Association to complete its fund-raising ($87,000 by the end of 1847). This Monument appropriately enough, commemorated the Hero not in any human form, however godlike, but in a geometric obelisk of abstract perfection.

The Sacred Name. In the United States the very name of Washington has been honored uniquely. In 1791, while the Hero himself was still alive, the commissioners for the proposed capital, although they had no legal authority to name the city, christened it the City of Washington. Despite the prevailing partisan bitterness, their choice was not effectively disputed. Washington, too, was the only person after the colonial period whose name was given to a state. "There has been but one Washington upon earth," observed

a member of Congress in 1853, during the debate on the organization of Washington Territory (later to become the State of Washington), "and there is not likely to be another, and, as Providence
has sent but one, for all time, let us have one State named after
that one man." In mid-twentieth century Washington, leading all
others, appeared in the name of at least 121 post offices. He was
far ahead, too, in the number of counties named after him; thirty-
two states have Washington counties. Of the states which have no
such counties, as George Stewart remarks, six were among the
smaller of the thirteen original colonies and thus already had their
counties named before 1775; and most of the rest were states in
the Far West which were not organized until after the Civil War,
when the Washington cult had declined.

Selected Bibliography

The most thorough biography of Washington is Douglas Southall Freeman's monumental six-volume *George Washington*, completed in a seventh volume by John A. Carroll and Mary Wells Ashworth: I and II, *Young Washington* (1948); III, *Planter and Patriot* (1951); IV, *Leader of the Revolution* (1951); V, *Victory with the Help of France* (1952); VI, *Patriot and President* (1954); VII, *First in Peace* (1957). Freeman has a good summary of Washington as a young man of twenty-six (II, 381–399), a concise appraisal of him when he assumed command of the Continental Army at the age of forty-three (III, 443–452), and a careful assessment of his military career at the end of the Revolution when he was fifty-one (V, 478–501).

The best brief surveys have been written by Englishmen: Marcus Cunliffe, *George Washington: Man and Monument* (1958), and Esmond Wright, *Washington and the American Revolution* (1957). A major three-volume biography is being written by James Thomas Flexner. The first two volumes take Washington through the Revolution: *George Washington: The Forge of Experience, 1732–1775* (1965) and *George Washington in the American Revolution, 1775–1783* (1968). Among the older biographies, the best is Paul Leicester Ford, *The True George Washington* (1896), reissued in 1924 as *George Washington*. Others include the adequate one-volume life by Shelby Little (1929), the two-volume study by Nathaniel W. Stephenson and Waldo H. Dunn, thorough but in the demigod tradition (1940), and the three-volume debunking account by Rupert Hughes (1926–1930). John C. Fitzpatrick, editor of Washington's *Writings*, sticks close to the documents in his biography, *George Washington Himself* (1933). Marcus Cunliffe has recently edited Mason L. Weems's *Life of Washington*, with a lengthy introduction about the author and his work (1962). For two perceptive articles, see Bernard Mayo, "Washington: 'Freedom's Myth' and 'More than Man,' " in his *Myths and Men* (1959), and Carl Russell Fish, "George Washington, the Man," Illinois State Historical Society, *Transactions*, XXXIX (1932), 21–40.

Historians and biographers in recent years have also singled out major aspects of Washington's life for specialized study. For his youth in Virginia and his interest in the West, the following are most useful: Bernhard Knollenberg, *George Washington: The Virginia Period, 1732–1775* (1964); Hugh Cleland, *George Washington in the Ohio Valley* (1955); Thomas P. Abernethy, *Western Lands and the American Revolution* (1937); and Charles H. Ambler, *George Washington and the West* (1936). A classic work on Washington and the movement for independence is Curtis P. Nettels' *George Washington and American Independence* (1951). In addition to the evaluations of Washington as a military leader by Freeman and Flexner, the following are helpful: Marcus Cunliffe's essay on "George Washington's Generalship," in George A. Billias, ed., *George Washington's Generals* (1964), which includes sketches of eleven other American commanders; R. Ernest Dupuy and Trevor N. Dupuy, *The Compact History of the Revolutionary War* (1963), especially the appendix on "The Historians and the Generalship of George Washington," 474–480; Bernhard Knollenberg, *Washington and the Revolution: A Reappraisal* (1940), the most critical of recent studies; Thomas G. Frothingham, *Washington: Commander in Chief* (1930), laudatory; Charles Francis Adams, *Studies Military and Diplomatic, 1775–1865* (1911), one of the earliest criticisms of Washington; and Louis C. Hatch, *The Administration of the American Revolutionary Army* (1904), still the standard account.

There is no satisfactory study of Washington's Presidency. In addition to Vol. VI by Freeman and Vol. VII by Carroll and Ashworth, the best brief account is in John C. Miller, *The Federalist Era, 1789–1801* (1960). Claude G. Bowers, *Hamilton and Jefferson: The Struggle for Democracy* (1925) downgrades Washington; Nathan Schachner, *The Founding Fathers* (1954), though less lively than Bowers, is better balanced. James Hart, *The American Presidency in Action, 1789* (1948), is a detailed investigation of the constitutional aspects of the Washington Presidency in its first year of activity, and Leonard D. White, *The Federalists: A Study in Administrative History* (1948) is a full-scale examination of Washington's administrative skills. There is an incisive, though critical, account of Washington in Joseph Charles, *Origins of the American Party System* (1956). Both Thomas A. Bailey, *Presidential Greatness* (1966), and Clinton Rossiter, *The American Presidency* (1960), rate Washington highly as President. For a fascinating explanation of the reasons why the Federalist financial program came to be designated as the Hamiltonian, rather than the Washingtonian, system, see Freeman W. Meyer, "A Note on the

Origins of the 'Hamiltonian System,' " *William and Mary Quarterly,* Series 3, 21 (1964), 579–588, which emphasizes the Congressional law creating the Treasury Department.

Washington's concept of foreign policy has received most attention from Samuel Flagg Bemis. His *Jay's Treaty* (1923) and *Pinckney's Treaty* (1926) remain superb studies in early American diplomatic history. His article on "Washington's Farewell Address: A Foreign Policy of Independence," *American Historical Review,* XXXIX (1934), 250–268, is also a standard. Felix Gilbert, *To the Farewell Address: Ideas of Early American Foreign Policy* (1961), is an intellectual history of the background of Washington's Farewell Address which overemphasizes Hamilton's role. Alexander DeConde presents a provocative analysis of the interaction between domestic politics and foreign affairs in his *Entangling Alliance: Politics and Diplomacy under George Washington* (1958). The only extended treatment of *George Washington and the French Revolution* is by Louis Sears (1960). Frederick Jackson Turner discussed "The Policy of France toward the Mississippi Valley in the Period of Washington and Adams" in the *American Historical Review,* X (1905), 249–279.

The personal side of Washington as farmer, businessman, and family man has also received considerable attention: Thomas J. Fleming, ed., *Affectionately Yours, George Washington: A Self-Portrait in Letters of Friendship* (1967); Francis Rufus Bellamy, *The Private Life of George Washington* (1951); Gilbert Chinard, *Washington as the French Knew Him* (1940); Halsted L. Ritter, *George Washington as a Business Man* (1931); Charles Moore, *The Family Life of George Washington* (1926); and Paul L. Haworth, *George Washington: Farmer* (1915), reissued with a new subtitle, *Country Gentleman* (1925). Washington's attitude toward slavery has been assessed by Walter H. Mazyck, *George Washington and the Negro* (1932) and by Matthew T. Mellon, *Early American Views on Negro Slavery* (1934). The only thorough account of *George Washington and Religion* is the study by Paul F. Boller, Jr. (1963).

The best piece on Washington's fondness for the drama is Paul Leicester Ford, *Washington and the Theatre* (1899). William A. Bryan has written an excellent literary history of the Washington legend in *George Washington in American Literature, 1775–1865* (1952); Samuel B. Shirk's *The Characterization of George Washington in American Plays Since 1875* (1949) is flat by comparison. Miscellaneous articles of interest include Dumas Malone, "Was Washington the Greatest American?" *New York Times Magazine,* February 16, 1958;

Reginald McGrane, "George Washington: An Anglo-American Hero," *Virginia Magazine of History and Biography,* LXIII (1955), 3–14; Saul K. Padover, "George Washington: Portrait of a True Conservative," *Social Research,* XXII (1955), 199–222; Marshall Smelser, "George Washington and the Alien and Sedition Acts," *American Historical Review,* LIX (1954), 322–334; Curtis Putnam Nettels, "The Washington Theme in American History," Massachusetts Historical Society, *Proceedings,* LXVIII (1952), 171–198; Everett S. Brown, "Washington and the Critical Period, 1783–1789," in his *The Territorial Delegate to Congress, and Other Essays* (1950); Bernhard Knollenberg, "John Adams, Knox, and Washington," American Antiquarian Society, *Proceedings,* LVI (1946), 227–237; and Max Farrand, "George Washington in the Federal Convention," *Yale Review,* XVI (1907), 280–287.

The United States George Washington Bicentennial Commission of 1932, directed by Congressman Sol Bloom, summarized its activities in a *History of the George Washington Bicentennial Celebration,* 4 vols. (1932), and in a fifth volume entitled *Report of the United States George Washington Bicentennial Commission* (1932). Wesley Frank Craven has an excellent chapter, "A Legend Debunked and Restored," in his thoughtful book, *The Legend of the Founding Fathers* (1956).

Washington's writings are most completely available in John C. Fitzpatrick, ed., *The Writings of George Washington,* 39 vols. (1931–1944). Fitzpatrick also edited *The Diaries of George Washington, 1748–1799,* 4 vols. (1925). Most of Washington's incoming correspondence has not been published except for the five volumes of *Letters to Washington and Accompanying Papers* edited by Stanislaus Murray Hamilton between 1898 and 1902. Selected portions of Washington's writings are available in Saxe Commins, ed., *Basic Writings of George Washington* (1948), and Saul K. Padover, *The Washington Papers* (1955). The basic works on the image of Washington captured by painters and sculptors are John H. Morgan and Mantle Fielding, *The Life Portraits of Washington and Their Replicas* (1931); Gustavus A. Eisen, *Portraits of Washington,* 3 vols. (1932); and Frances D. Whittemore, *George Washington in Sculpture* (1933). The most recent book is Clark Kinnaird, *George Washington: The Pictorial Biography* (1967), but the quality of the illustrations does not measure up to their quantity, about four hundred black-and-white reproductions of paintings, sketches, prints, and engravings. For "A Penetrating Characterization of Washington by John Trumbull," see the article by Edgar P. Richardson in *Winterthur Portfolio,* III (1967), 1–23.

JAMES MORTON SMITH received his doctorate in 1951 from Cornell University, where he is now Professor of American History. He has taught at Butler University, the Ohio State University, and the College of William and Mary and for eleven years was Editor of Publications at the Institute of Early American History and Culture at Williamsburg, Virginia. He has also served as Visiting Professor of History at Duke University, the University of Wisconsin, and Harpur College of the State University of New York. He is author of *Freedom's Fetters: The Alien and Sedition Laws and American Civil Liberties* and editor of *Seventeenth-Century America: Essays in Colonial History*. His other publications include a two-volume documentary history of American constitutional development, which he edited with Paul L. Murphy: I, *Liberty and Justice: Forging the Federal Union,* and II, *Liberty and Justice: The Modern Constitution.*

✪

AÏDA DIPACE DONALD holds degrees from Barnard and Columbia and a Ph.D. from the University of Rochester. A former member of the History Department at Columbia, Mrs. Donald has been a Fulbright Fellow at Oxford and the recipient of an A.A.U.W. fellowship. She has published *John F. Kennedy and the New Frontier* and *Diary of Charles Francis Adams.*